CU01572813

SIXTIES SPOTTING DAYS
AROUND THE SCOTTISH REGION

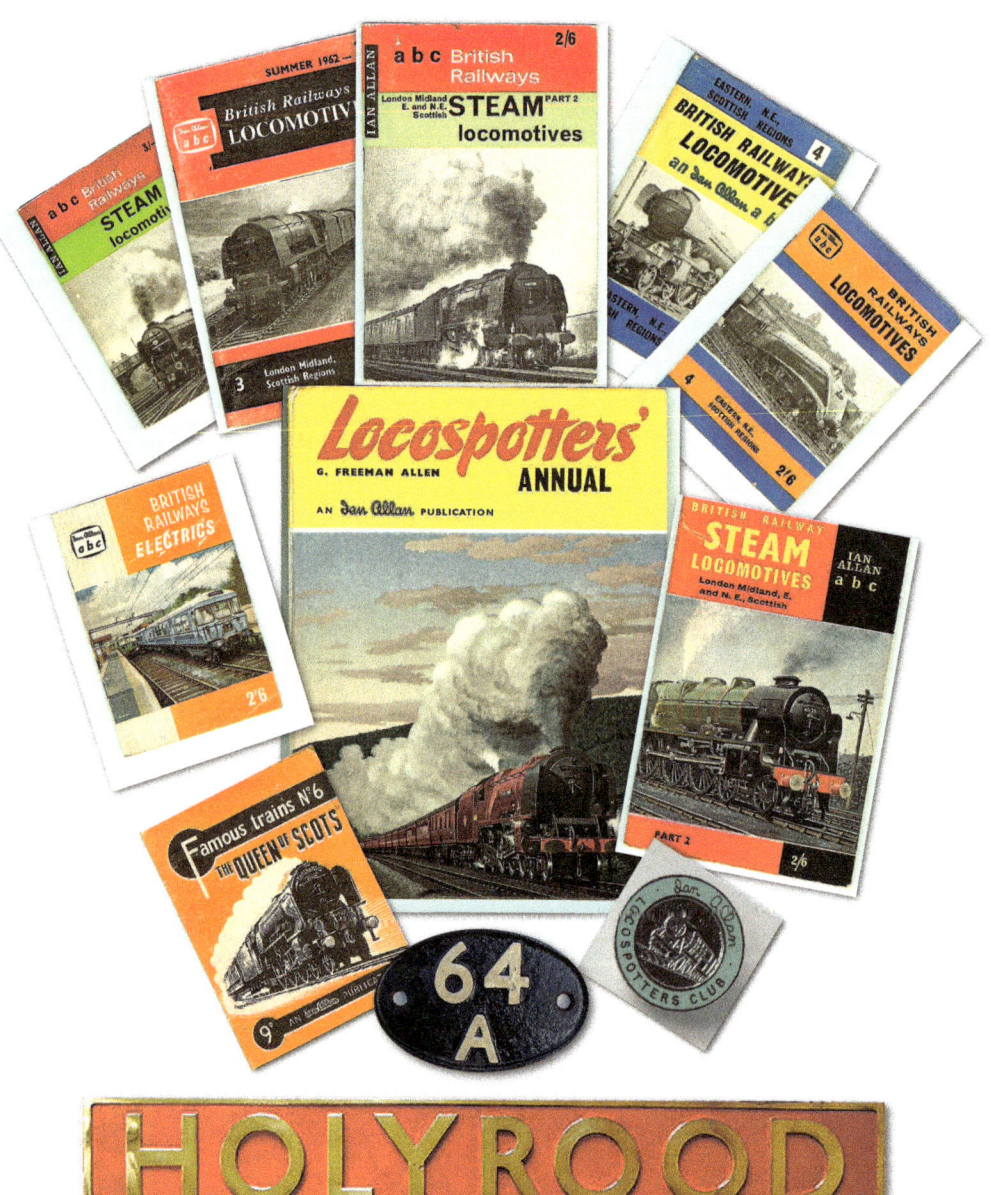

SIXTIES SPOTTING DAYS AROUND THE SCOTTISH REGION

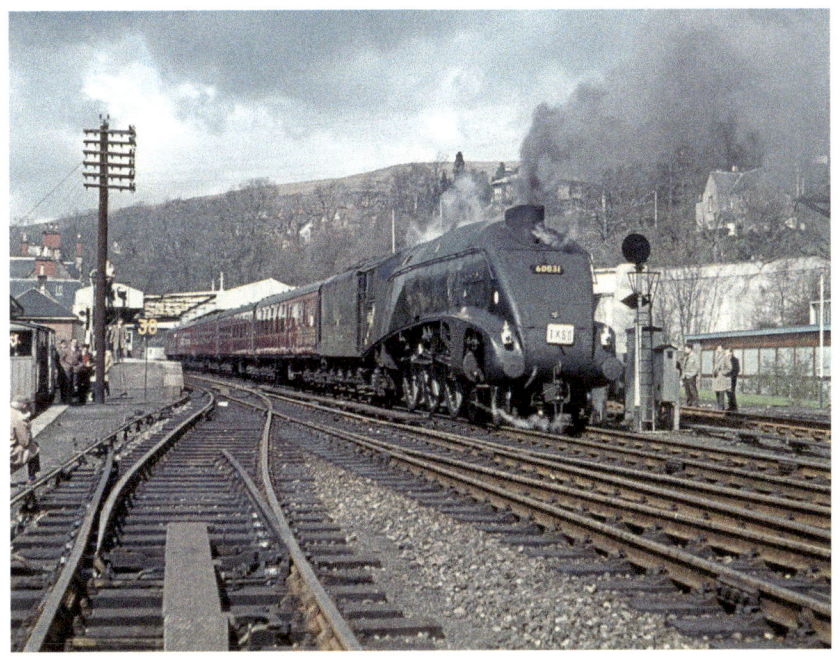

Kevin Derrick

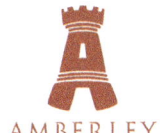

AMBERLEY

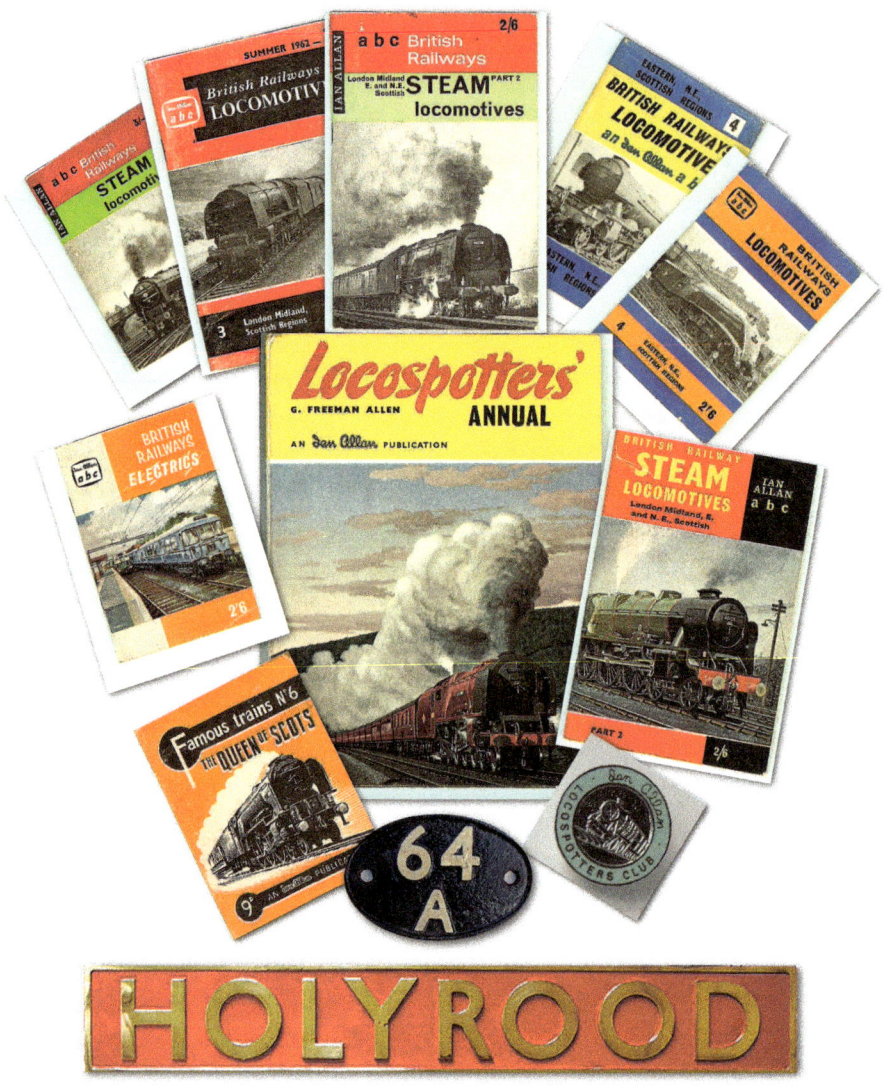

This edition first published 2016

Amberley Publishing
The Hill, Stroud
Gloucestershire, GL5 4EP

www.amberley-books.com

Copyright © Kevin Derrick, 2016

The right of Kevin Derrick to be identified as
the Author of this work has been asserted in
accordance with the Copyrights, Designs and
Patents Act 1988.

ISBN 978 1 4456 6079 0 (print)
ISBN 978 1 4456 6080 6 (ebook)

All rights reserved. No part of this book may be
reprinted or reproduced or utilised in any form
or by any electronic, mechanical or other means,
now known or hereafter invented, including
photocopying and recording, or in any information
storage or retrieval system, without the permission
in writing from the Publishers.

British Library Cataloguing in Publication Data.
A catalogue record for this book is available from
the British Library.

Typesetting by Amberley Publishing.
Printed in the UK.

Contents

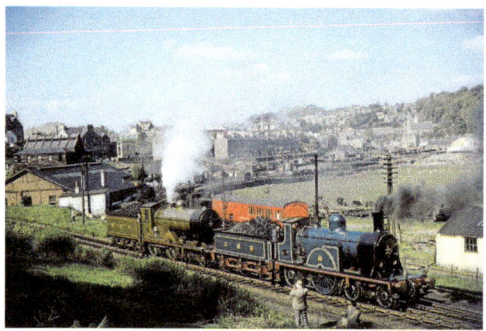 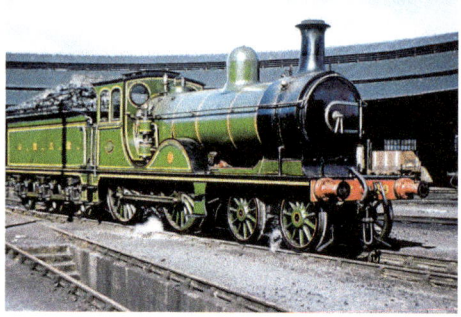

Left: Pre-Grouping glories are recalled with Caledonian 123 and North British 256 *Glen Douglas* at Oban. (Strathwood Library Collection)

Right: Great North of Scotland 49 *Gordon Highlander* reflects on the past in the Highland Railway's stronghold of Inverness. (Strathwood Library Collection)

Introduction

Was it the mix of superb Scottish scenery and the fascinating array of locomotive designs that drew enthusiasts from the south to attend those memorable extended Easter tours of the region during the sixties? Or simply the ease at which a spotter could be conducted around what was an almost foreign land? Certainly for many our photographers their experiences drew them back time and time again.

Much of what changed the world during the nineteenth century was either developed or built in Scotland; by the sixties much was in decline and the once mighty shipyards on the Clyde had one last hurrah when the RMS *Queen Elizabeth* 2, often referred to simply as the QE2, was built by the Upper Clyde Shipbuilders in the John Brown Shipyard in Clydebank. Her keel was laid down on 5 July 1965, as hull number 736, in the same plot that had been used to build iconic liners such as *Lusitania, Aquitania, Queen Mary* and *Queen Elizabeth*. She was launched and named on 20 September 1967 by HRH Queen Elizabeth II, using the same pair of gold scissors her mother and grandmother used to launch the *Queen Elizabeth* and *Queen Mary*, respectively. On 19 November 1968 she left John Brown's fitting out berth, and travelled down the River Clyde to the Firth of Clyde Dry Dock at Inchgreen, Greenock, for final trials and commissioning. Why is he carping on about shipping you may ask? Well, it was about the last great engineering feat being undertaken in Glasgow, which had once been the largest manufacturer of railway locomotives in the country within the various works of Sharpe Stewart, Neilson, Dubs and ultimately North British. However, the demise of steam around the world and within the United Kingdom killed off locomotive production, with the diesels and electrics produced by North British unfortunately not living up to the fine reputation the company once enjoyed, forcing the company to close completely, declaring bankruptcy on 19 April 1962.

If like us you enjoy a little bit of nostalgia join us in a good wallow again back in time within both the Sixties and Seventies Spotting Days series.

Kevin Derrick
Boat of Garten 2010

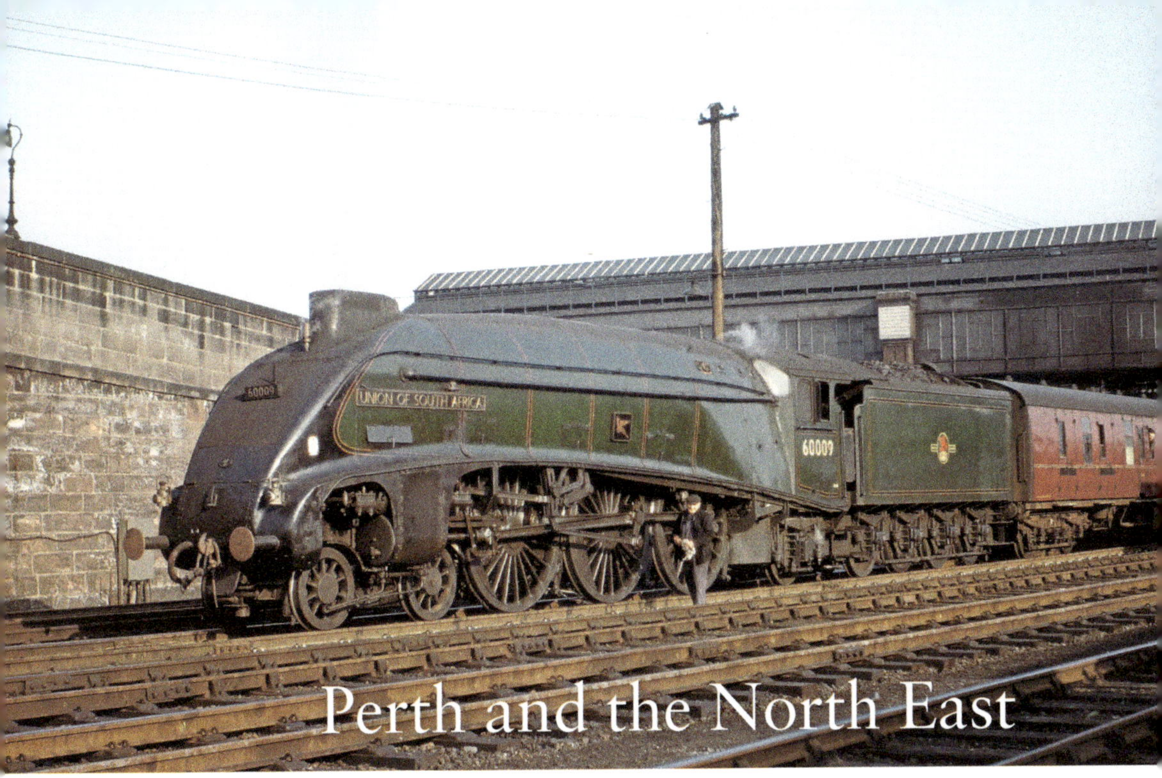

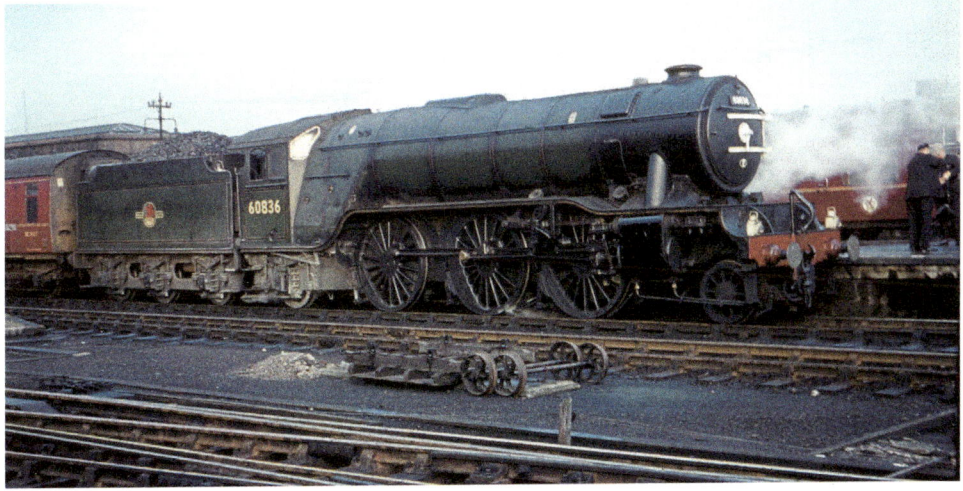

Perth and the North East

The classic view at Perth station in 1965 of a Gresley A4, No. 60009 *Union of South Africa*. This was the year that the book *No Easy Walk to Freedom* by Ruth First described how two young practising attorneys, Nelson Mandela and Oliver Tambo, were causing uproar in Johannesburg, as the name of their practise was written huge across the frosted window panes on the second floor of their scruffy office building. The letters stood out like a challenge; to white South Africa it was bad enough that two men with black skins should practise as lawyers, but it was indescribably worse that the letters also spelled out their political partnership. In time things would change… (John Rowe)

On Guy Fawkes Night 1966 Class V2 No. 60836, one of the last survivors of her 184-member class, waits patiently for the off with a full tender of coal for the onward journey. King William the Lion granted Perth burgh status in the early twelfth century; King Edward 1 of England, nicknamed Long Shanks, brought his armies there in 1296 where, with only a ditch for defence and little fortification, it fell quickly. (Strathwood Library Collection)

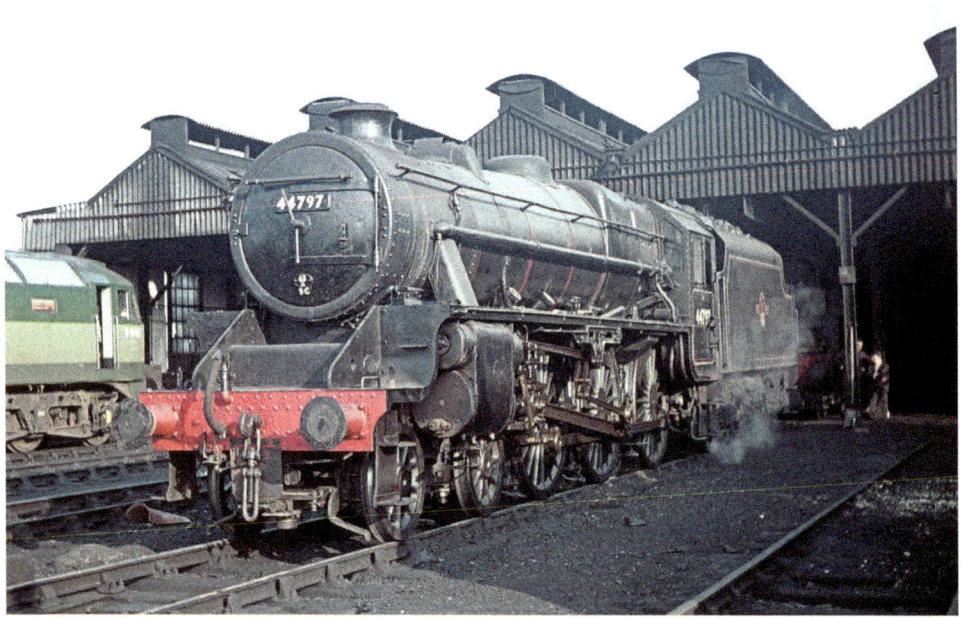

Perth shed was once blessed with the largest allocation of Stanier's Black Fives in the country; however by 10 June 1965 when No. 44797 was recorded diesels had seen most of them off. (Peter Coton)

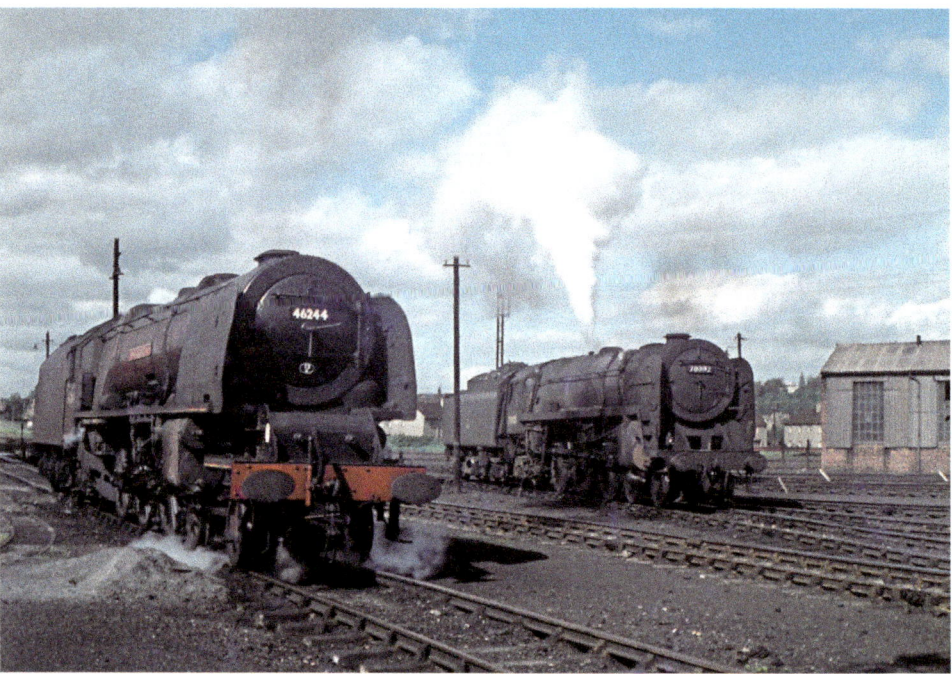

Visitors the previous summer would have been able to enjoy the presence of No. 46244 *King George VI* and No. 70002 *Geoffrey Chaucer*. (Douglas Paul)

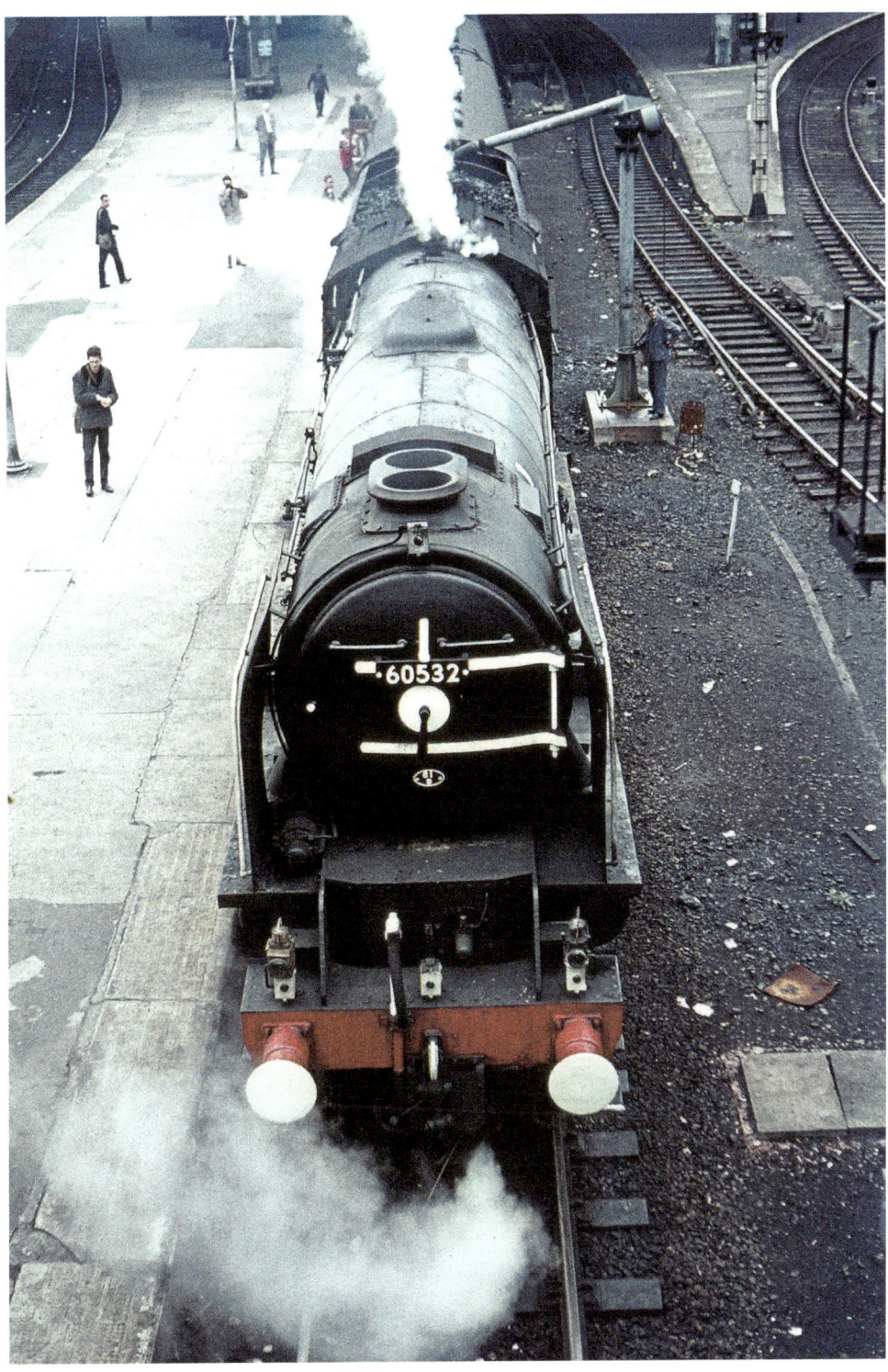

Championed by the children's television show of the same name at the end of the decade, Class A2 No. 60532 *Blue Peter* was slaking her thirst in the station on 30 August 1966. (Strathwood Library Collection)

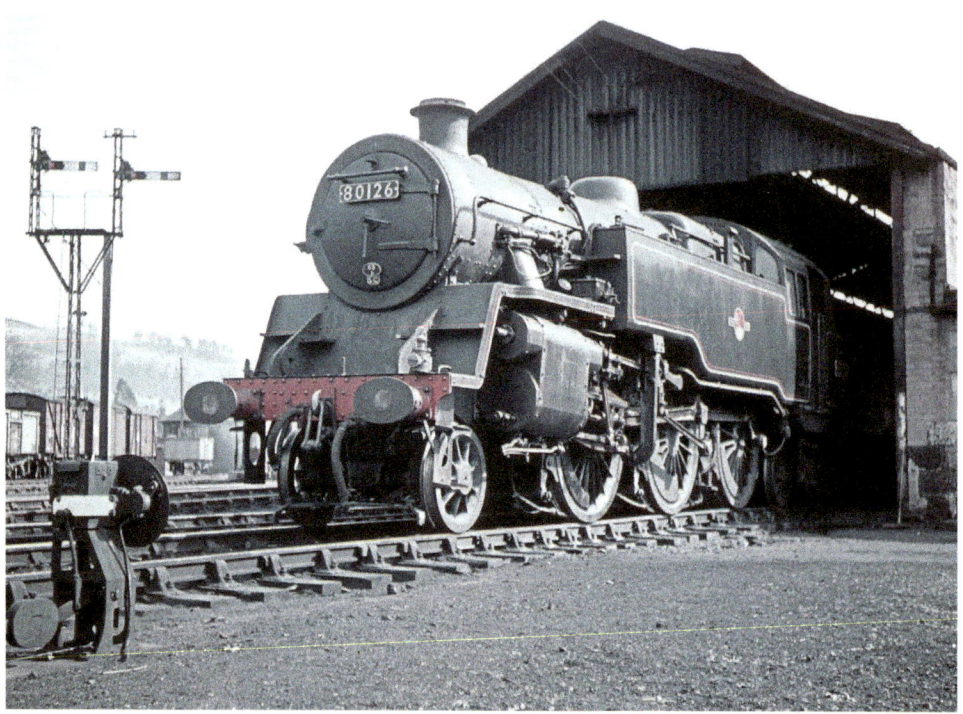

Back on Perth shed between spells on the Killin branch was Standard 4MT No. 80126 during a visit in April 1961. (Late Vincent Heckford/Strathwood Library Collection)

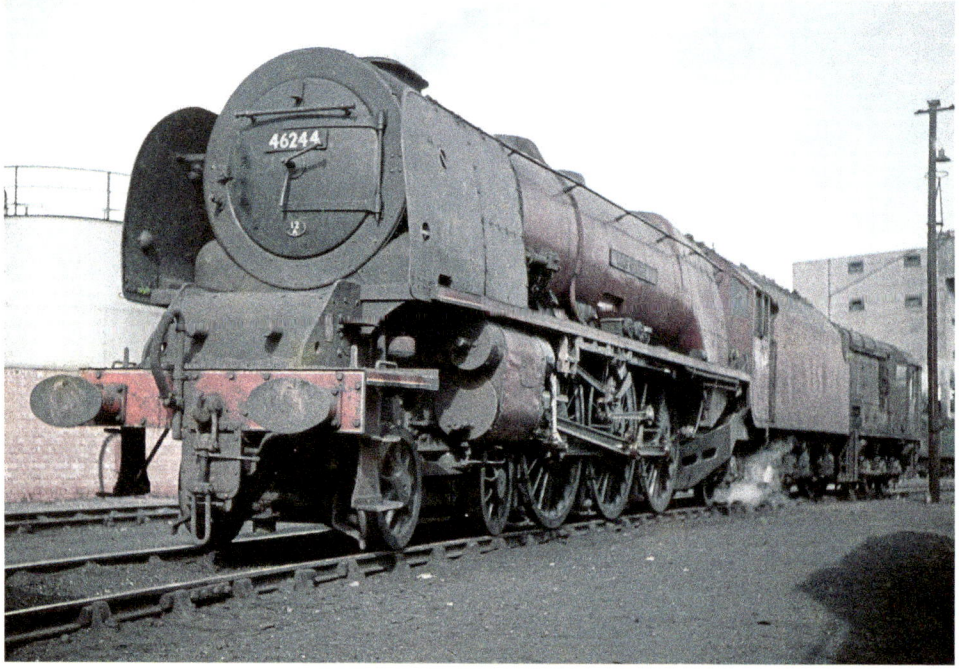

Stanier royalty on shed again in the form of No. 46244 *King George VI* the same day. (Late Vincent Heckford/ Strathwood Library Collection)

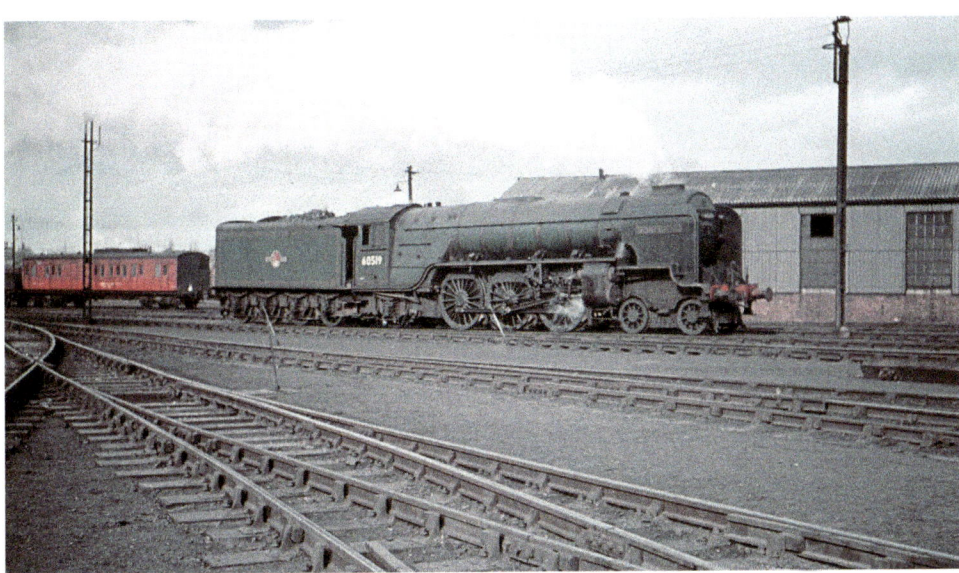

With mainline services reaching far and wide, Perth enjoyed a healthy variety of motive power at the beginning of the sixties such as Class A2/3 No. 60519 *Honeyway* in April 1961. This locomotive was named after the winning horse of the 1946 Champion Stakes, owned by Lord Milford. When Wogan Philipps became the second Lord Milford in 1962, he arrived at the House of Lords to be mobbed by all his old chums from Eton and Oxford, receiving cheers of welcome, offers of help, invitations for a drink. 'Then I gave my maiden speech,' he remembered. 'I proposed the abolition of the place. None of them ever spoke to me again.' (Late Vincent Heckford/Strathwood Library Collection)

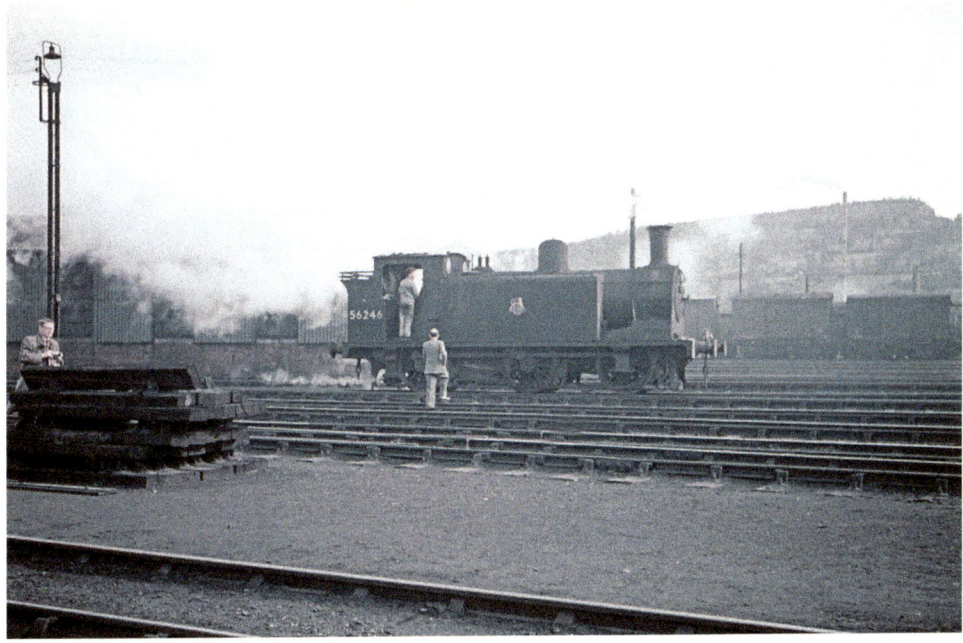

Much more humble tank locomotives such as ex-Caledonian Railway McIntosh Class 3F No. 56246 on the that same shed bash in April 1961. This was the engine's last month in traffic and it was scrapped a few weeks later inside Inverurie Works. (Late Vincent Heckford/Strathwood Library Collection)

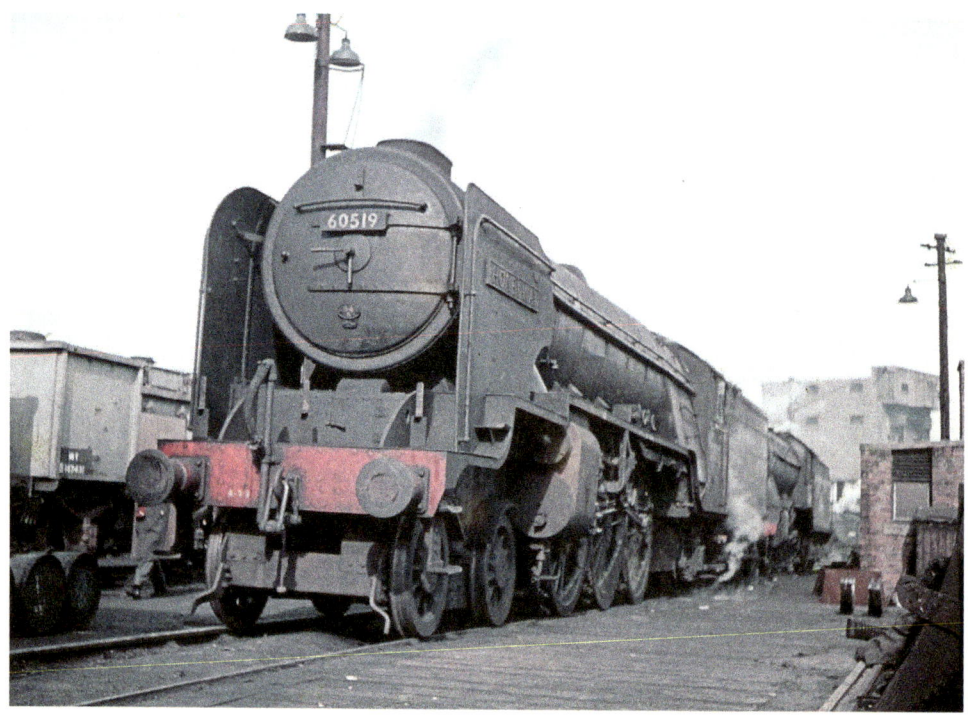

Honeyway has now made her way to be stabled next to a Class V2 to await her next duty south from Perth. (Late Vincent Heckford/Strathwood Library Collection)

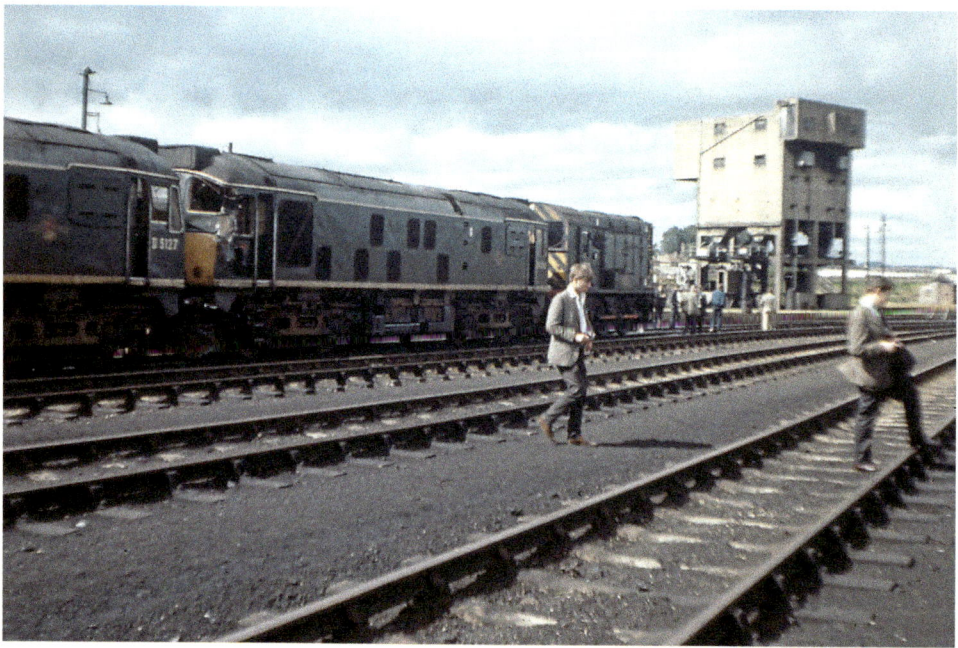

Closed officially to steam on 29 May 1967, Perth shed (63A) held D5127, D5132, and D3541 a few months later on 17 August. It would close completely in October 1969 by which time The Archies went to number one for eight weeks with 'Sugar Sugar', selling over six million copies worldwide. (Michael Patterson)

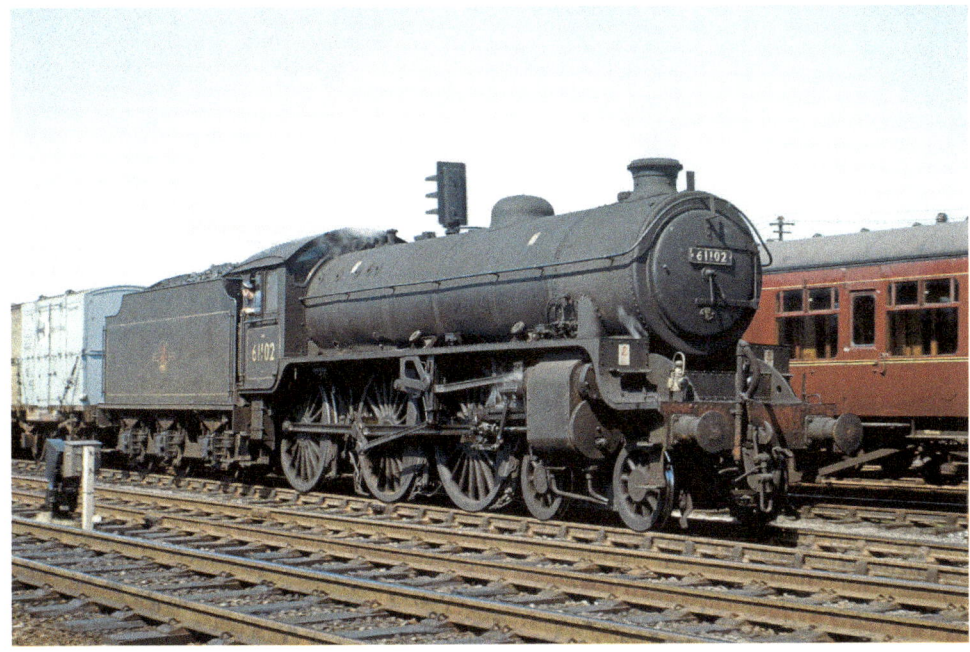

A long term 62B (Dundee Tay Bridge) engine was 61102, which was seen getting away with a train of refrigerated containers for the south at Perth in 1965. This B1 was just one of a large number to be built by North British in Glasgow, this one entering service in December 1946 and giving just over twenty years' service to the railway. (John Rowe)

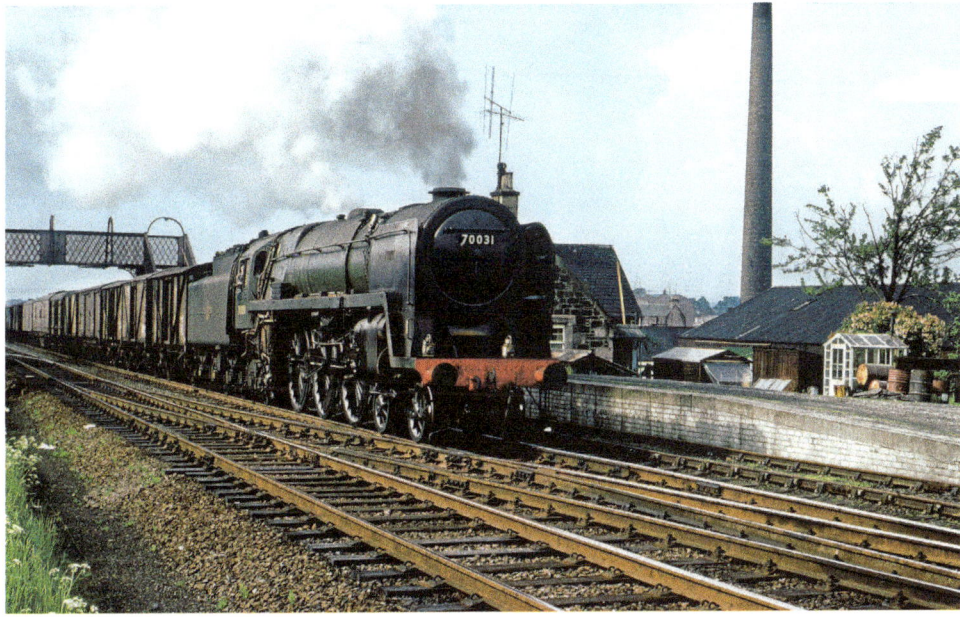

Whereas Britannia No. 70031, now devoid of its *Byron* nameplates; could only be given fifteen years in traffic as we see it accelerating hard away from Perth in 1966. Over in Las Vegas the world-famous Caesar's Palace hotel and casino opened and would become an American icon, with all of the famous names in show business playing there at one time or another. (John Rowe)

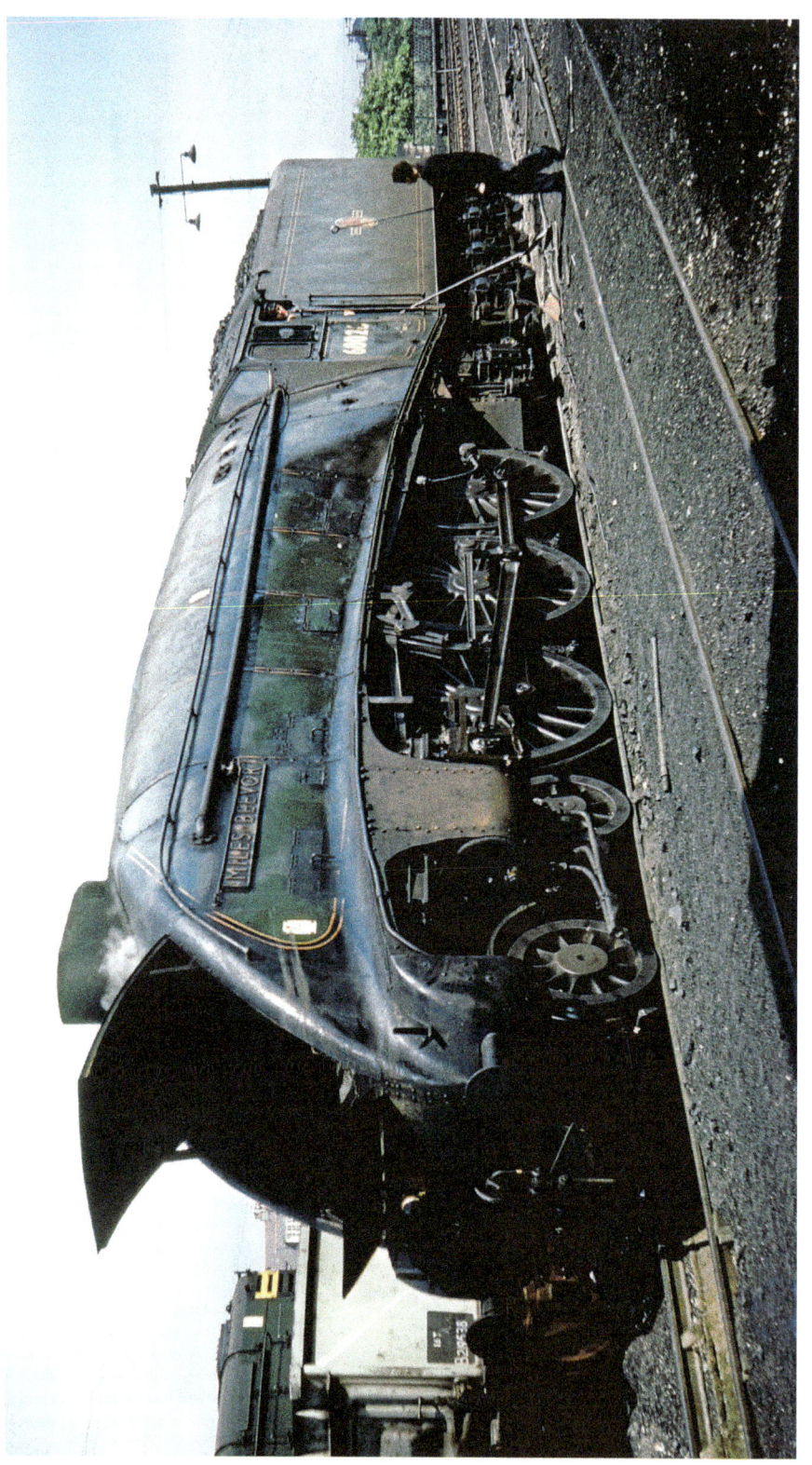

Preparation duties for shed staff at Aberdeen Ferryhill in June 1965 on No. 60026 *Miles Beevor*. The dubious honour of being the last A4 to be scrapped would fall to this locomotive in January 1968, at the hands of the cutters in the employ of Hughes Bolckows Ltd at Blyth after being stripped of usable parts within Crewe Works during 1967. (Win Wall/Strathwood Library Collection)

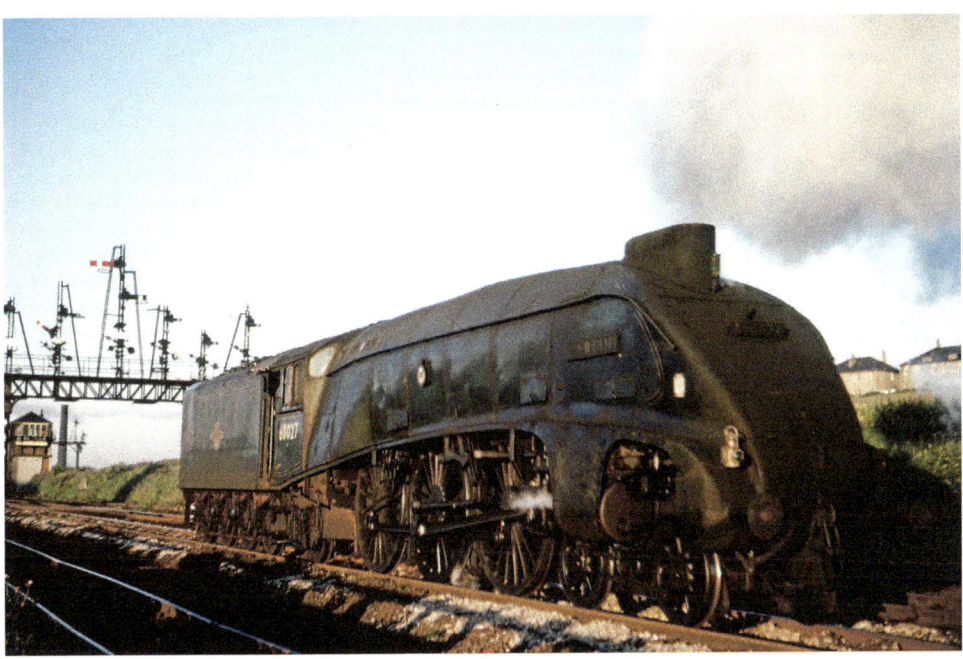

Running light near Ferryhill in 1963 was No. 60027 *Merlin*, proudly bearing the badge of HMS *Merlin*. These crests carried on the boiler casing were of the Naval Air Station located at Donibristle, Fife. On 3 May 1946 the locomotive was brought in to HMS *Merlin* via a rail connection from the East Coast main line and the crest was unveiled by the Air Station's commanding officer, Captain Chatwin. (Strathwood Library Collection)

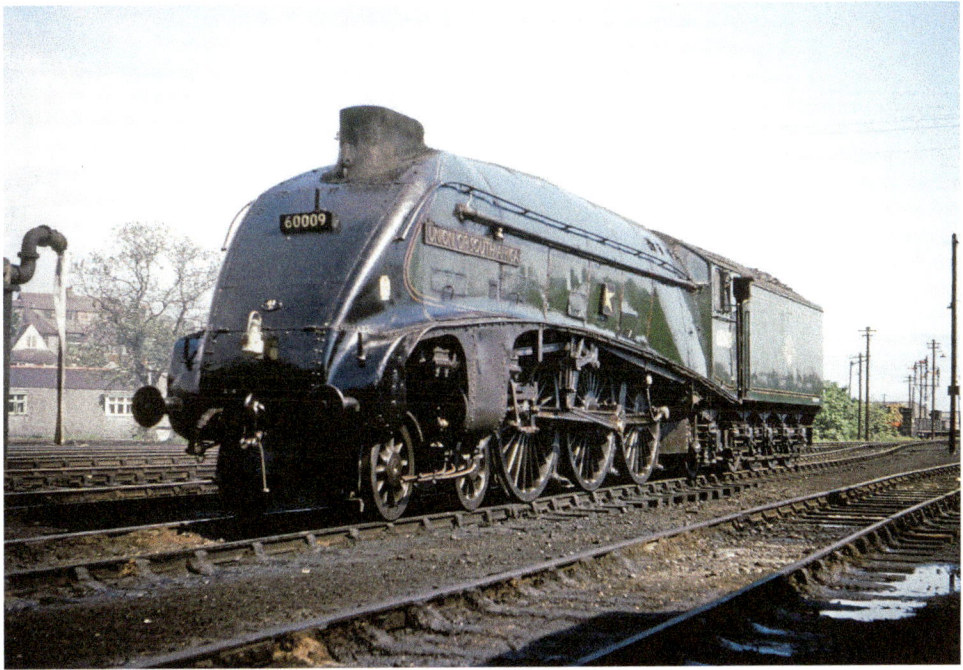

The engraved stainless steel plaque fitted to No. 60009 *Union of South Africa*, seen at Ferryhill in June 1965, had been carried since April 1954. (Win Wall/Strathwood Library Collection)

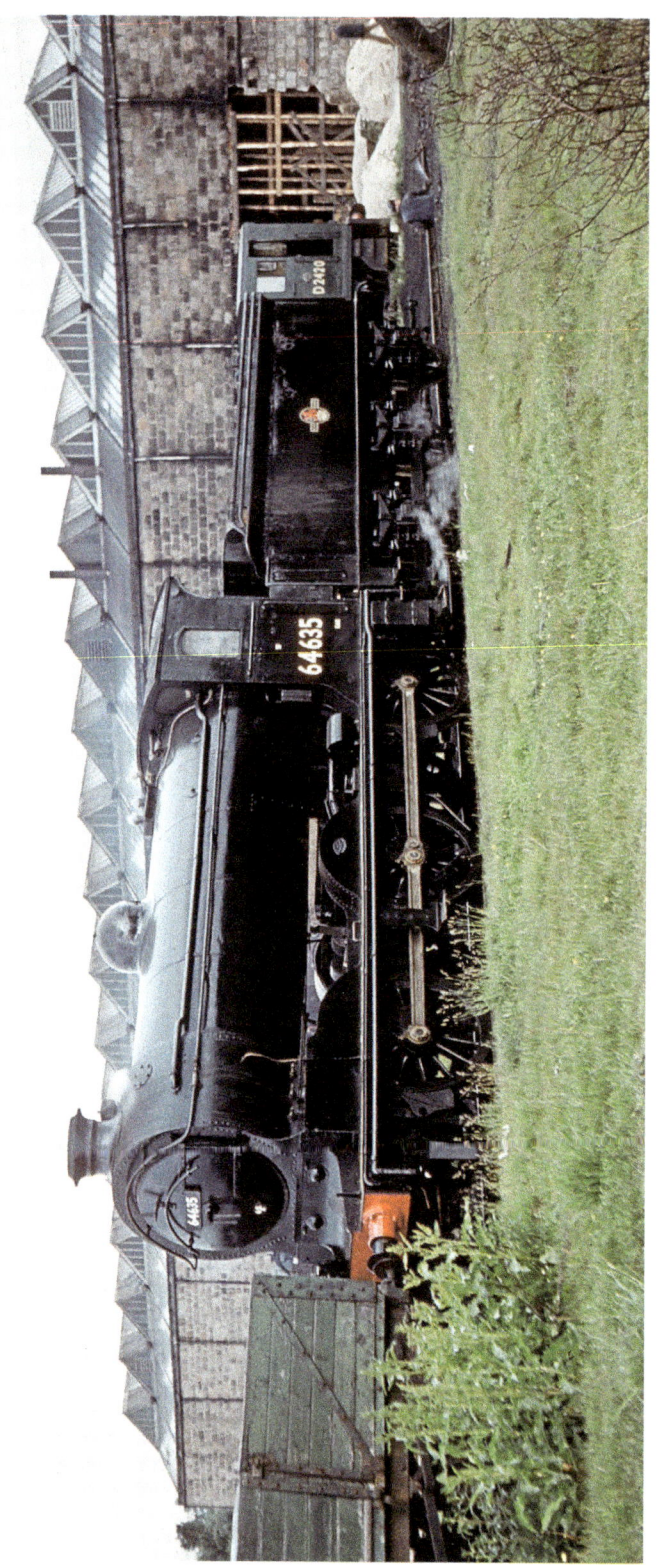

In 1960 Inverurie Works was proudly sending out ex-works locomotives such as Class J37 64635. By 1968 the local MP, Mr James Davidson, was fighting against the closure in the House of Commons stating, 'The works employs about 580 men, one in four of the insured population of the Royal Burgh of Inverurie. Of those men, 224 are skilled and 204 are semi-skilled. There are 100 salaried staff, and the rest are unskilled, including 40 apprentices. There are slight variations from month to month, so those figures may be marginally out of date. When it is appreciated that the population of Inverurie is only 5,267, it may be seen that it is a real railway town.' Sadly his pleas were only given polite attention as the works closed in 1969 after being established by the Great North of Scotland Railway in 1903. (Frank Hornby)

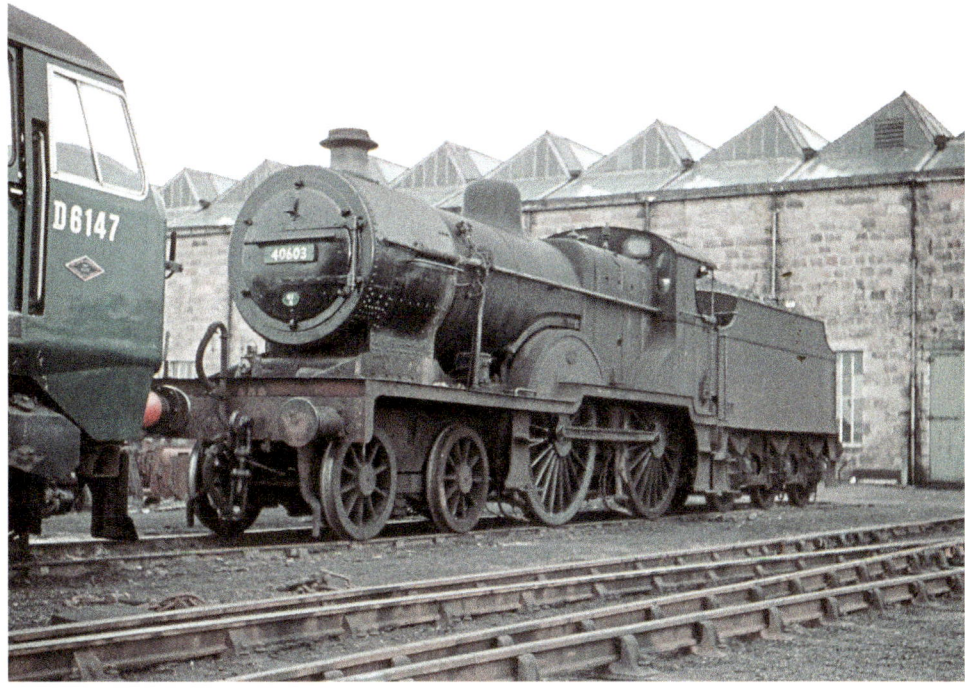

The North British-built D6147 had arrived for repairs in April 1961 whilst the withdrawn Class 2P No. 40603 would be scrapped at Inverurie at the end of that summer. (Late Vincent Heckford/Strathwood Library Collection)

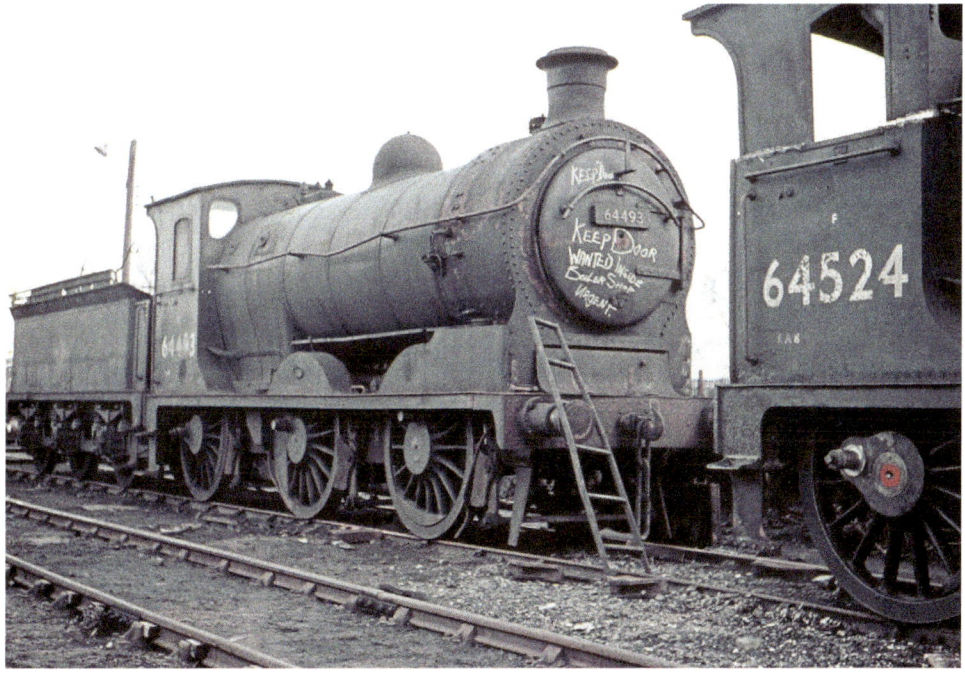

Making room for the unfortunate 40603 would be Class J35s Nos 64493 and 64524 during this Easter Scottish shed bash in 1961. (Late Vincent Heckford/Strathwood Library Collection)

Old King Coal

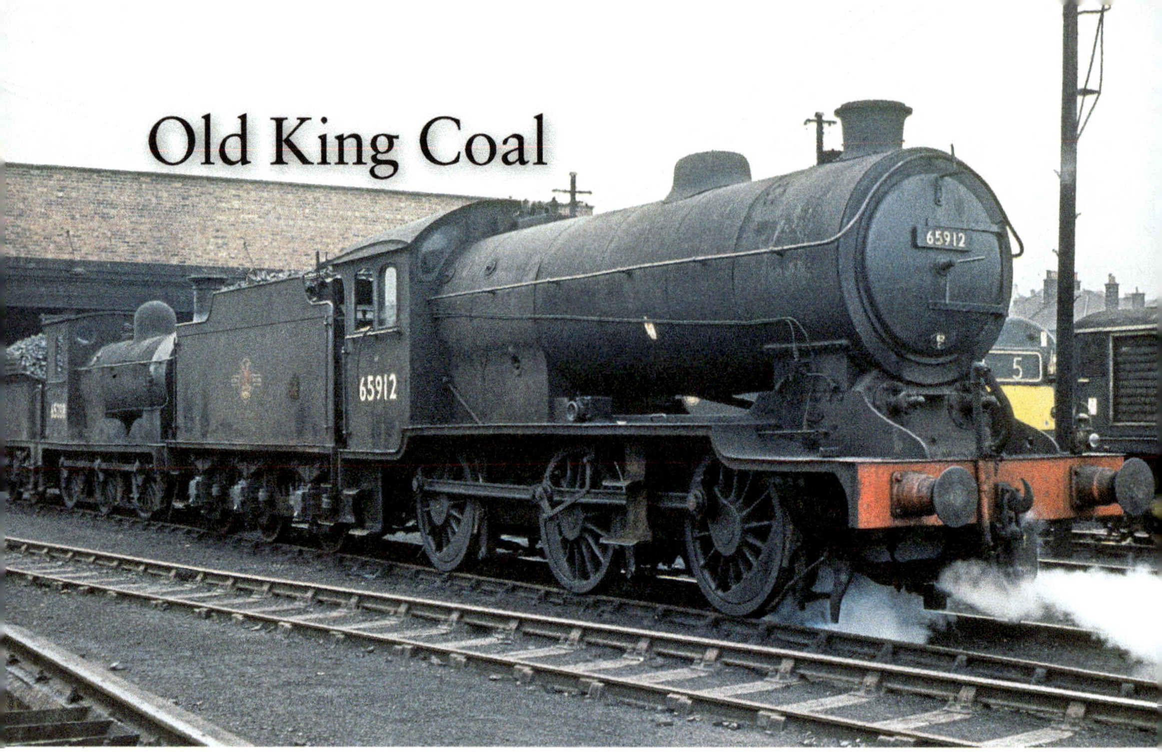

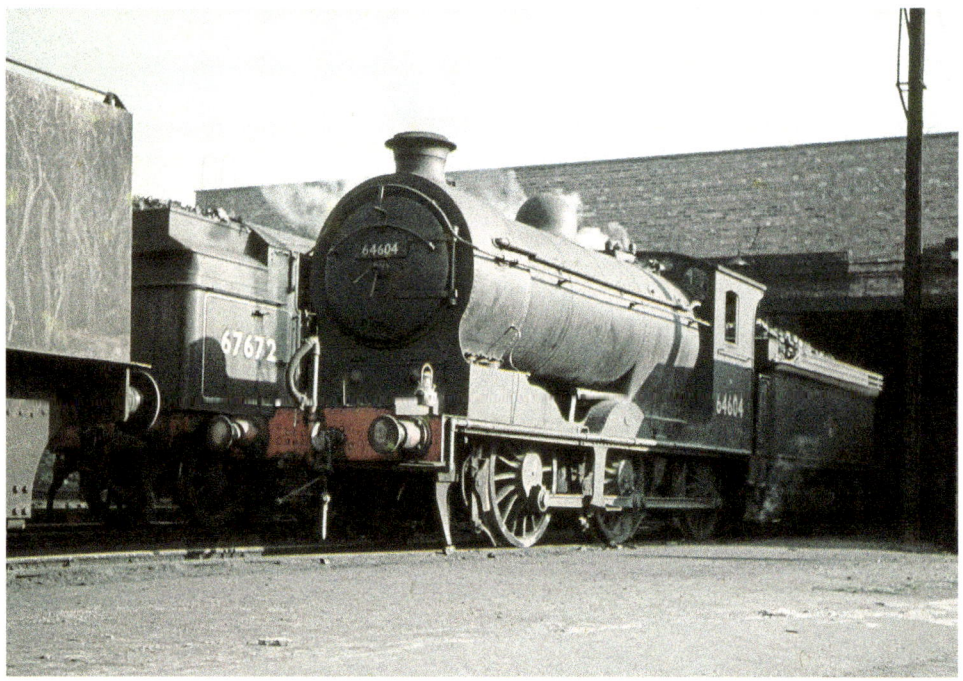

Those troublesome Claytons are on shed along with Class J38 No. 65912 at 62C (Dunfermline) on 24 September 1966; steam finished here on 5 June the following year, 1967, with a number of Claytons being withdrawn themselves in 1968. (Win Wall/Strathwood Library Collection)

An Austerity and Class V3 were accompanying Class J37 No. 64604 on shed at Dunfermline in April 1961. On the twelfth of the month Major Yuri Gagarin became the first man in space, to the consternation of the West at the time. (Late Vincent Heckford/Strathwood Library Collection)

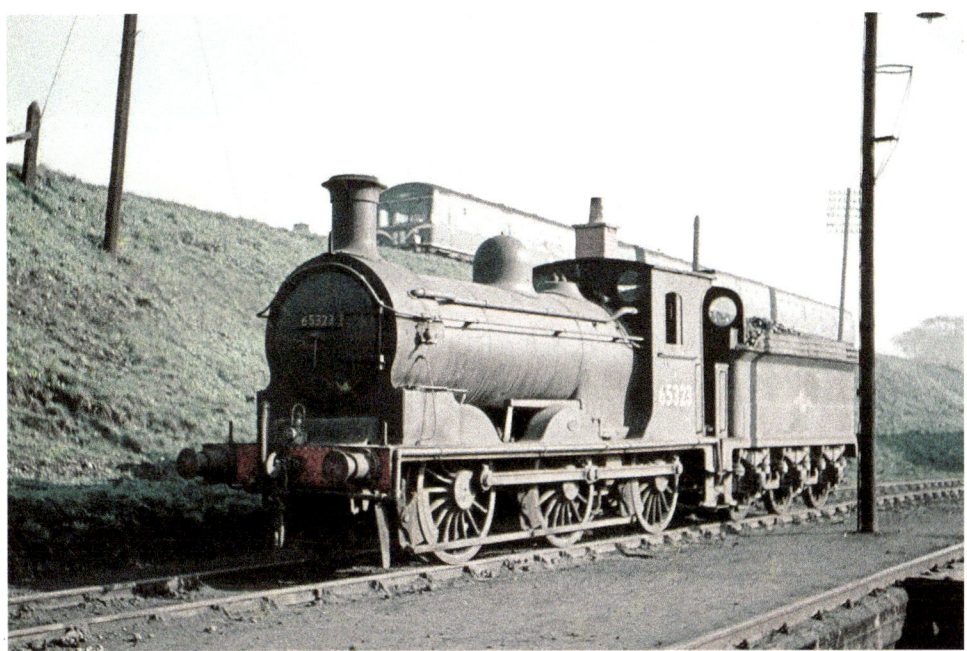

Within the Kingdom of Fife, Dunfermline was one of a number of once busy sheds occupied in supplying locomotives for the movement of coal from the many mines in the area. Among these was Class J36 No. 65323 in April 1961 whilst a Metropolitan Cammell DMU clatters past the shed yard. (Late Vincent Heckford/ Strathwood Library Collection)

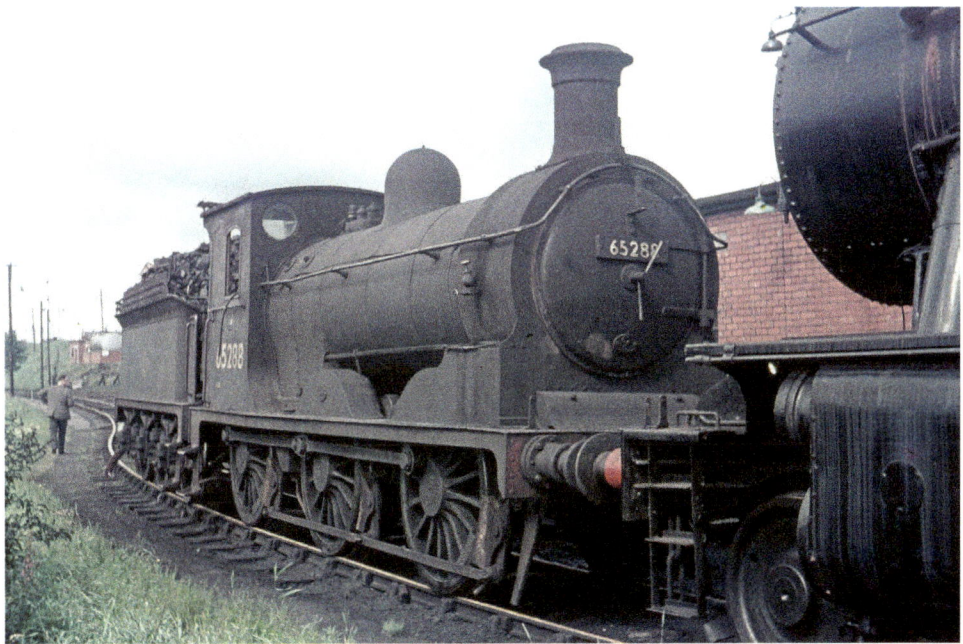

Coaled and ready for duty the next day on 1 August 1965 was Class J35 No. 65288, again at Dunfermline. This example was built at Cowlairs whilst others would be constructed at both Nielson's and Sharpe Stewart's works in the last few years of the nineteenth century. (Dave Down)

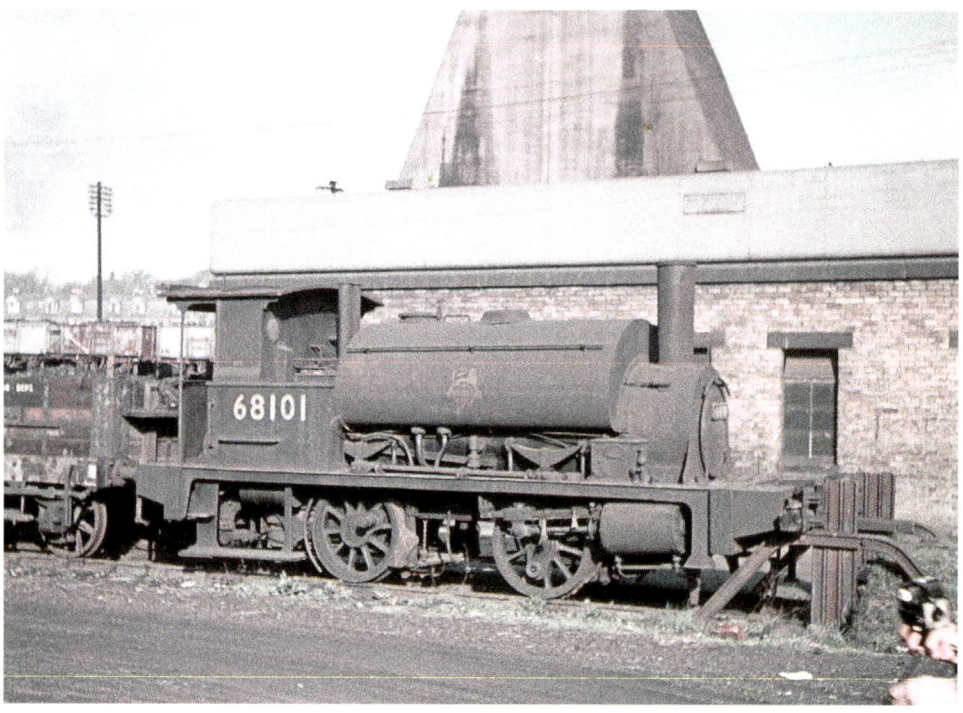

Built in 1889, also at Cowlairs Works, was Class Y9 No. 68101, seen without its rods at Dunfermline in 1961, although it was not withdrawn until October 1962. (Late Vincent Heckford/Strathwood Library Collection)

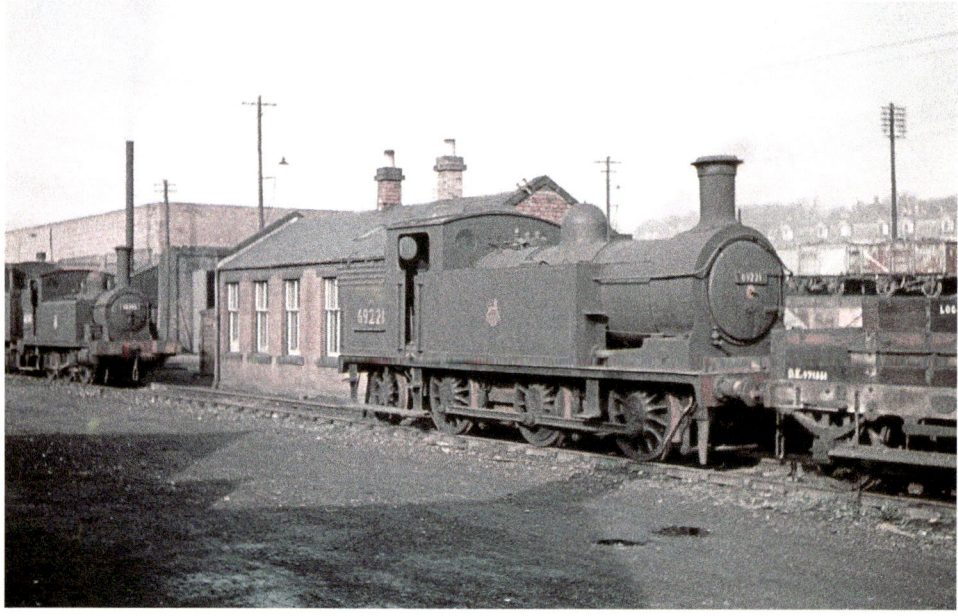

Another product from Cowlairs was Class N15 No. 69221, emerging from the works in March 1924. By the time of this extensive Easter shed bash at Dunfermline in 1961 it looked to be out traffic, officially withdrawn in July and swiftly despatched through Inverurie's cutters by September. (Late Vincent Heckford/Strathwood Library Collection)

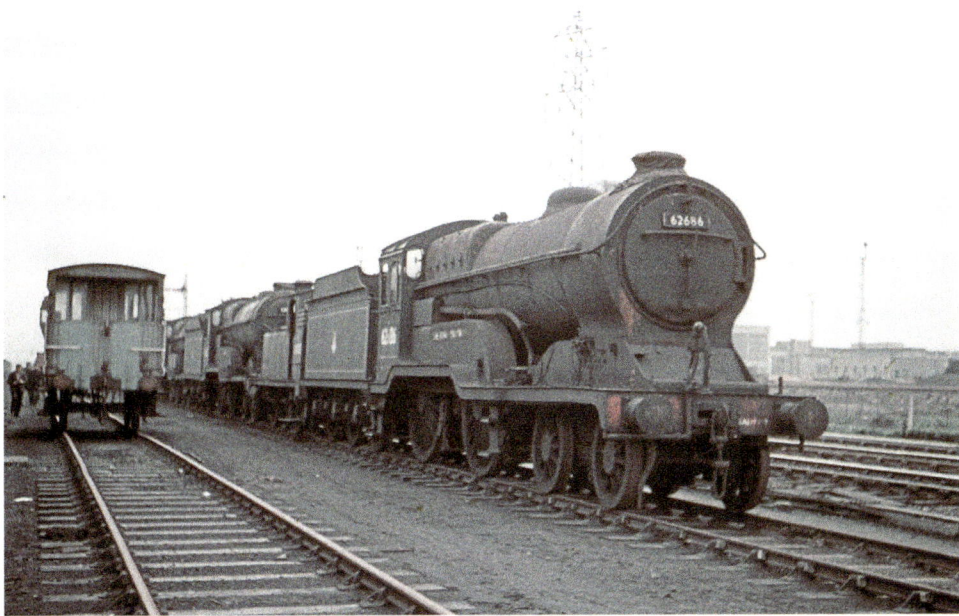

From the mid-1950s various dumps of withdrawn or stored locomotives existed across Scotland, with most sheds having something set aside somewhere. Among these was Thornton Junction, which offered a line of redundant Class D11s headed by No. 62686 *The Fiery Cross* in 1961. This distinctive name was one of many drawn from Sir Walter Scott's novels and poems, this one being Highlander Roderick Dhu's mobilisation signal to all Clan Alpine. This particular D11 went to Cowlairs Works in 1962 to meet its fiery end. (Late Vincent Heckford/Strathwood Library Collection)

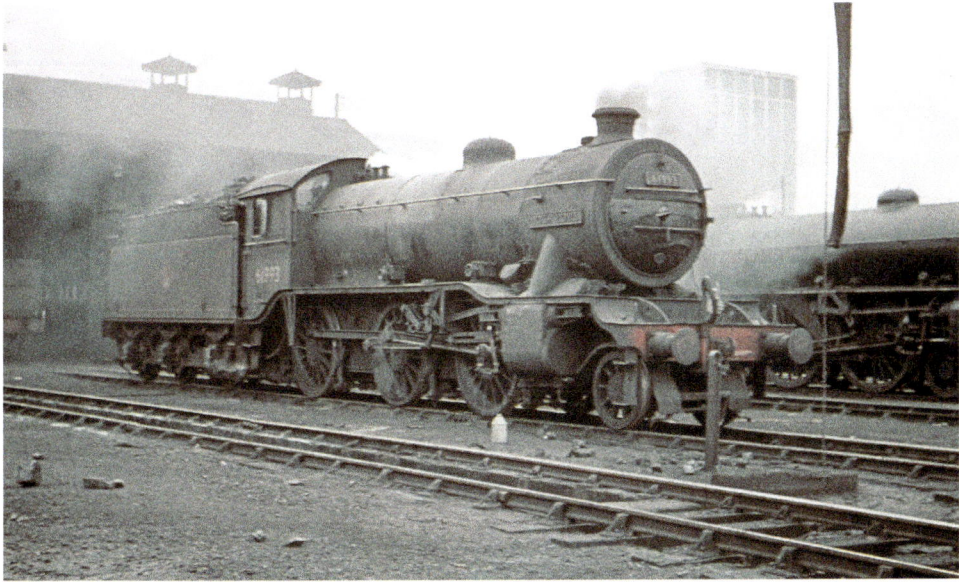

Built south of the border at Darlington Works in January 1937 was Class K1 No. 61993 *Loch Long*, seen the same day at Thornton Junction; this would be its last year in service, being withdrawn that October. Over in Paris that troubled October the French police massacred over 200 Algerian protesters on the streets during a peaceful protest against the war that had been ongoing since 1952. (Late Vincent Heckford/Strathwood Library Collection)

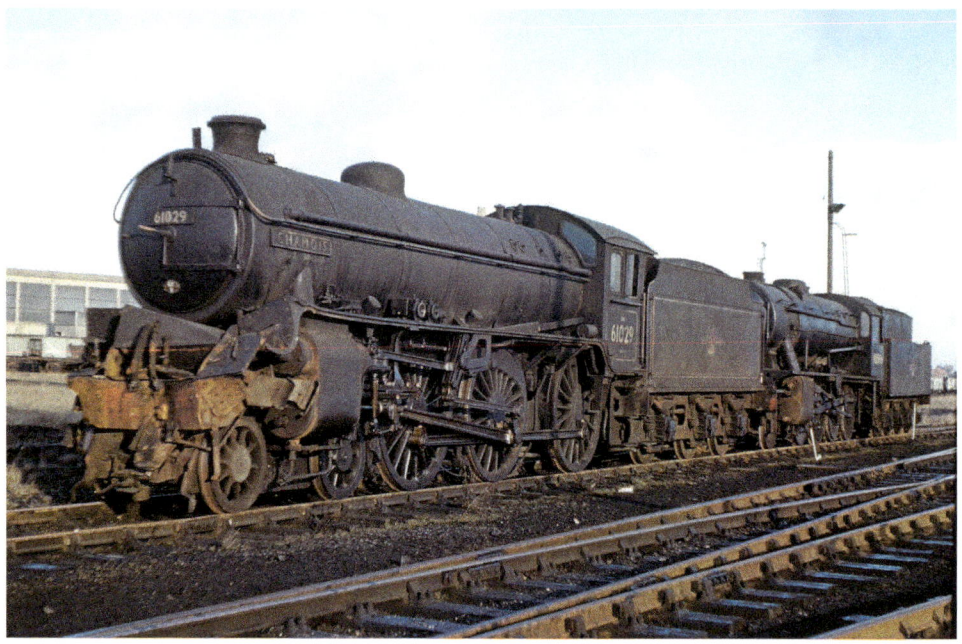

There would be no repairs for Class B1 No. 61029 *Chamois* when seen at Thornton Junction in January 1967. It had been withdrawn a few weeks before and, remarkably, still bore its nameplates. (Jerry Beddows)

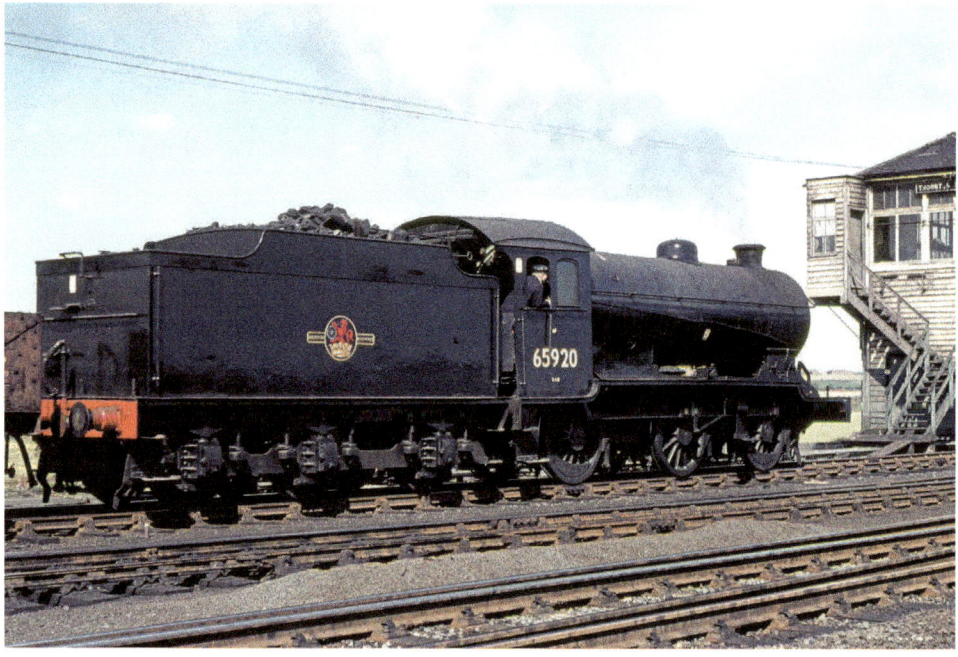

Recently out shopped was Class J38 No. 65920, making its way through Thornton Junction during 1965. This Darlington-built engine lasted forty years in service, from March 1926 until November 1966. By this time the cinemas across the country were playing perhaps the ultimate 'Spaghetti Western'; the basic story of *The Good, the Bad and the Ugly* is a simple treasure hunt, and remarkably there is no dialogue at all for the first ten minutes of the film. (Strathwood Library Collection)

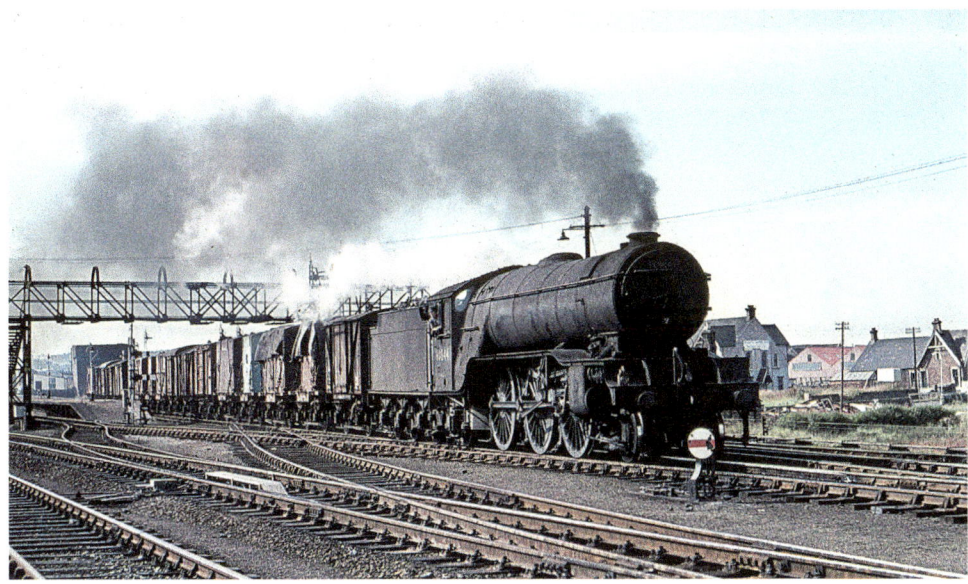

Running confidently across the point work at Thornton Junction in 1965 was Class V2 No. 60844, although there were a number of speed restrictions in the area due to mining subsidence. During the first part of the twentieth century, Thornton railway station was situated on the Aberdeen to London main line at the far end of the village, at the end of Station Road. The village boasted the largest railway marshalling yard in Scotland during the 1950s. In 1957 the Rothes Pit was opened to mine the coal underlying the village. The planned long-term benefits were to be huge, and the driver for economic regeneration for central Fife. In 1961, four years after opening, the huge investment was written off and the mine run down because of unstemmable flooding. Ironically, miners who'd worked in older deep pits in the area had fore-warned against the development of the Rothes Pit for this very reason. The state-of-the art engineering and design was closed, leaving the huge enclosed concrete wheel-towers standing at Thornton for many years as a forlorn symbol of the collapse until 1993, when the towers were destroyed. (Strathwood Library Collection)

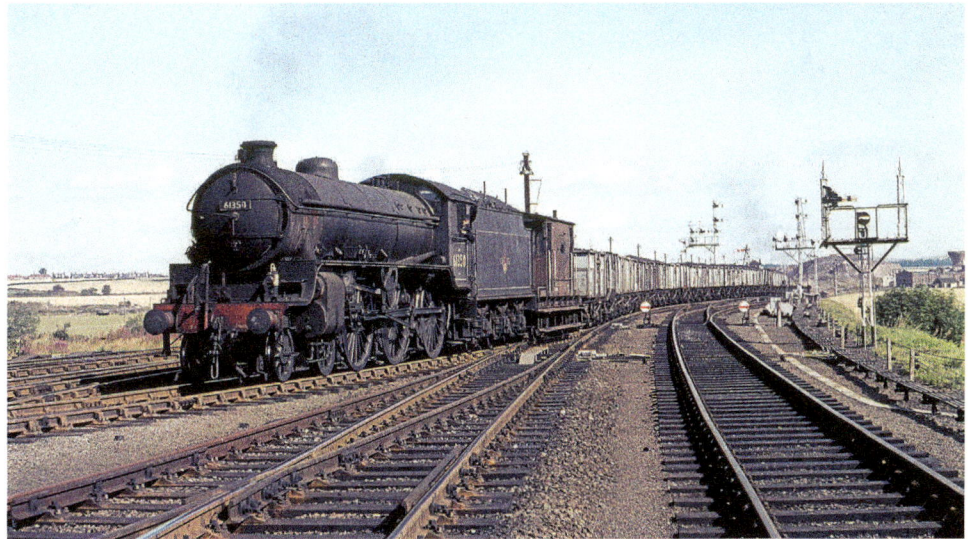

Bringing another rake of coal trucks into Thornton Junction the same day was No. 61350. This Class B1 emerged from Darlington Works in British Railways ownership during July 1949. (Strathwood Library Collection)

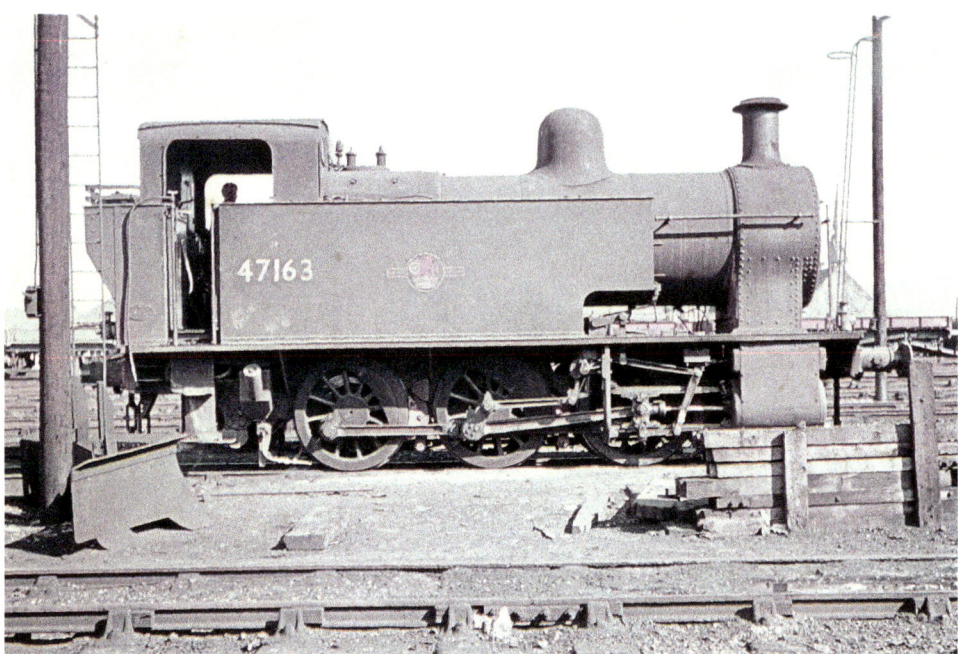

The short wheel-base of 9 feet 6 inches is most apparent in this side on view of Fowler Dock Tank No. 47163 at Ladybank in April 1961. This was a sub shed of Thornton Junction which continued to stable locomotives until 1973. (Late Vincent Heckford/Strathwood Library Collection)

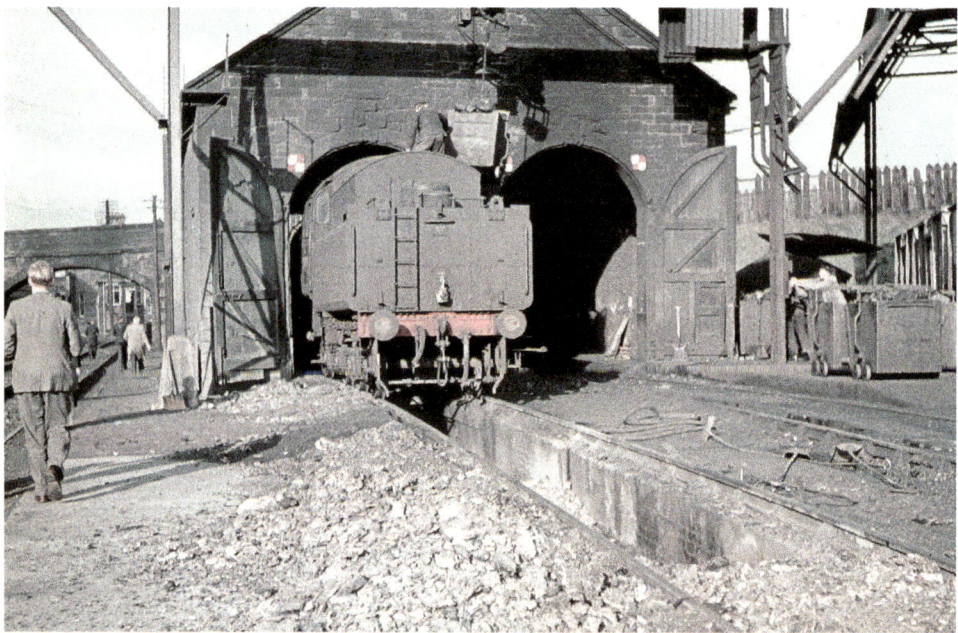

A small two-road shed existed at Alloa as a sub shed of Dunfermline and closed in January 1967. During this visit it yielded Standard 4MT No. 76109 being coaled in what looks like an operation that could bring on a sweat for one operator and bruised shins for the other. Nervous Health and Safety officers should look the other way! (Late Vincent Heckford/Strathwood Library Collection)

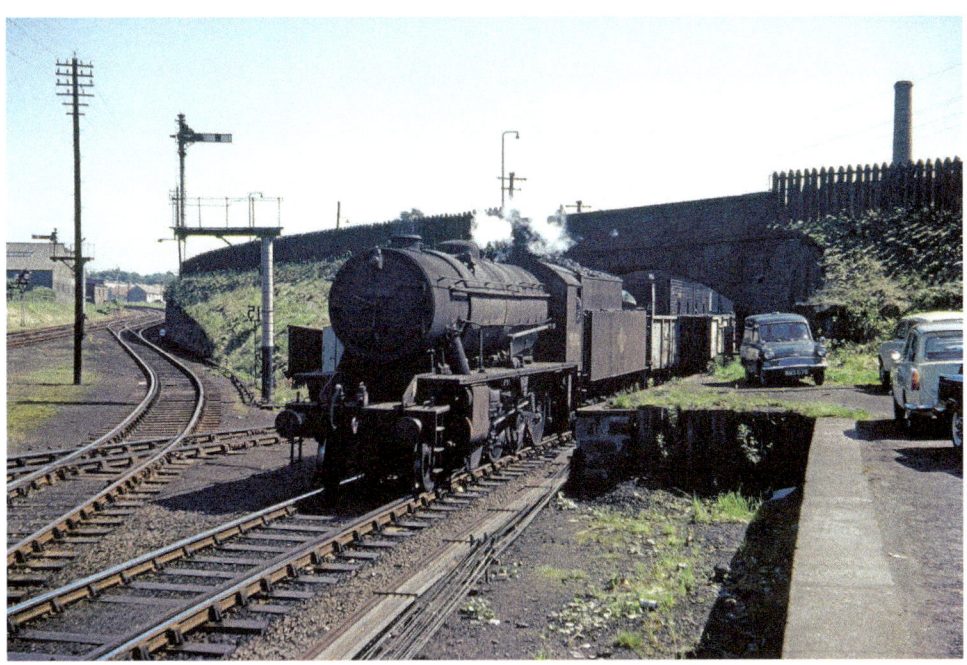

Running into the station at Alloa on 29 June 1966, Austerity No. 90386 has a rake of empties well in hand. (Michael Beaton)

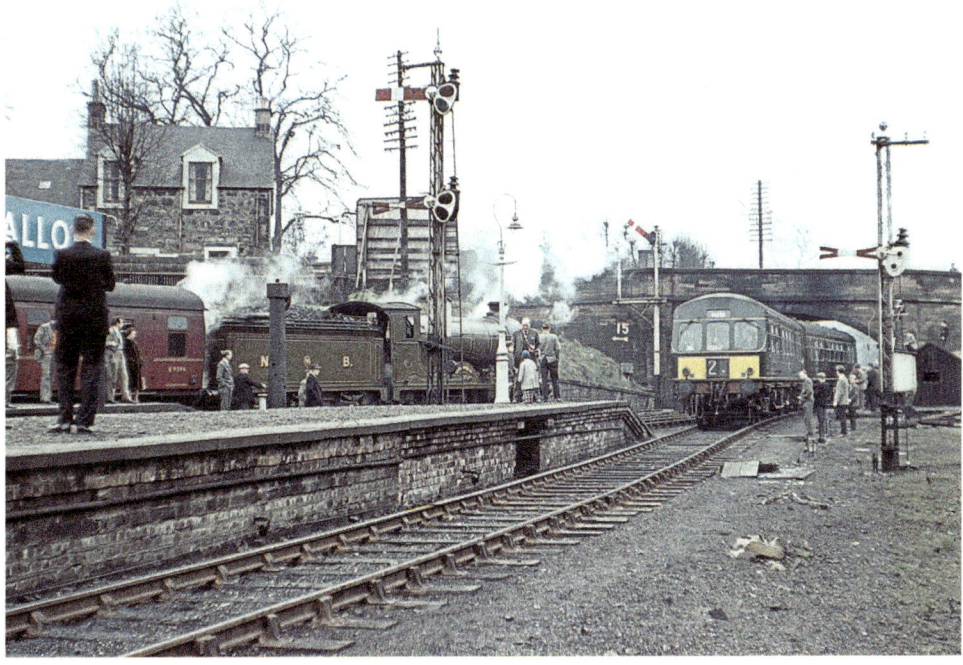

Enthusiasts have spilt onto the trackside to get their views of preserved Class D34 No. 256 *Glen Douglas* at Alloa on 13 April 1963. (Richard Icke)

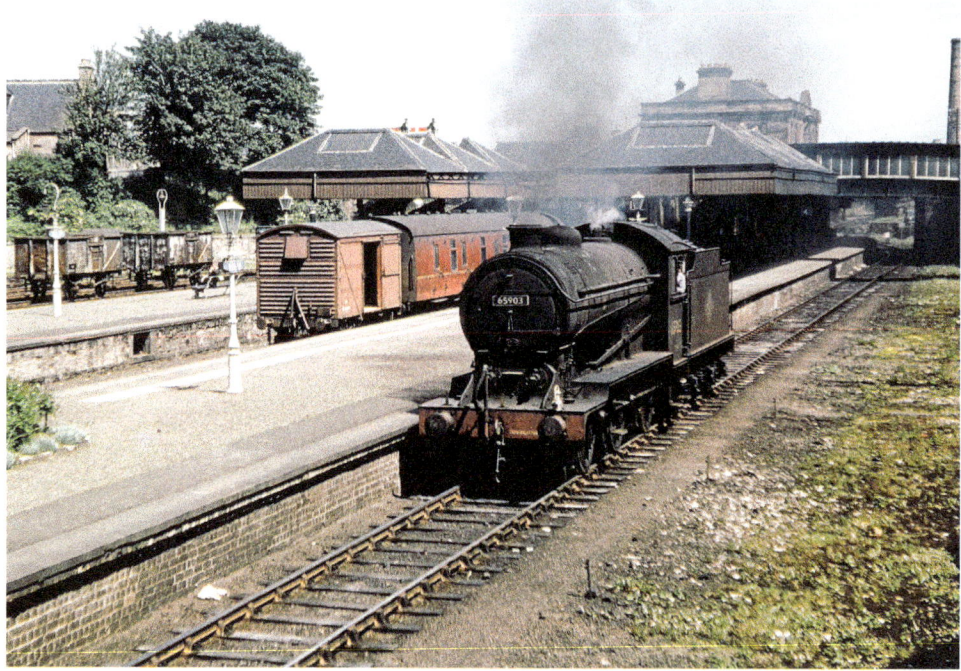

A short, light engine movement for Class J38 No. 65903 through the platforms at Alloa on 29 June 1966. During the same year, while waiting at a bus stop, Ralph Baer, an inventor with Sanders Associates, wrote a four-page document which laid out the basic principles for creating a video game to be played on a television: the beginning of a multi-billion pound industry. (Michael Beaton)

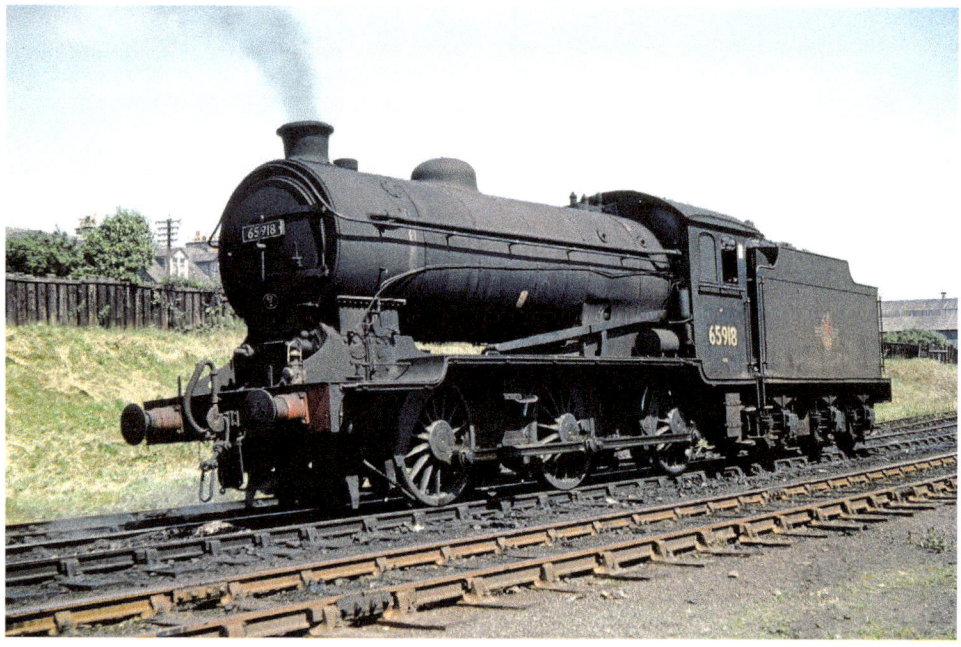

Another light engine movement through Alloa the same warm day in June 1966: another Class J38, No. 65918. (Michael Beaton)

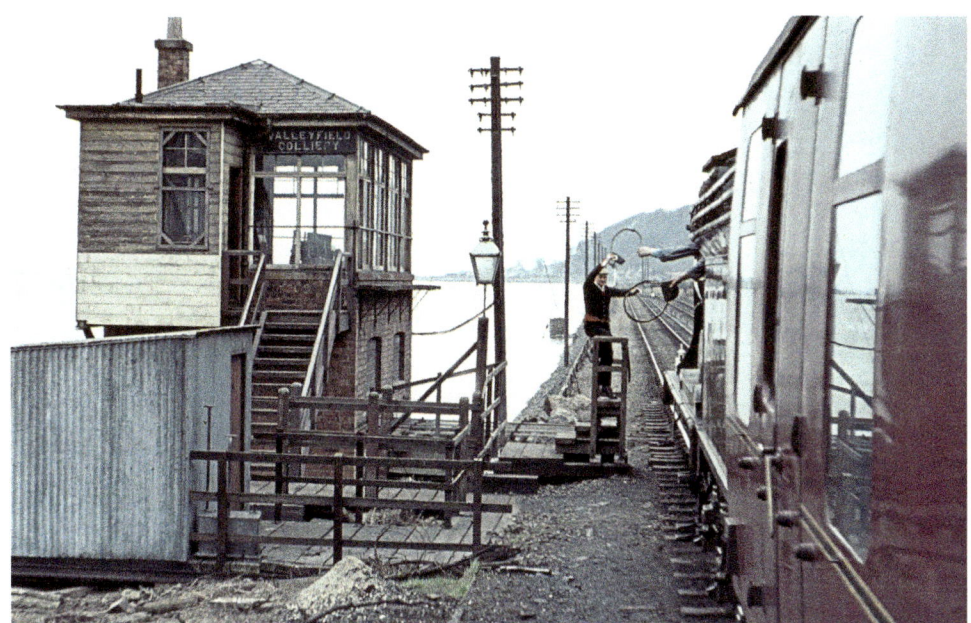

Above: An exchange of tokens at Valleyfield Colliery on 13 April 1963 as No. 256 *Glen Douglas* takes a jointly organised Stephenson Locomotive Society and Branch Line Society Scottish Rambler No. 2 rail tour forward. (Richard Icke)

Right: On 22 August 1966 Class J37 No. 64618 bangs away from Dysart with coal from Dubby Colliery after a rainstorm. (Jerry Beddows)

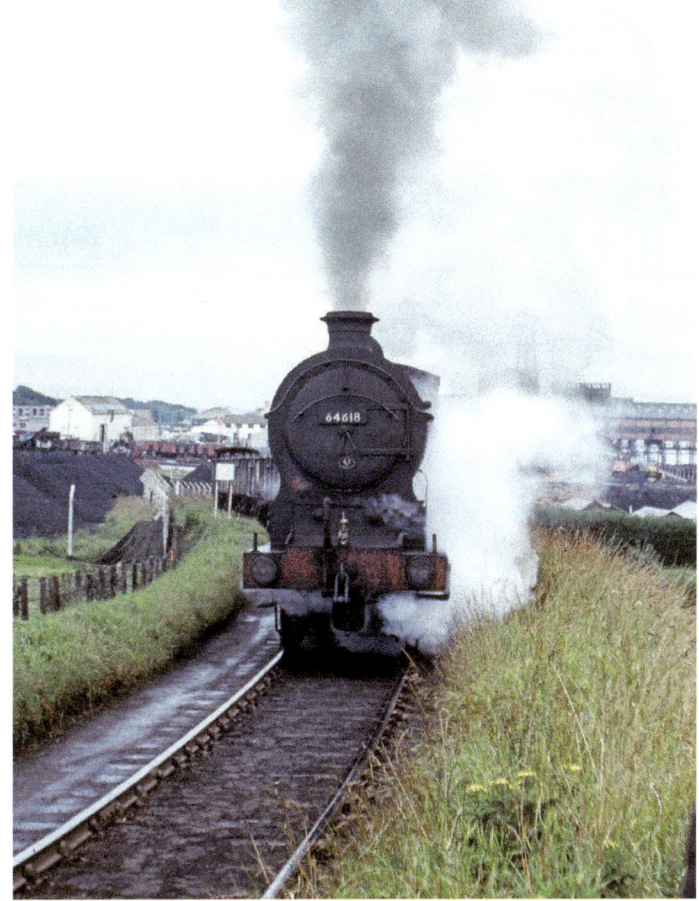

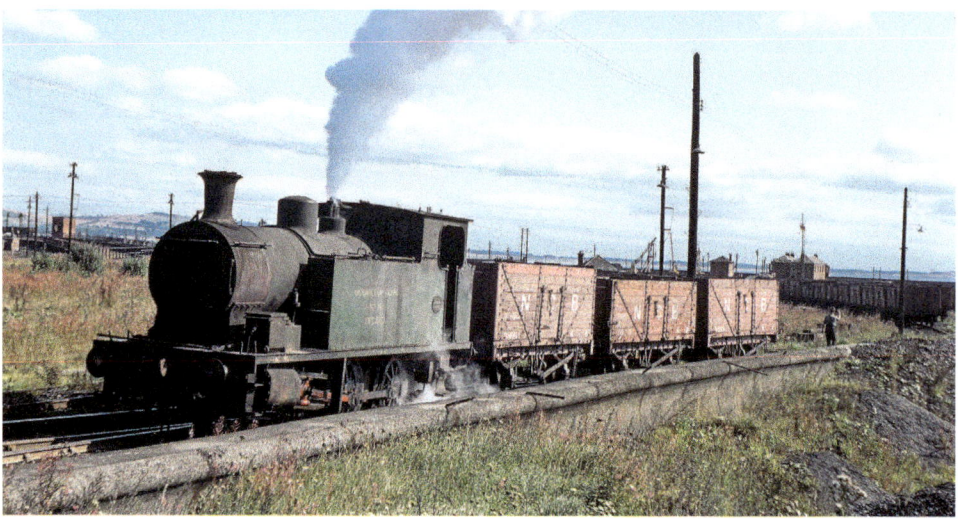

Steam could be found in isolated pockets until the end of the decade in Scotland. One of these was the Weymss Private Railway serving Methil Docks, where a visit in August 1969 showed the NCB's 10 and WPR 15 both in action. (Both Jerry Beddows)

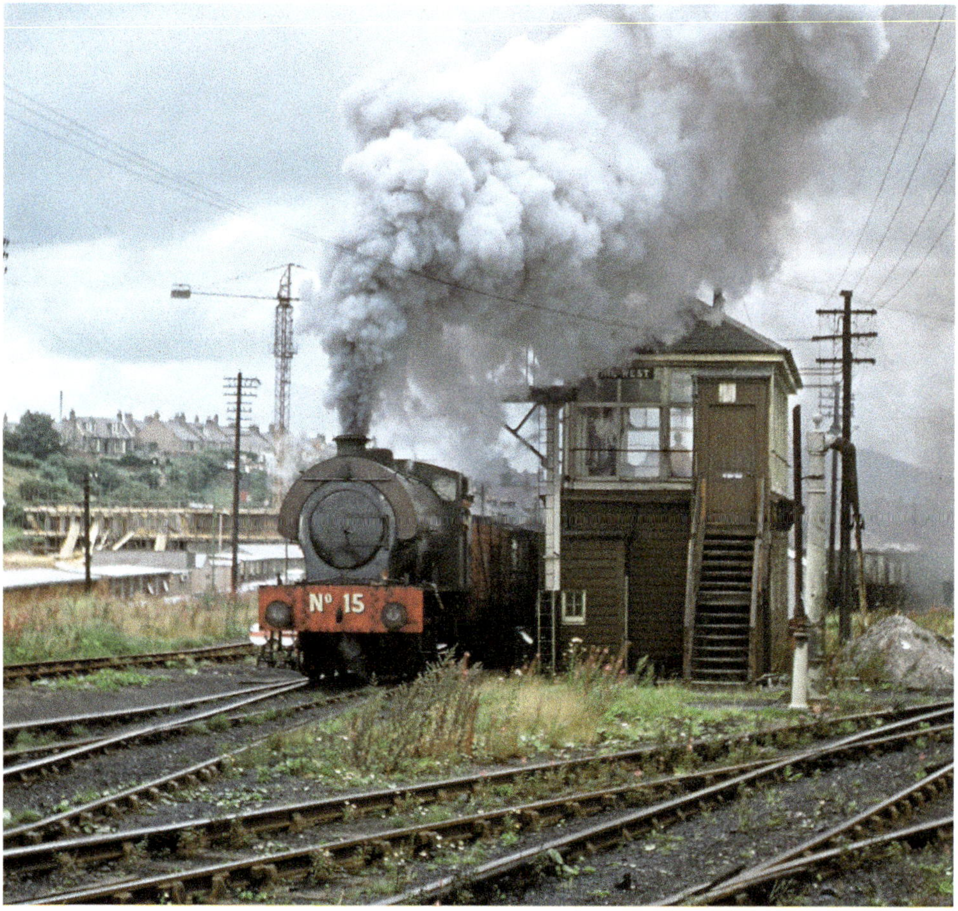

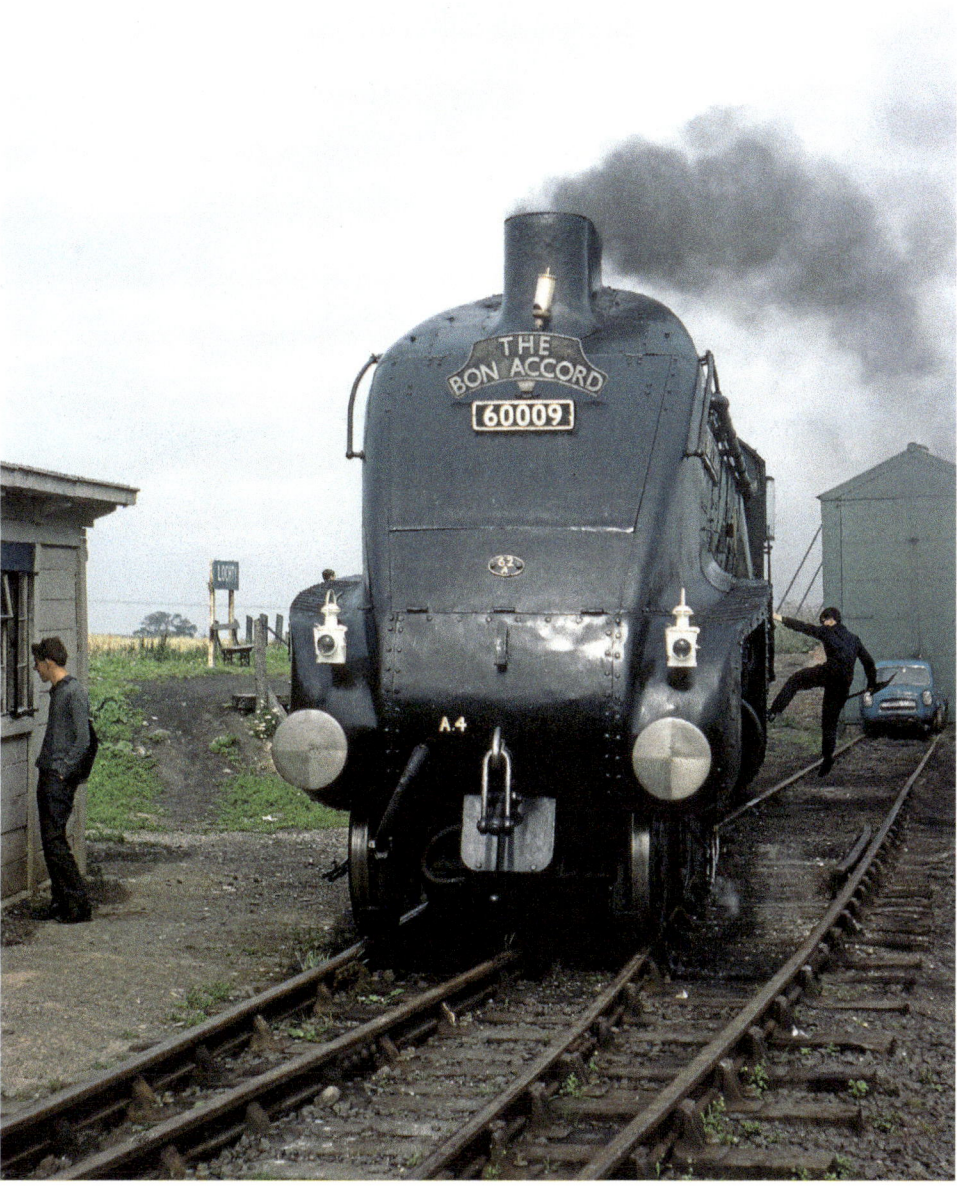

The Lochty Private Railway Company was formed in 1966 by John Cameron, with himself and Mrs Cameron as directors and friends as shareholders. It was at this time that the full significance of his newly acquired Lochty Farm occurred to John Cameron, as across its land ran the trackbed of the last 3/4 mile of the former East Fife Central Railway, a line which was built about 1898 to serve coal pits and agricultural interests in the area. Rumour has it that it was in fact built to keep the 'Caley' out of Fife!

By 1967 a large shed was built to house the preserved Class A4 No. 60009 *Union of South Africa* and 3/4 mile of track was relaid: one pair of points and one line leading into the shed, the other to the old loading bank, which was modified to serve as a platform. During the summer months on Sundays the A4 was steamed, running up and down the line for the benefit of the many photographers and public spectators.

The old Ford Popular converted to rail use looks interesting in the background of this view taken on 24 August 1969. (Jerry Beddows)

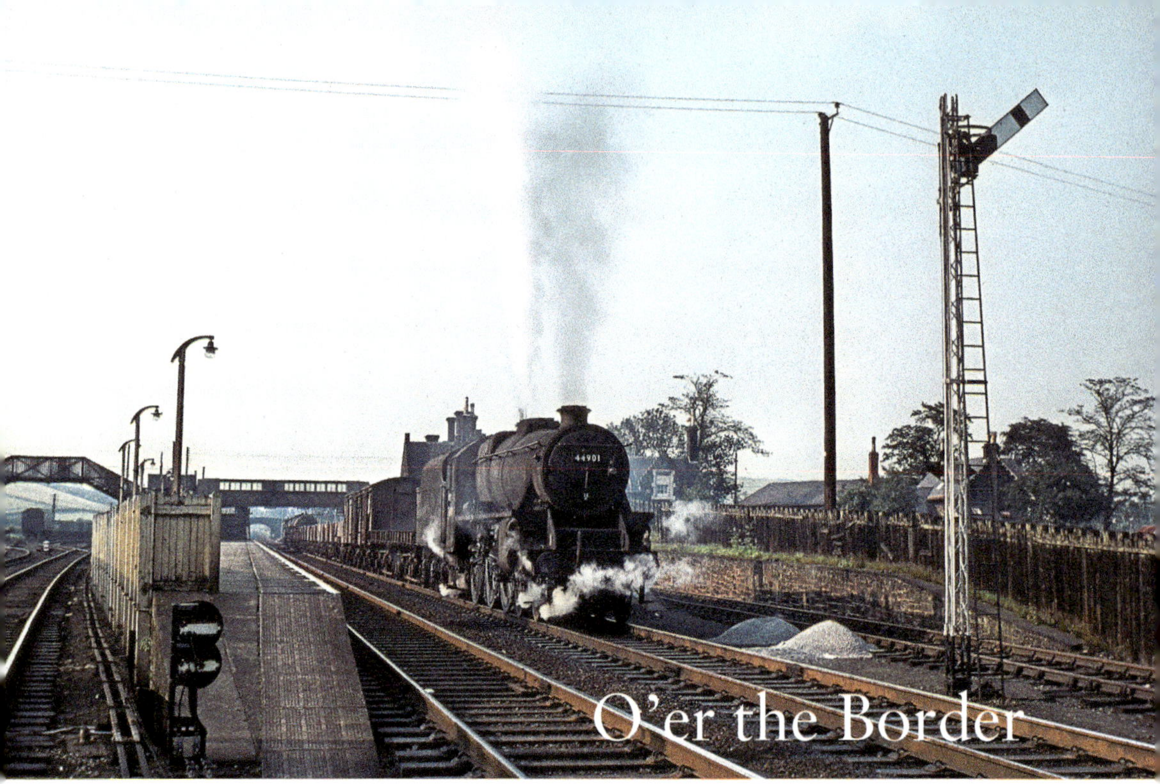

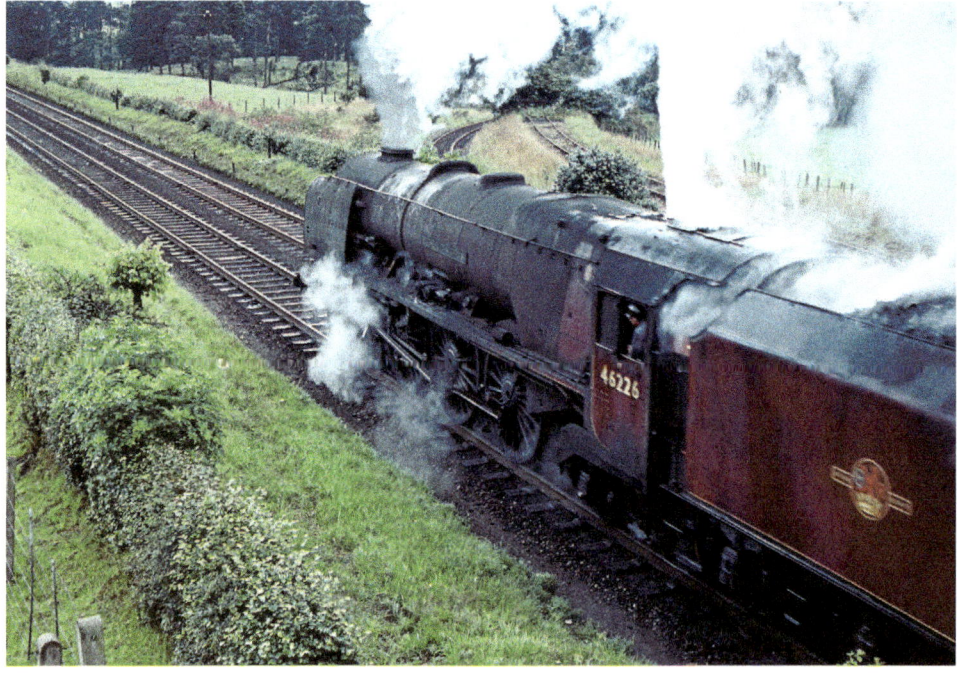

O'er the Border

A clear run through Beattock station for Black Five No. 44901 on 3 September 1964. In the news the following day was the opening of the new Forth Road Bridge by Her Majesty Queen Elizabeth II. (Strathwood Library Collection)

The full steam fury of No. 46226 *Duchess of Norfolk* is unleashed while departing north from Beattock in 1960. (Strathwood Library Collection)

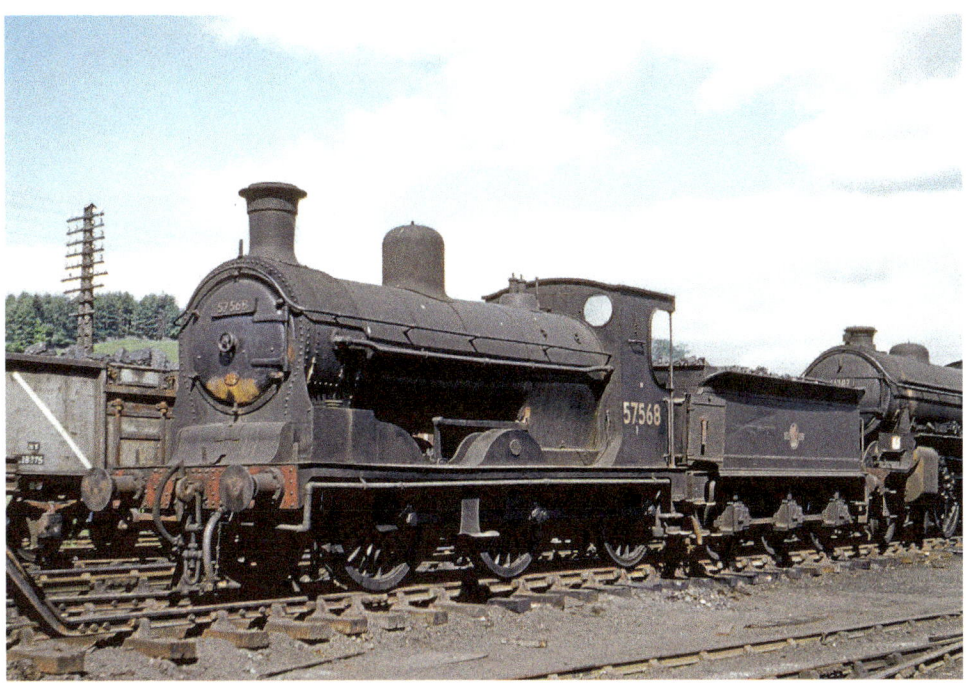

Meanwhile, on 10 June 1962 all is quiet and peaceful in the sunshine at 68D (Beattock shed) with McIntosh Class 3F No. 57568 standing idle. A few weeks later on 8 July the shed code would be changed to become 65F, which it remained until closure in 1967. (Frank Hornby)

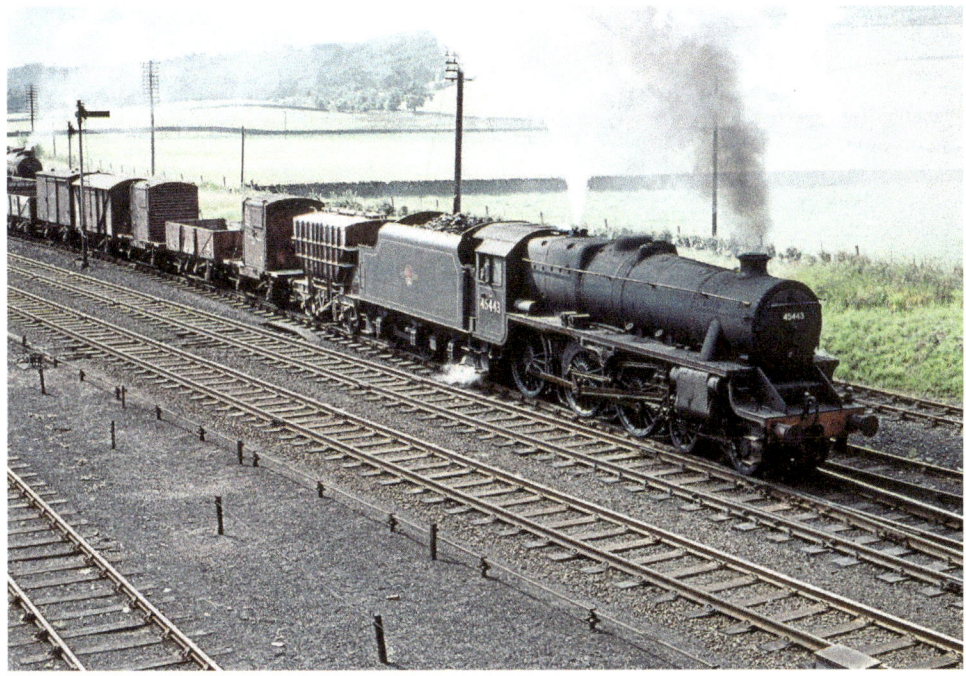

Black Five No. 45443 moves its goods working away from Beattock's once-busy yard in 1960. (Strathwood Library Collection)

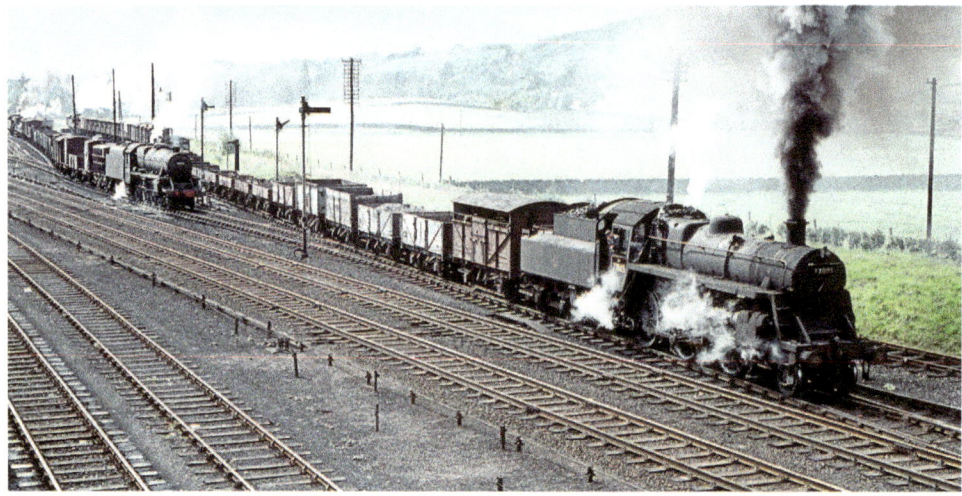

Getting away on the same day in 1960 before No. 45443 in the background was Standard 3MT No. 77005. Released the same year was the movie *The Magnificent Seven*. This epic Western was a remake of Akira Kurosawa's *Seven Samurai*. Swap seventeenth-century Japan for nineteenth-century Mexico and pick cinema's most sinister baldy to lead some of the decade's top male leads and you've got a sure fire hit! Steve McQueen, James Coburn, Charles Bronson, and Robert Vaughan were amongst the motley crew, led by Yul Brynner as the lead. (Strathwood Library Collection)

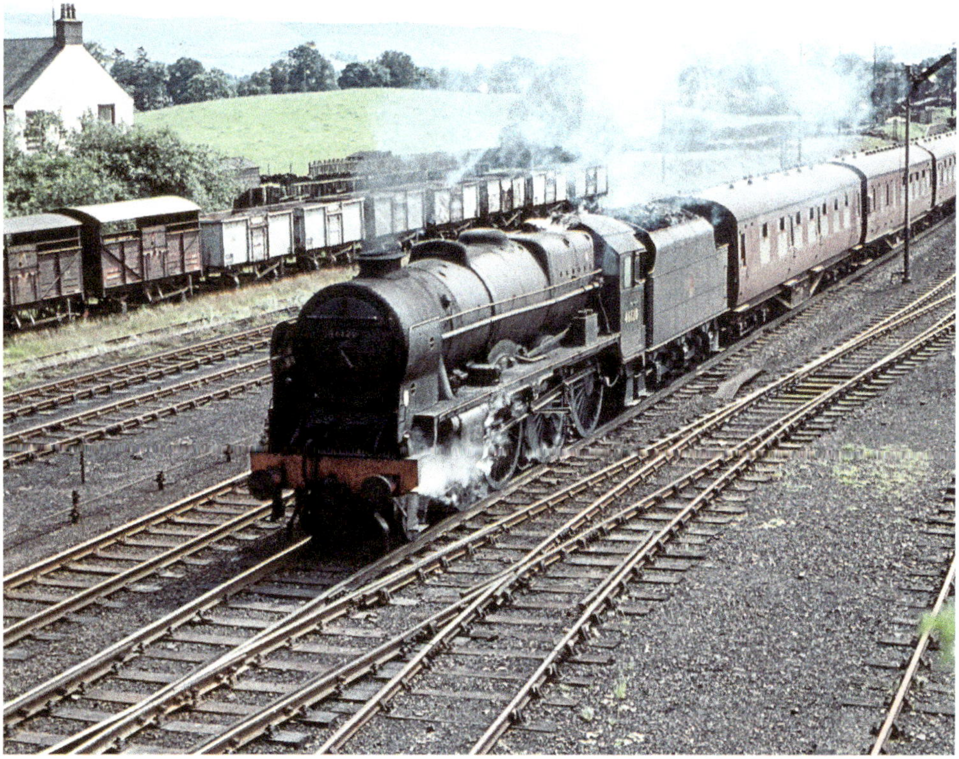

Also heading north in 1960 was Royal Scot No. 46120 *Royal Inniskilling Fusilier*, one of the North British-built batch from 1927. (Strathwood Library Collection)

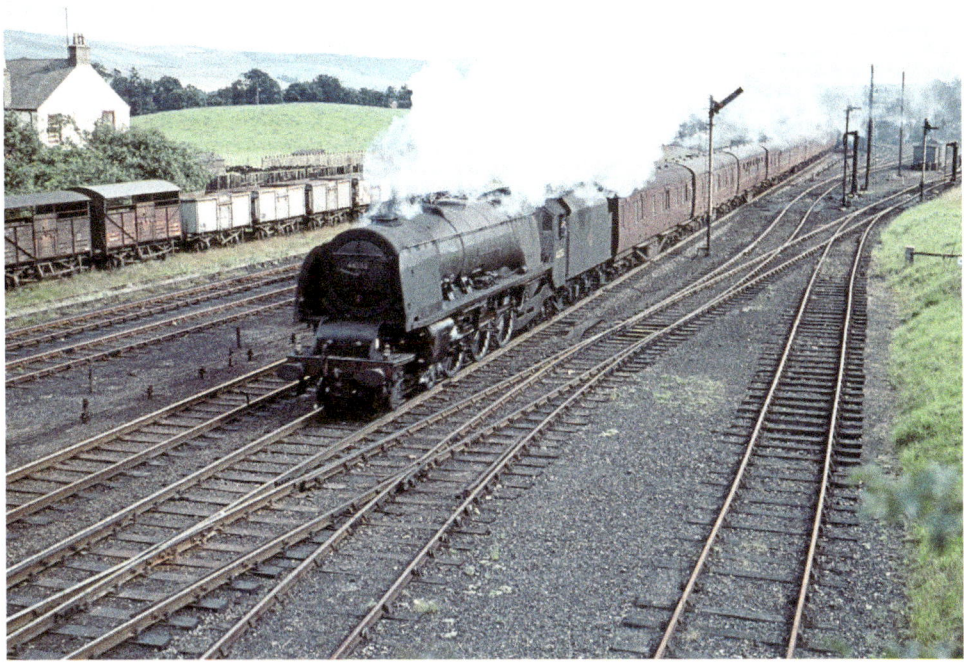

Later the same afternoon, the driver of No. 46253 *City of St Albans* was in no mood to be stopping to pick up a banker. (Strathwood Library Collection)

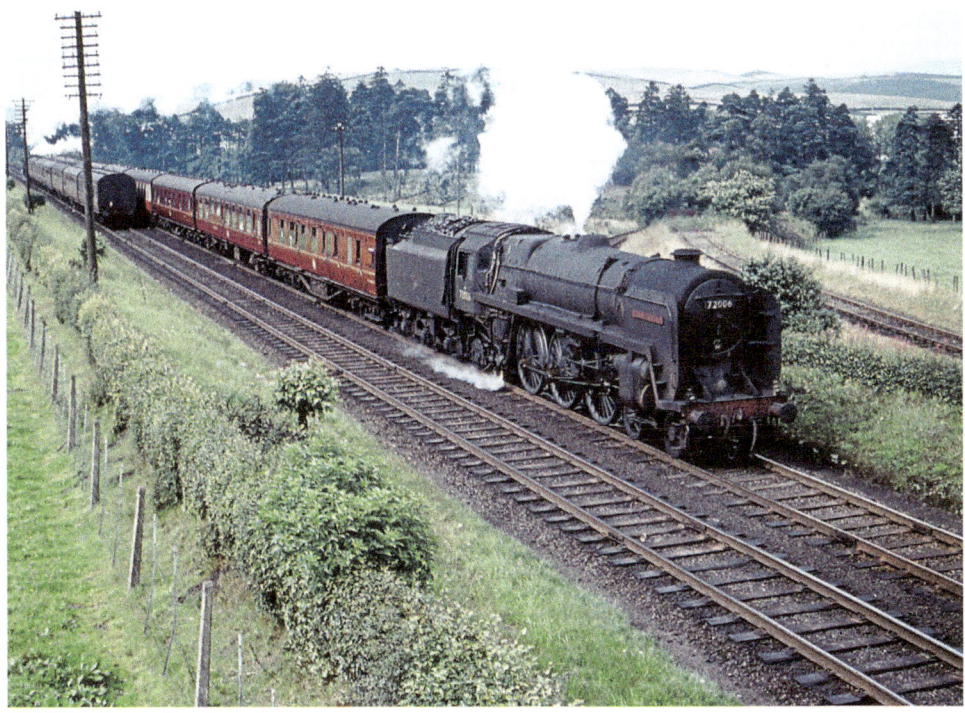

A down train heads north as No. 72006 *Clan Mackenzie* arrives on the up line for a stop at Beattock, again in 1960. (Strathwood Library Collection)

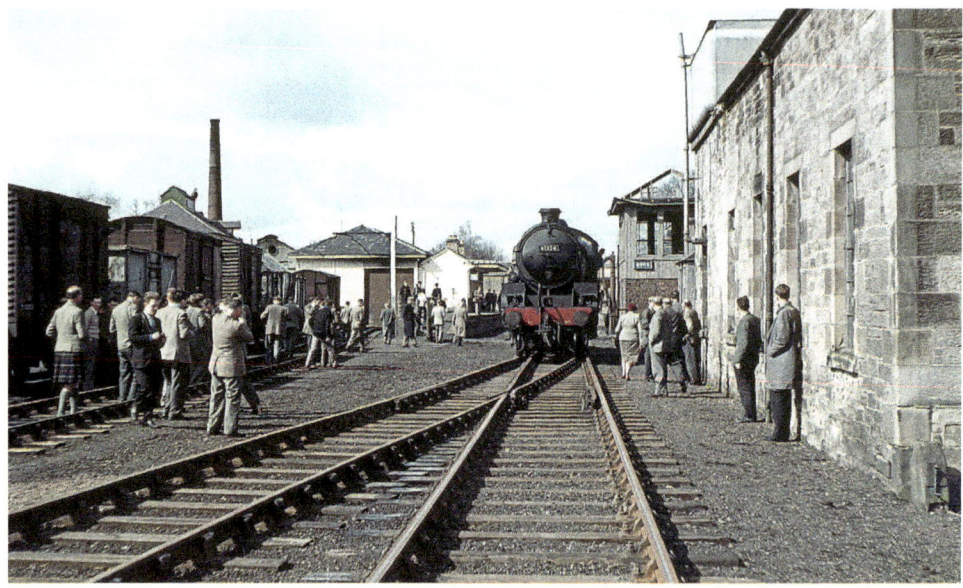

As part of the epic Scottish Rambler No. 2 excursion in 1963, Class B1 No. 61324 worked various legs of the four-day tour including one to Duns on the morning of 14 April. This was a through station on the former North British Railway route from Reston on the East Coast Main Line to St Boswells, which closed to passengers in 1951. (Richard Icke)

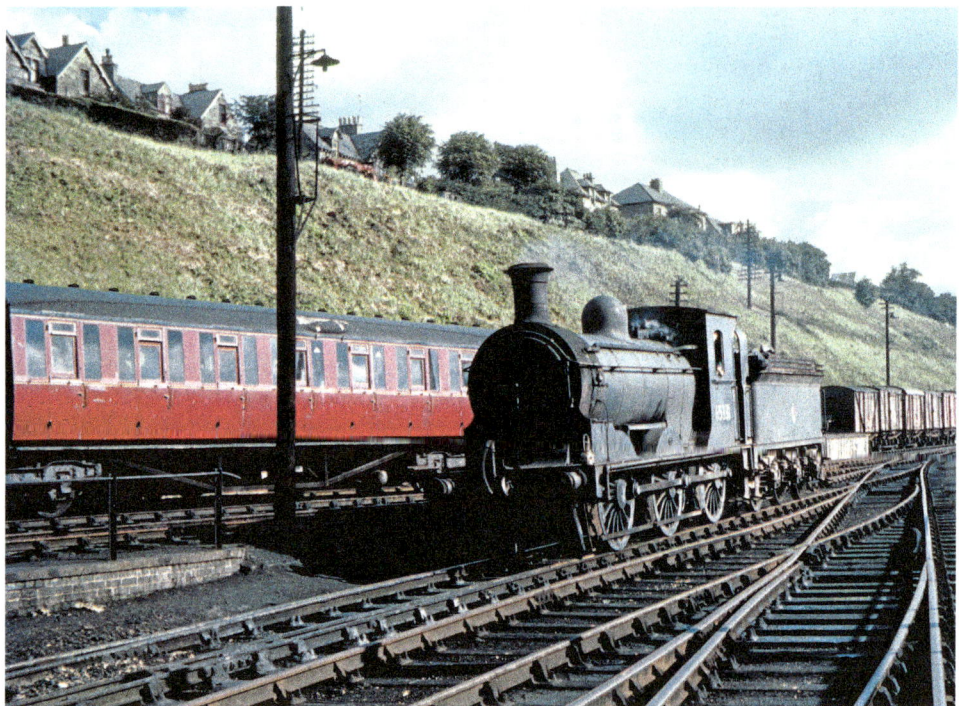

Heading south along the Waverley Route from St Boswells was Hawick, which would lose its rail connections in 1969. However, at the start of the decade in 1960 things looked much rosier when Class J36 No. 65331 was making its way on to the shed. (Stuart R. Harris)

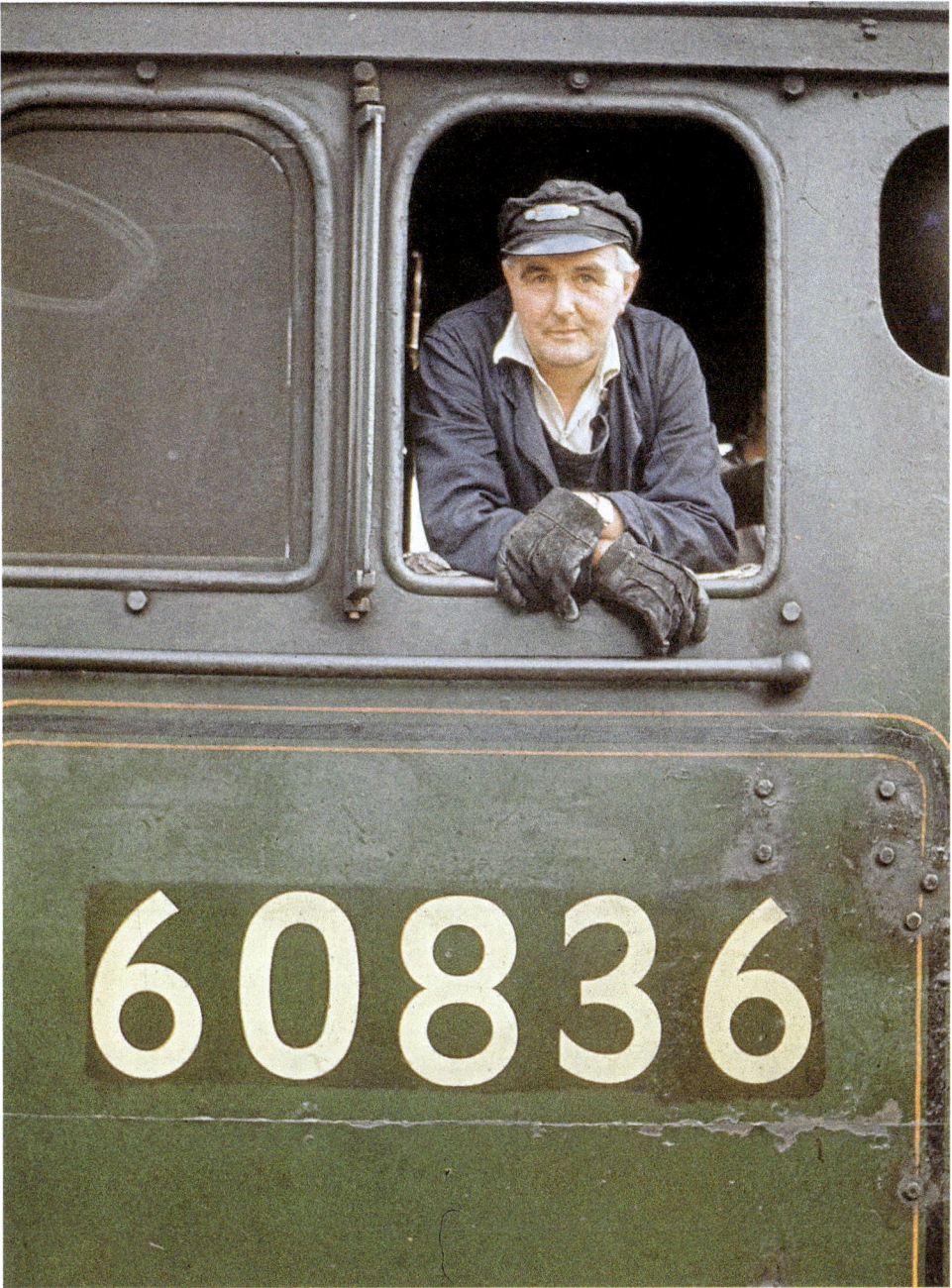

Over 3 and 4 September 1966 The South and West Railway Society ran their Granite City from Euston to Aberdeen via the Waverley Route and back the next day down the East Coast Main Line to Kings Cross. One of the crew on board Class V2 No. 60836, which covered the leg from Carlisle to Edinburgh Waverley, rests during the stop at Hawick in the afternoon of 3 September 1966. New in 1966 was the game Twister; was this the ideal free love hippy game where you could entangle yourself with as many other people as humanly possible, all in the name of good clean fun? When Milton Bradley first released the game, some argued it was like selling 'sex in a box'. But perhaps that's why it became a household name. (Late Alan Marriott/ Strathwood Library Collection)

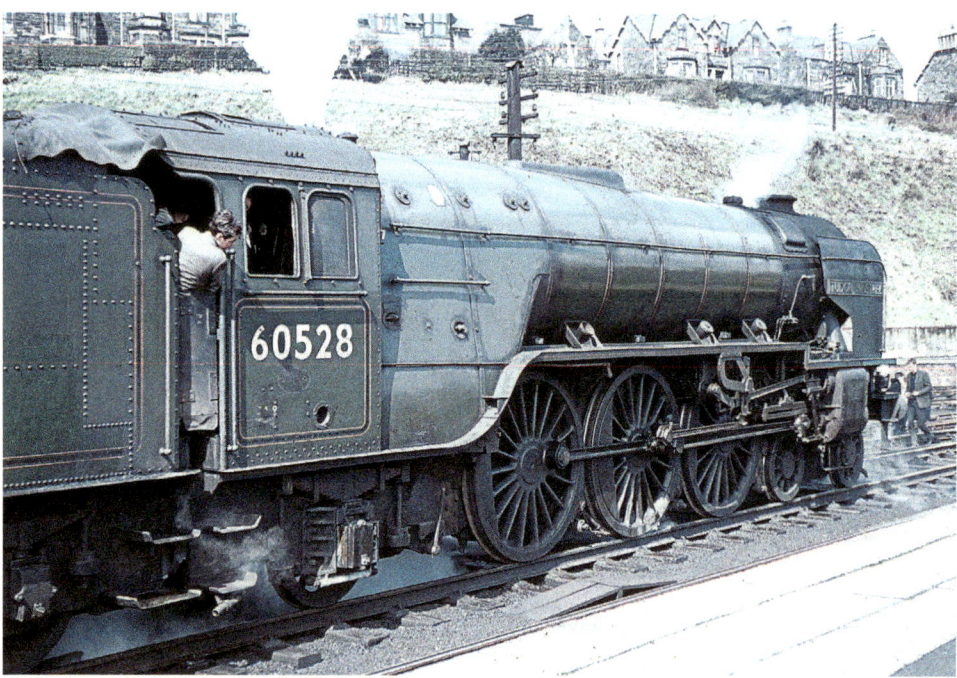

A number of specials ran over the lamented Waverley Route during the sixties including this one on 23 April 1966, halted at Hawick behind Class A 2 No. 60528 *Tudor Minstrel*. (Strathwood Library Collection)

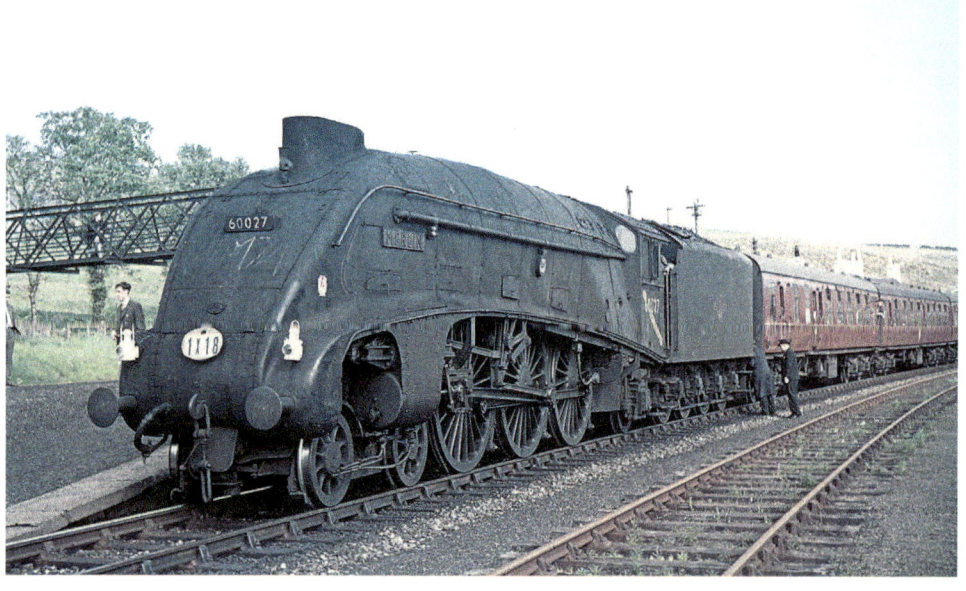

Another traversed the route on 5 June 1965, with a very scruffy No. 60027 *Merlin* paused for photographs at Riccarton Junction. The A4 was a hastily called upon replacement for No. 60052 *Prince Palatine*, which was well turned out for the day but failed with a hot box at Carlisle, leaving the Streak to take the train north over the Waverley Route. (Peter Coton)

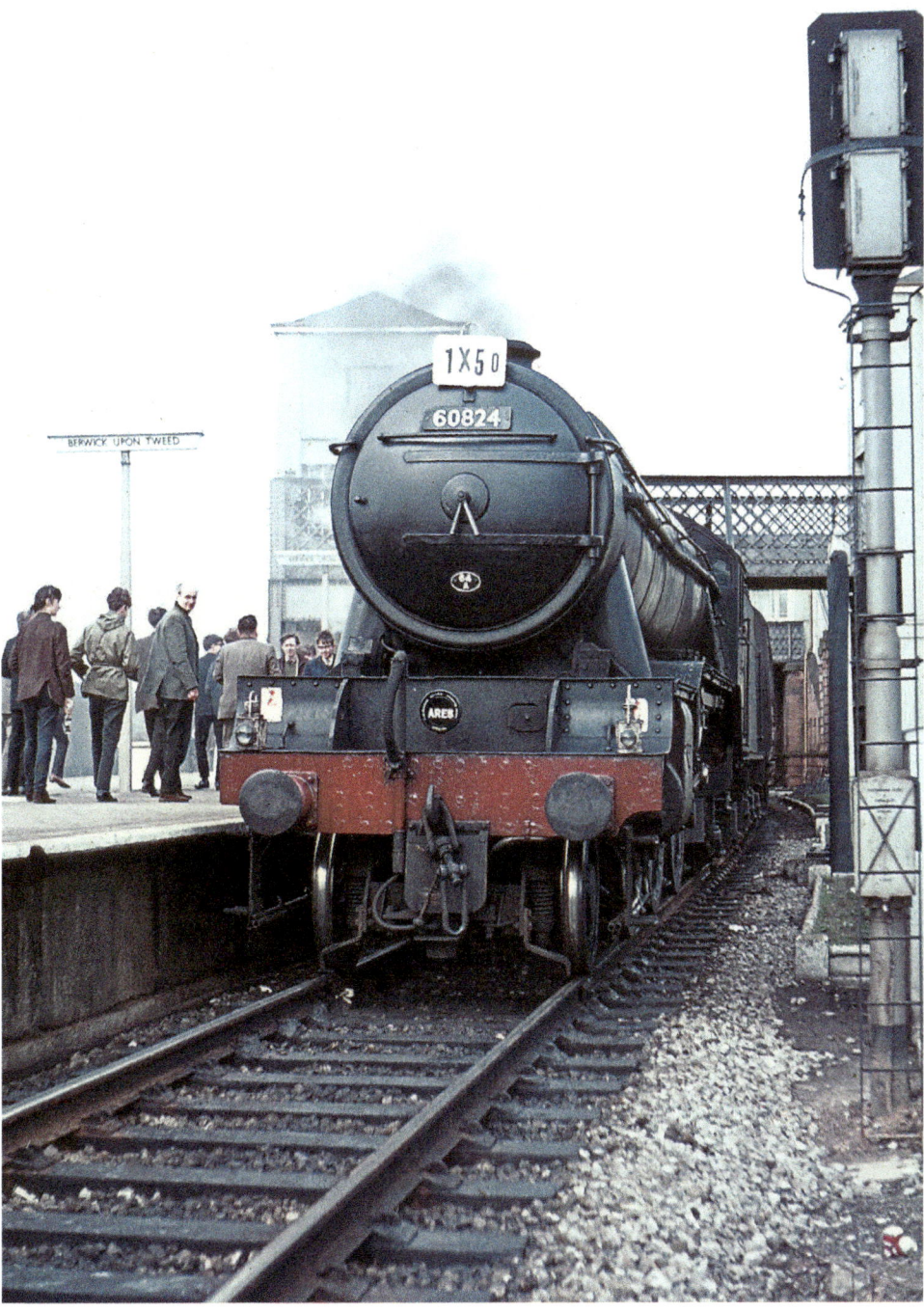

Back to 23 April 1966 and No. 60824 has just taken over from fellow V2 No. 60836 for the run down to York from Berwick-upon-Tweed, where it will give over in turn to No. 45565 *Victoria* for the return to Manchester Victoria. The 1966 Scottish Cup Final would be contested between Celtic and Rangers in front of 126,552 people for a 0-0 draw on this day. Replayed four days later before 98,202 Glaswegians, Rangers came away with the spoils 1-0. (Strathwood Library Collection)

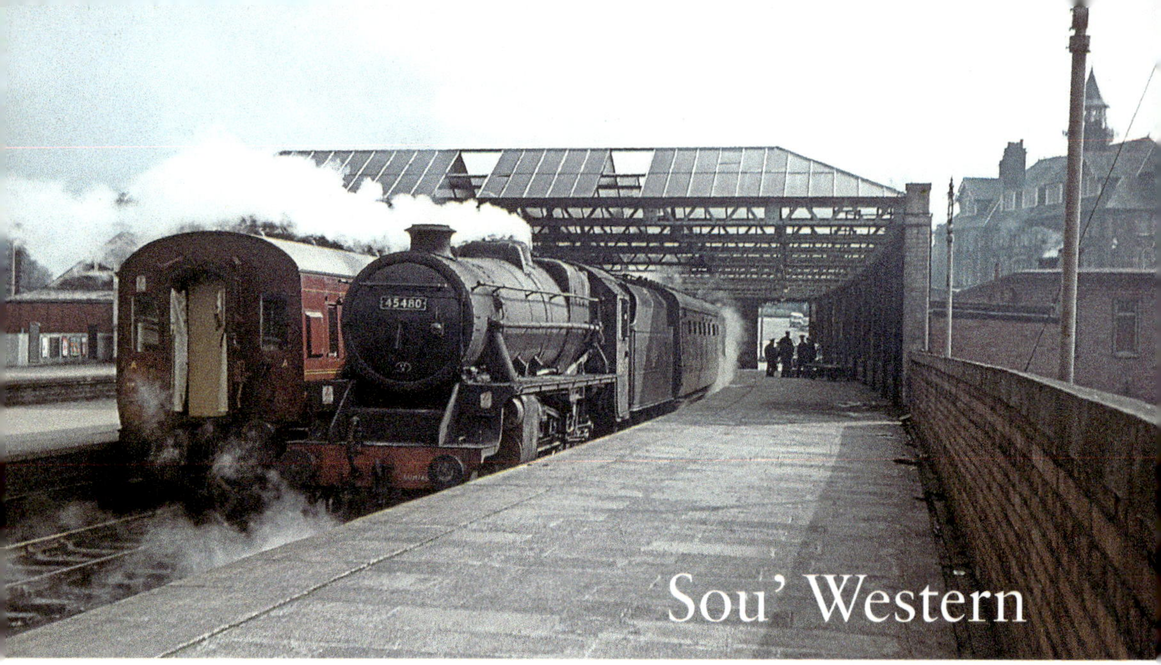

Sou' Western

There was still regular passenger traffic along the former Glasgow & South Western Railway's line from Dumfries to Stranraer during 1965. Waiting to leave for Kircudbright with the 2.50 p.m. departure from Dumfries on 27 March 1965 was Black Five No. 45480. This was exactly two years after the publication of the infamous Beeching Plan which went on to devastate railways across the mainland but particularly north of the border, isolating many large communities whose voices would not be heard in Westminster. (Late Roy Hamilton)

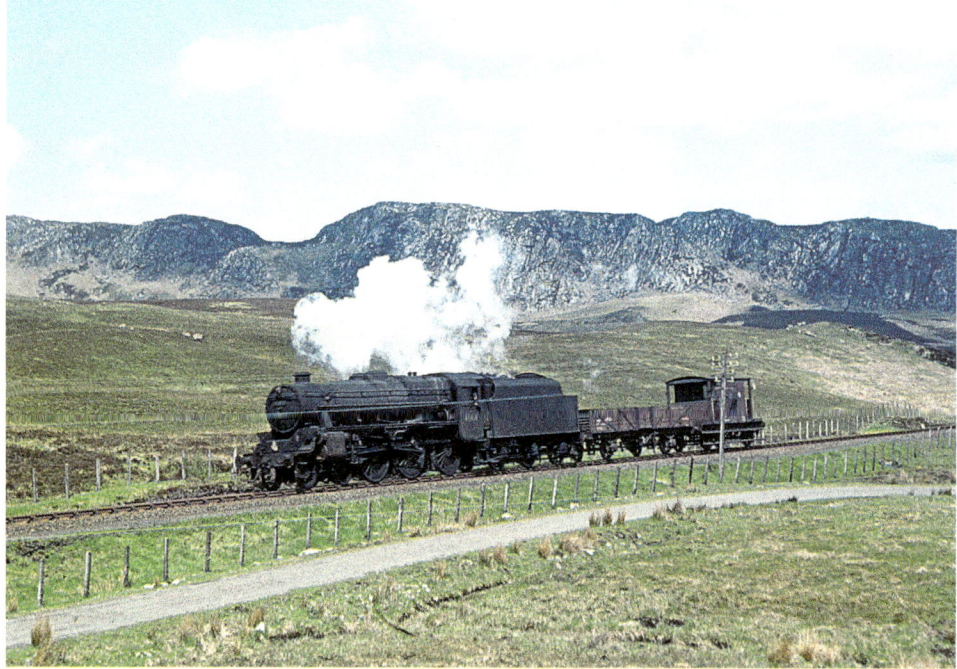

Some justification perhaps when we see, on 29 May 1965, Black Five No. 45471 with very little in tow near Gatehouse of Fleet, heading west towards the major port of Stranraer. The closure of this route would prove to be very short-sighted in following years judging by the volume of traffic forced to be taken by road from Stranraer heading to and from Northern Ireland in the following decades. (Late Roy Hamilton/Strathwood Library Collection)

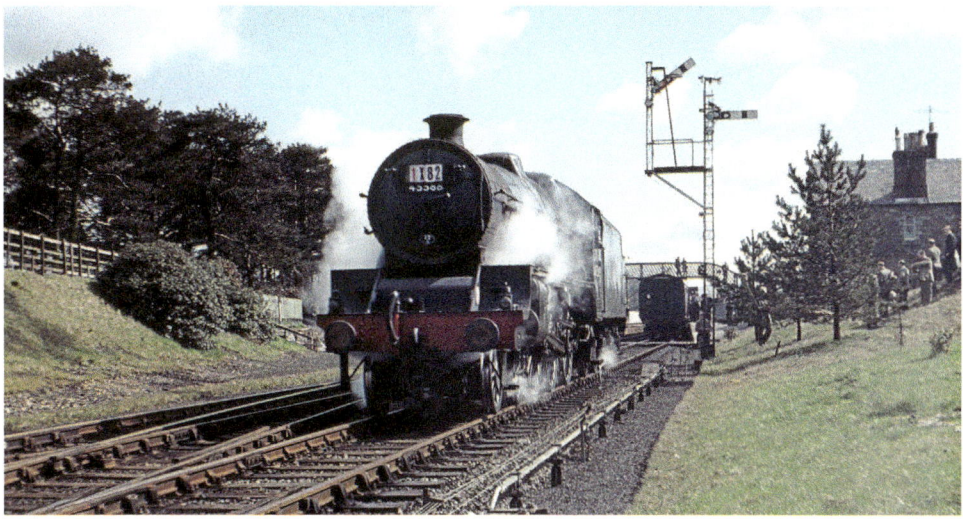

Back to the marathon Scottish Rambler No. 2 Railtour in April 1963 and Jubilee No. 45588 *Kashmir* was used for three legs of the tour on the fourth day. This included the run from Carlisle to Castle Douglas, where it came off for Standard 4MT No. 80023 to take the participants down the branch to Kircudbright and back. (Richard Icke)

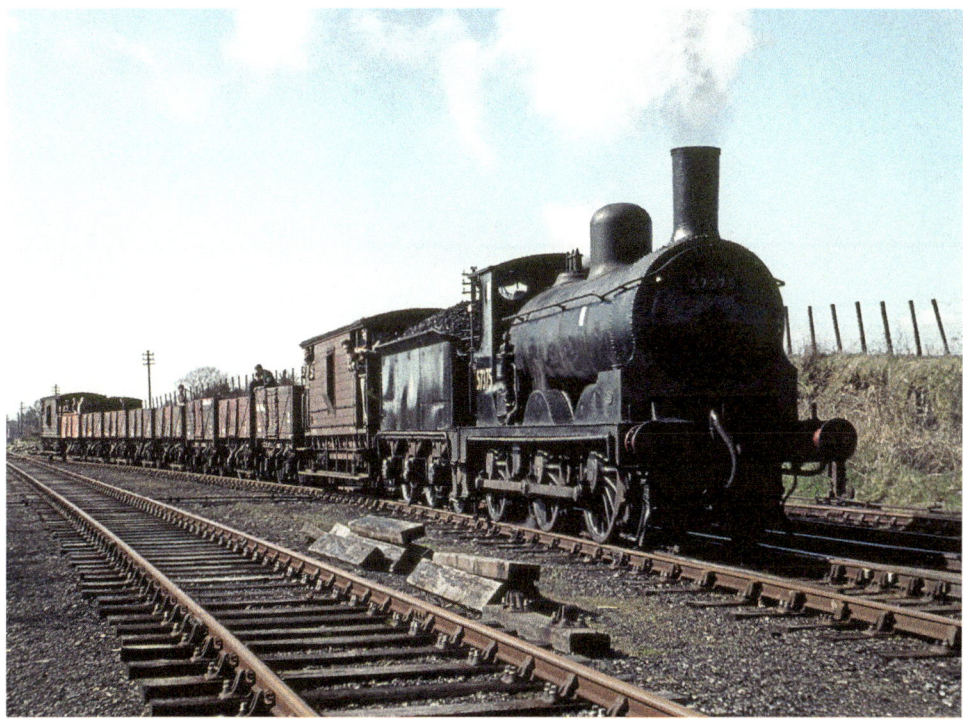

Afterwards the Jubilee was put back on to the train again at Castle Douglas to take the stock forward to Newton Stewart, which was the junction for the branches to Whithorn and Garlieston. The nature of the track work precluded the use of coaching stock by this date, so the regular engine for the branches, then a Drummond 2F, was cleaned up and assembled with a rake of open wagons, hopefully swept out, to take the enthusiasts along the branches, where we see the stock during a stop at Millisle. (Richard Icke)

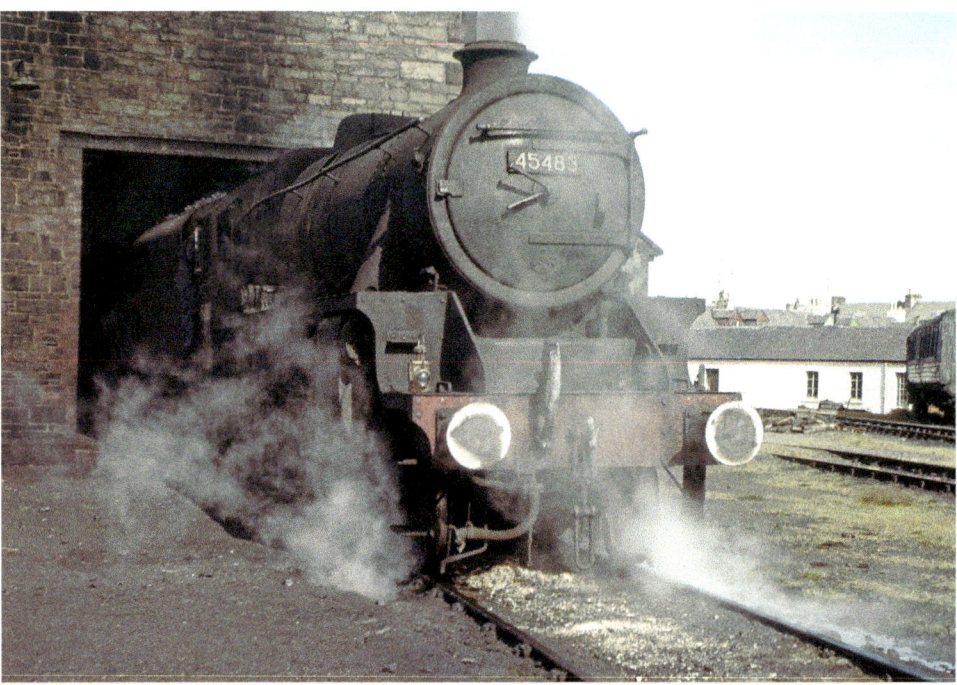

After the route to Stranraer from Dumfries closed in 1965 the town was still served by the line from Ayr in the north, which continued to bring steam to the port until the shed became diesel only after 27 November 1967. The year before, on 24 July, Black Five No. 45483 was in residence at the small shed, coded 67F after 1962. (Strathwood Library Collection)

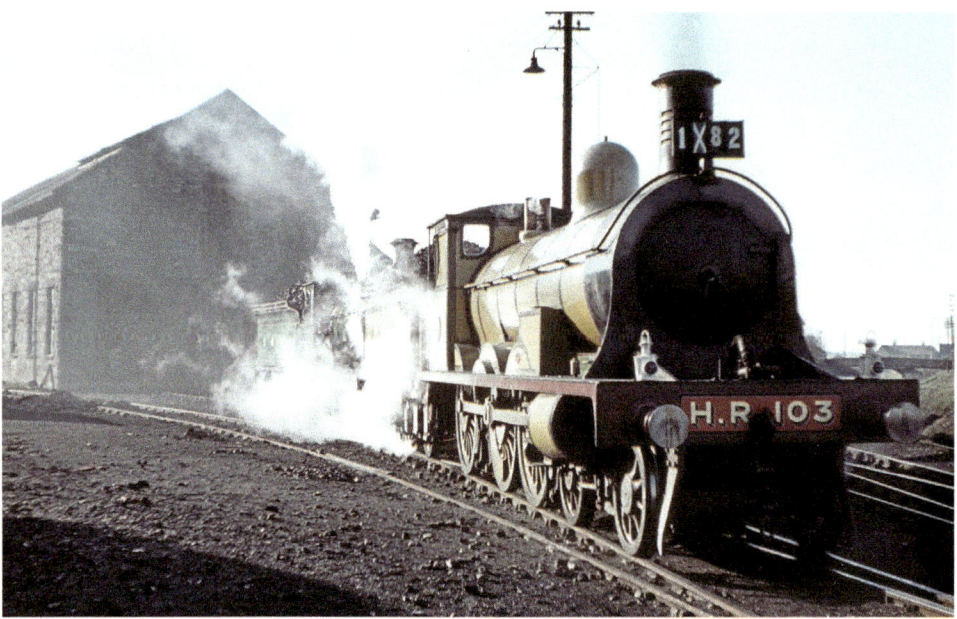

Returning to the Scottish Rambler No. 2 in April 1963 and the ex-Highland Railway 103 along with ex-Great North of Scotland Railway 49 *Gordon Highlander* would be mustered at Stranraer to take over from No. 45588 for the run along the Glasgow & South Western's tortuous route back to Glasgow St Enoch. (Richard Icke)

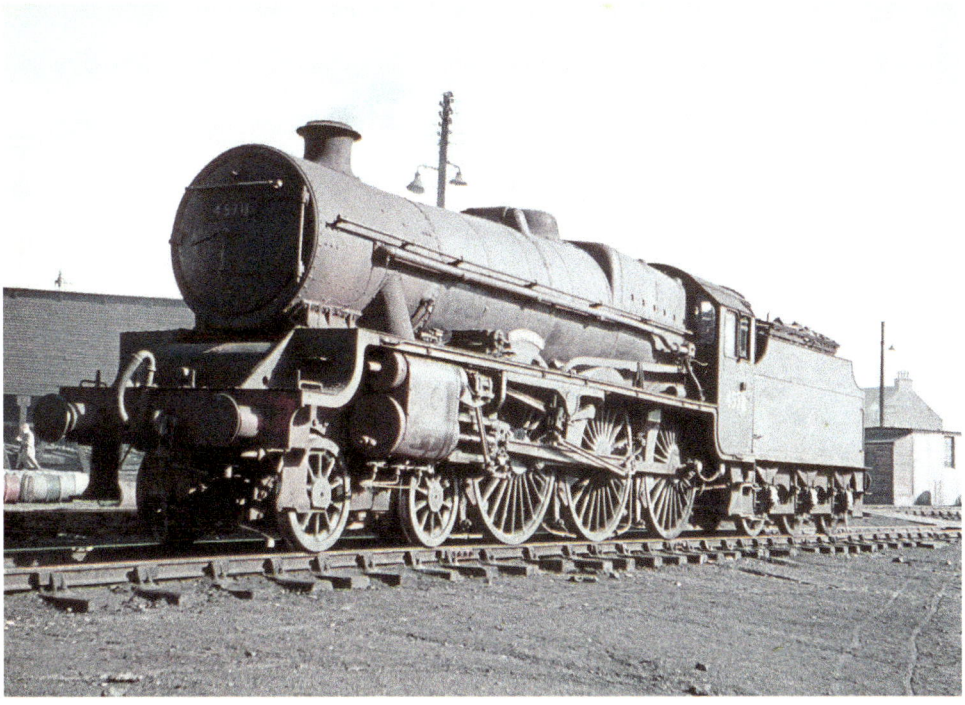

Several of the regular Jubilees along this route are virtually unrecorded in colour, including No. 45711 *Courageous*, seen on shed at Ayr in April 1961. (Late Vincent Heckford/Strathwood Library Collection)

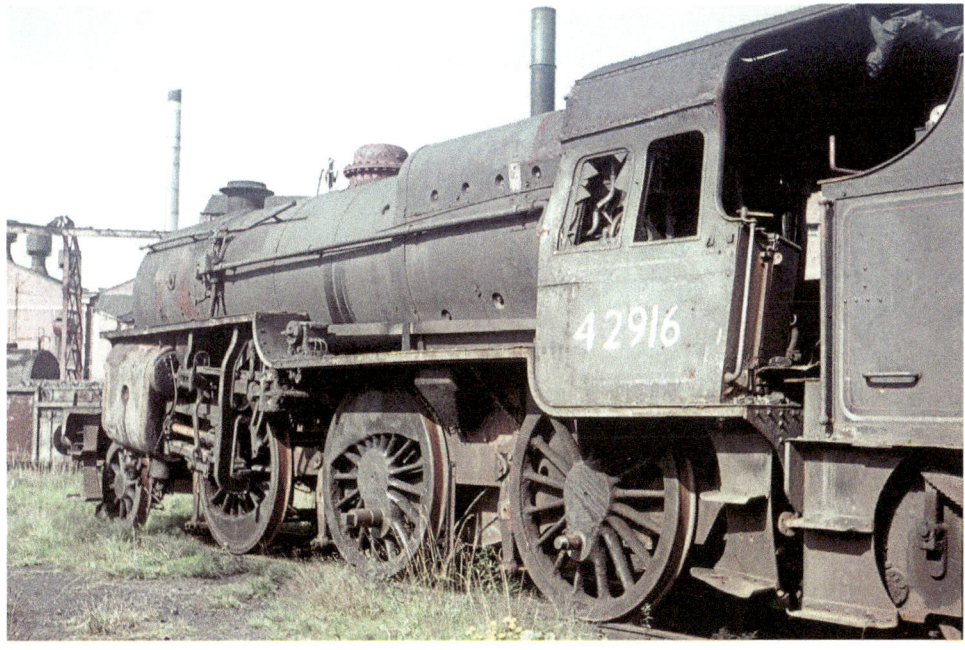

There is no future for Crab 42916 aside from the breakers when seen at Ayr on 2 August 1965. This long-term resident of Ayrshire would be sent to Motherwell Machinery & Scrap at Wishaw to be disposed of rather than making the shorter trip to the local breakers, West of Scotland Shipbreaking at Troon. (Dave Down)

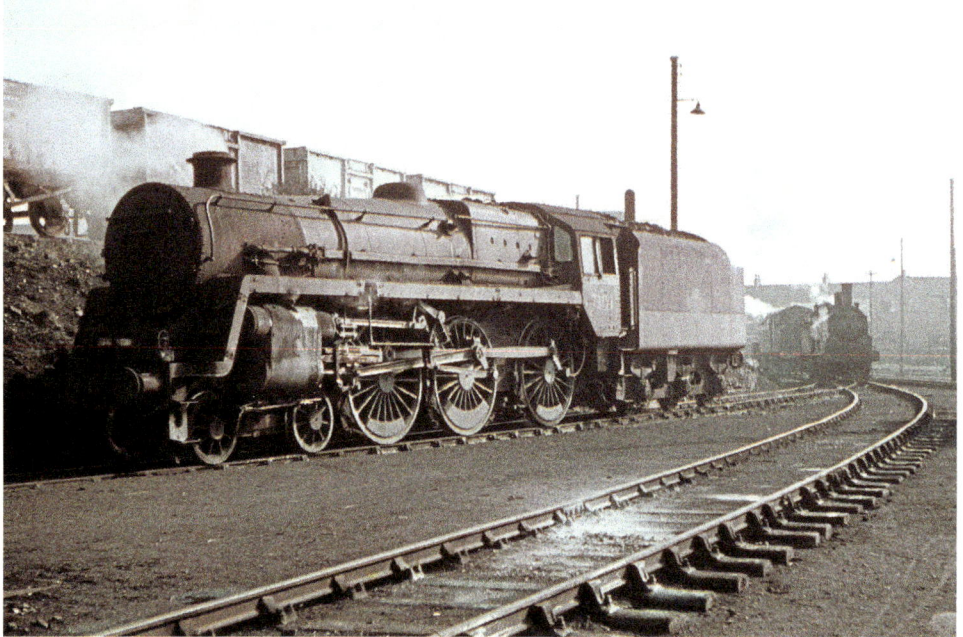

The arrival of a number of Standard designs to the routes to and from Ayr in the 1950s did not halt the arrival of diesels, in spite of some incredible performances by local crews, often described by the late Derek Cross, who lived in the area. Imposing on an old timer, Drummond 2F No. 57262, at Ayr in 1961 was Standard 5MT No. 73121. (Late Vicnent Heckford/Strathwood Library collection)

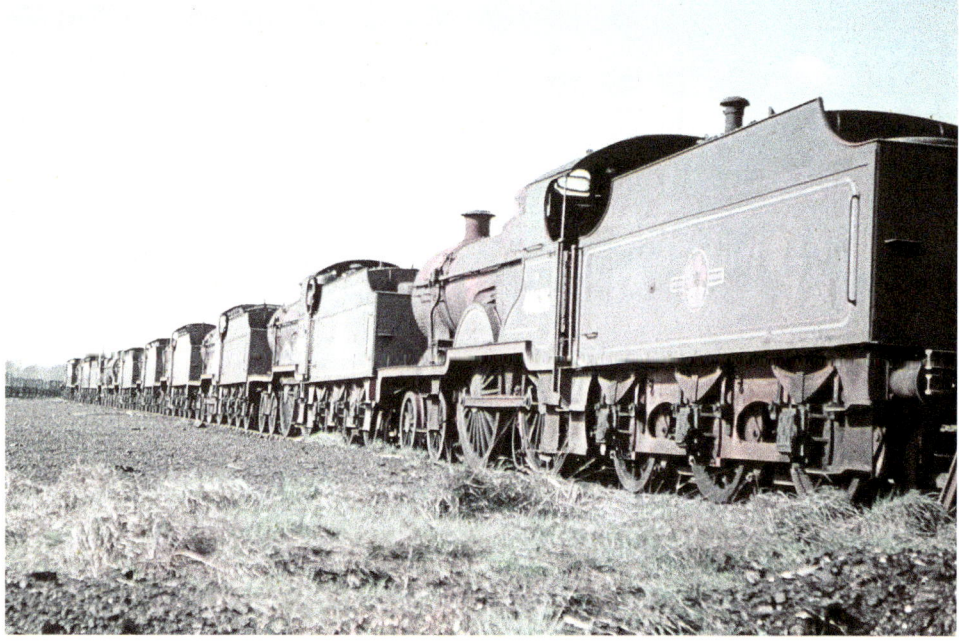

Another long line of redundant steam engines await their fates at Hurlford the same month with Nos 40626, 40599 and 40645 being noted. The nearby railway works at Kilmarnock had built up a reputation for disposing of a large number of engines in preceding years. (Late Vincent Heckford/Strathwood Library Collection)

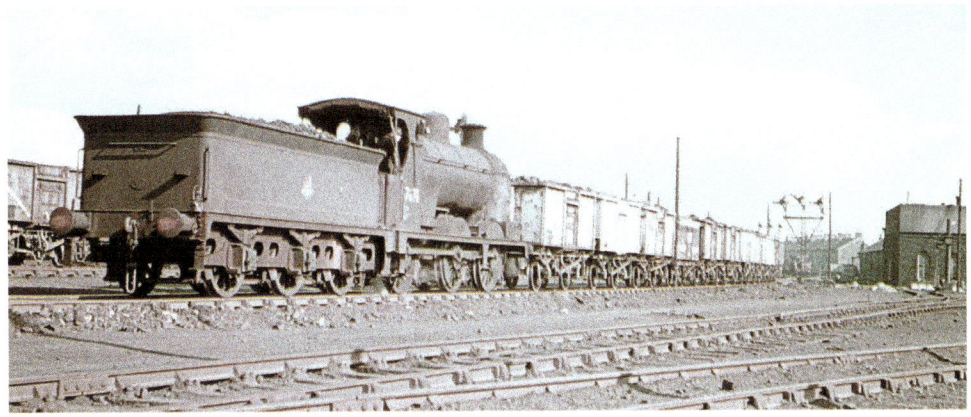

Moving on to Hurlford, we find one of Pickersgill's 3Fs, No. 57671, ambling past the shed with a long rake of trucks.

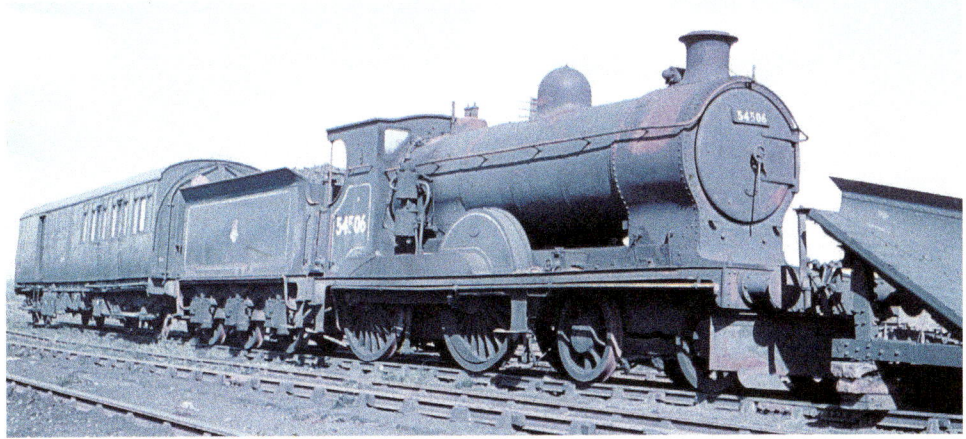

More signs of unwanted 4-4-0s at Ardrossan with another of Pickersgill's designs for the Caledonian Railway, with No. 54506 laid up.

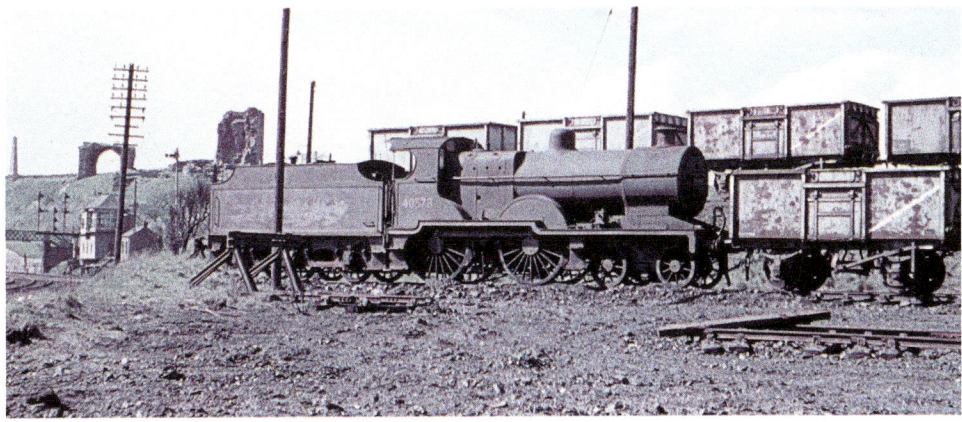

Also set aside at Ardrossan was No. 40578 from the LMS, built in 1928 at Derby, awaiting the chop in April 1961. (All: Late Vincent Heckford/Strathwood Library Collection)

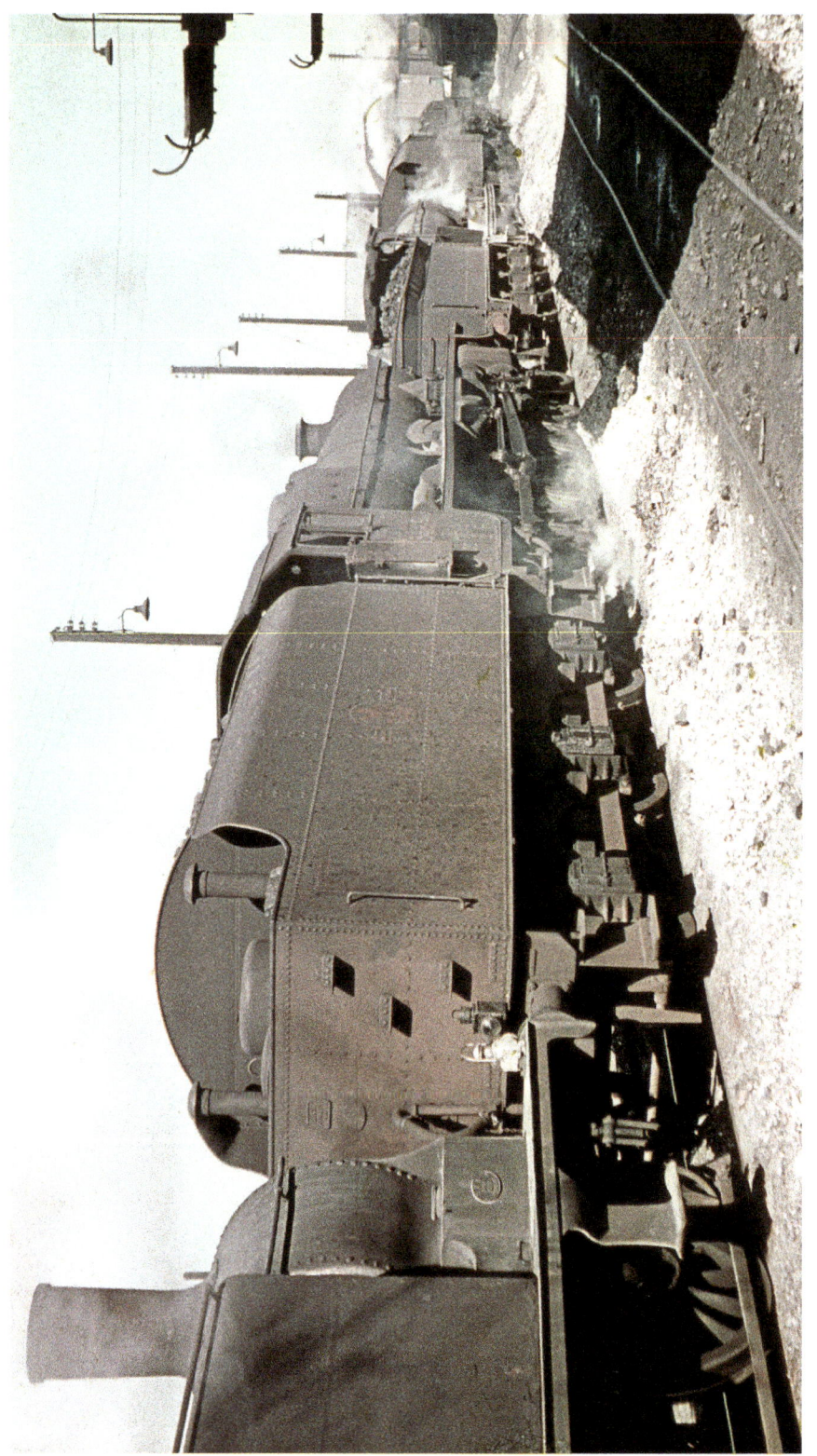

Another of Corkerhill's famed Jubilees, No. 45665 *Lord Rutherford of Nelson*, rests awhile at Ardrossan at Easter in 1961. It was set aside in June 1962 at Lugton and withdrawn officially in October that same year before making a final journey to Campbells of Shieldhall, who set to work with the torches in December 1963. (Late Vincent Heckford/Strathwood Library Collection)

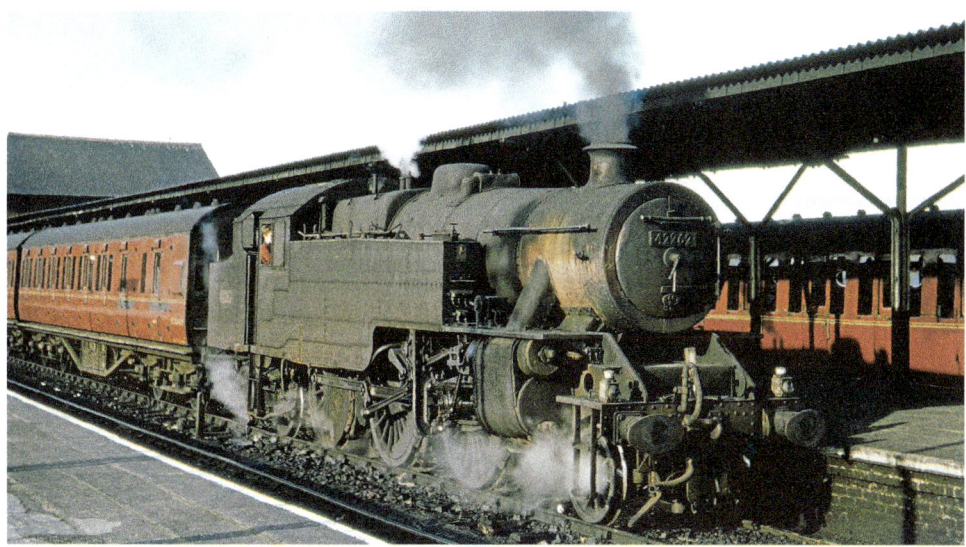

Waiting at the head of a local passenger set at Gorock in September 1964 is No. 42262, itself just days away from coming out of service. (Strathwood Library Collection)

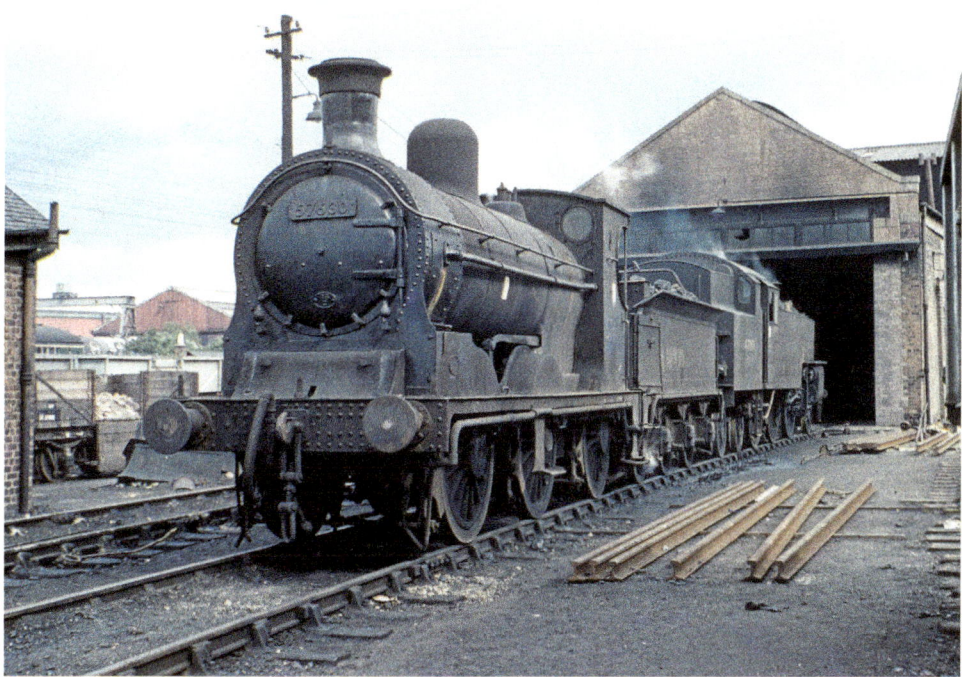

Hamilton would be given over to the maintenance of DMUs after the demise of steam on 10 November 1962. When this shot of Nos 57660 and 42165 was recorded in July 1962 the writing was firmly on the wall here. The first of the James Bond films, *Dr No*, starred little-known Scottish actor Sean Connery as the suave, yet – by modern standards – hopelessly politically incorrect, spy. Others rumoured to have been considered for the part included Christopher Lee, Roger Moore and David Niven. Moore was already committed to filming *The Saint*, but his chance would come again in the seventies. (Strathwood Library Collection)

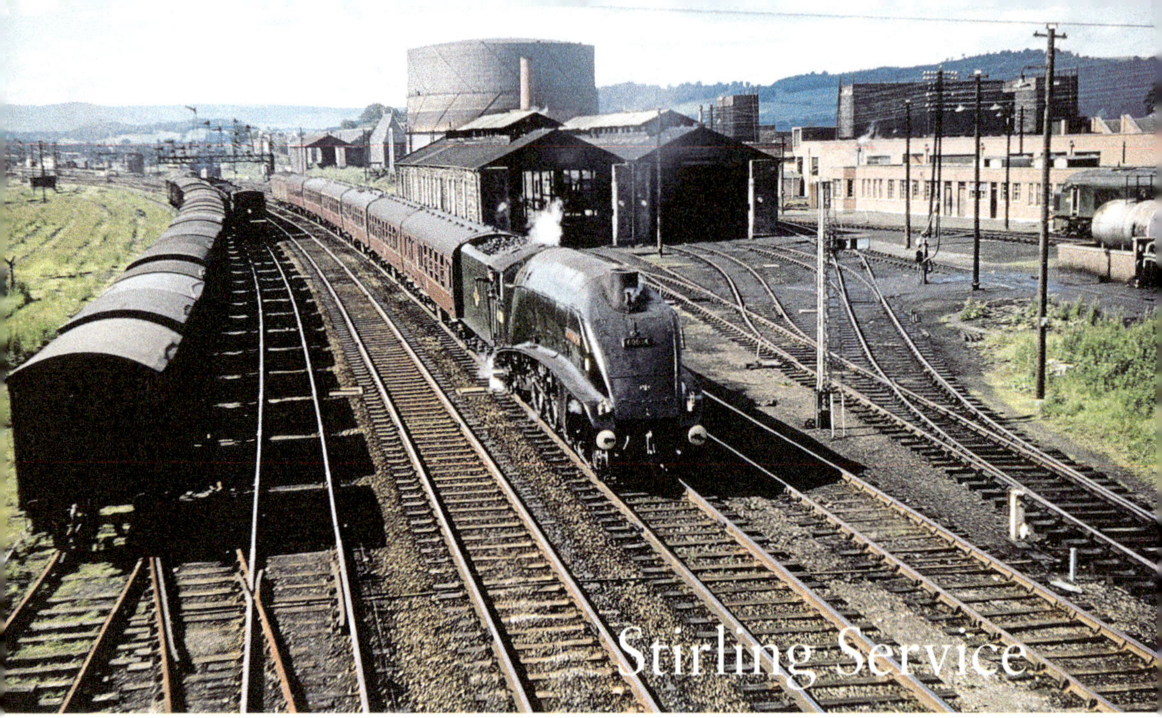

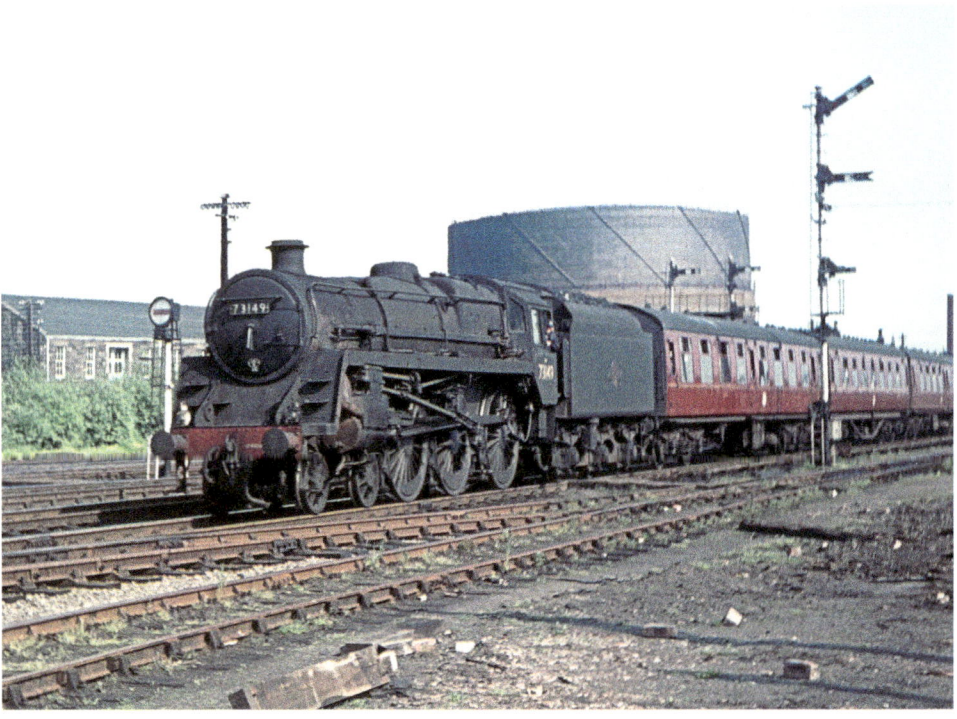

A lonesome Peak is about all that was on shed at Stirling on 28 June 1966 when No. 60024 *Kingfisher* made its way past. The shed here was coded as 65J as of 18 June 1960, having been previously 63B. (Michael Beaton)

The gasworks in the background was a familiar landmark to many photographs taken at Stirling over the years as Standard 5MT No. 73149 arrives on 10 June 1965. On television that evening you could have tuned in to watch Alan Freeman host *Top of the Pops* with guests including the Rolling Stones and the Who. (Peter Coton)

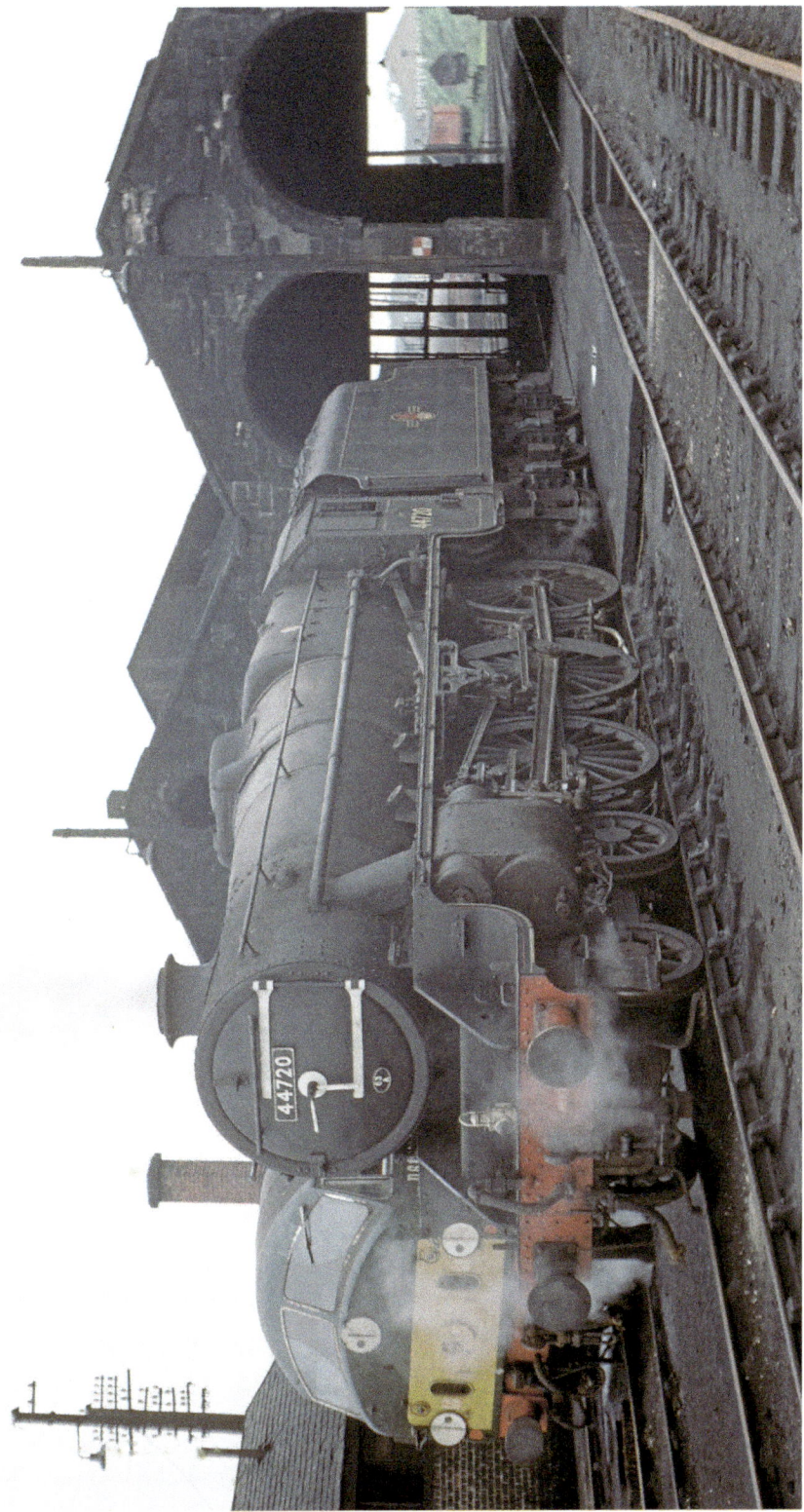

One of the North British-built Bo-Bos waits for something to do alongside Black Five No. 44720 outside the shed buildings at Stirling on 7 June 1966. On 20 June the French President Charles De Gaulle started a state visit to Russia; great team players as they were during the Cold War, on the last day of the month France would pull out officially from NATO. (Jerry Beddows)

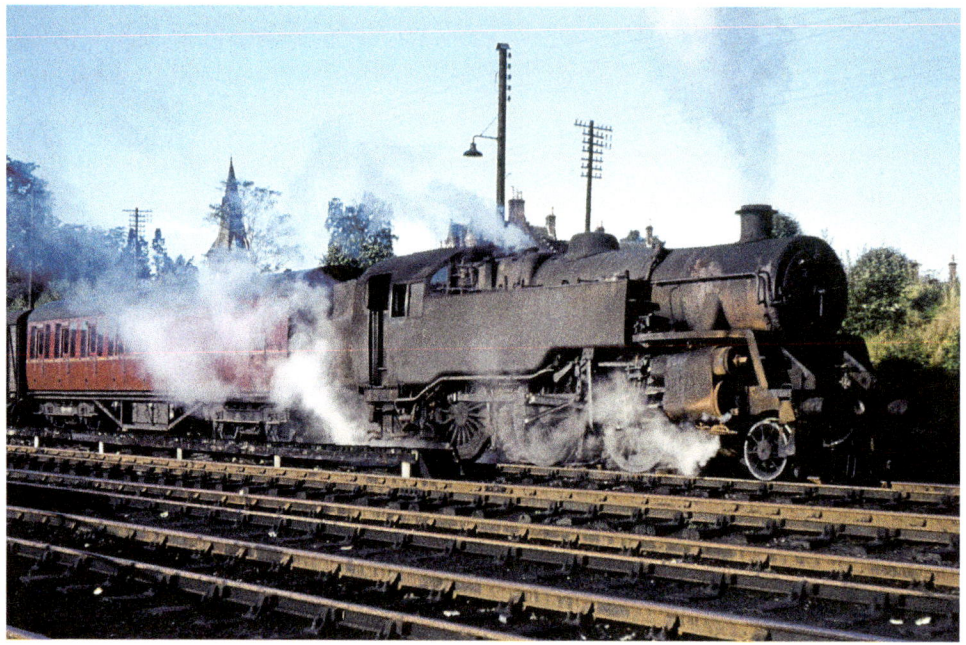

Stirling was once the junction with the mainlines to Perth and the north for the route to Callander and Oban. Standard 4MT No. 80092 warms through a coach from the Killin branch train stock at Stirling in 1965, the last year of the service. (Strathwood Library Collection)

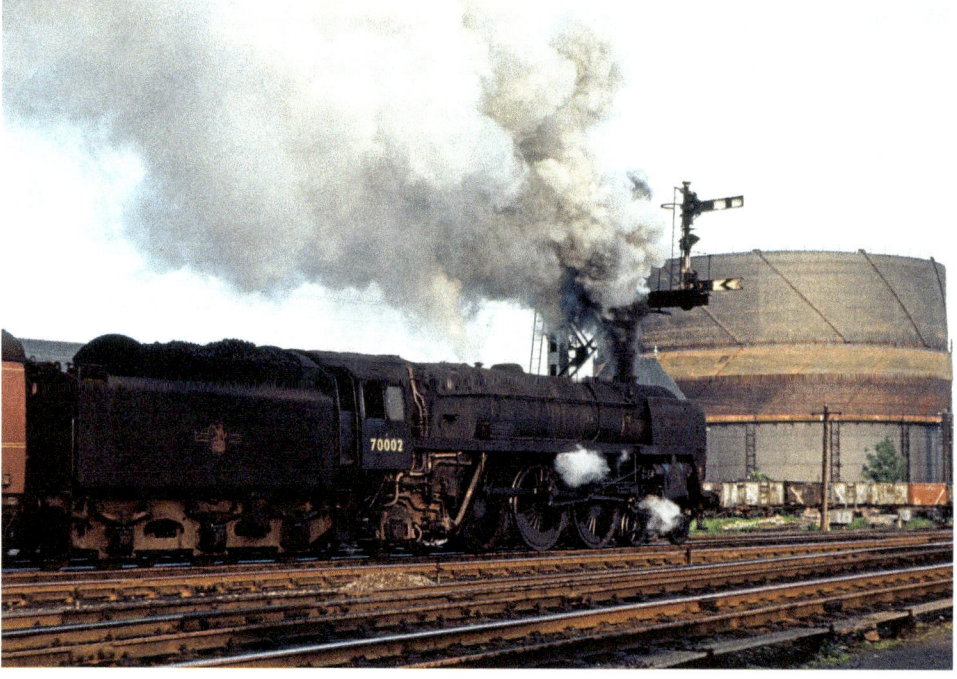

Storming away past the Stirling gas holder a full decade before gas was drawn from the North Sea, when the country relied upon Towns Gas manufactured from coal, was Britannia 70002, once named *Geoffrey Chaucer*, in June 1965. (Strathwood Library Collection)

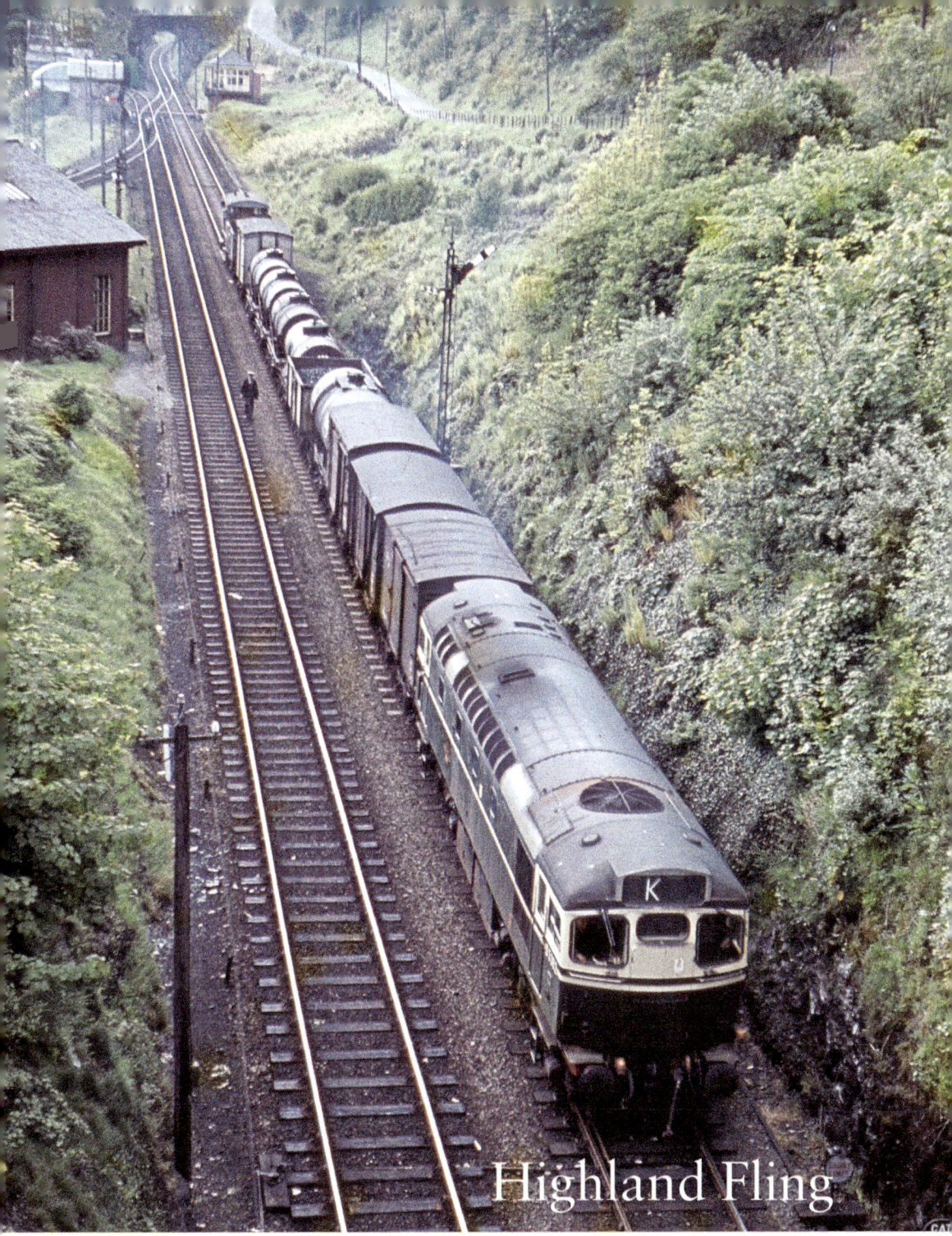

Highland Fling

Diesels took over on the routes to Oban in the early sixties. Among these was Birmingham Railway Carriage & Wagon Company-built D5362, moving past the sheds at Oban with a short goods on 25 June 1962. Sent from its makers at Smethwick in November 1961 to take up service from 65A (Eastfield), it would remain allocated there its entire working life, which ended in 1983 when it suffered one fire too many and was withdrawn. (Winston Cole)

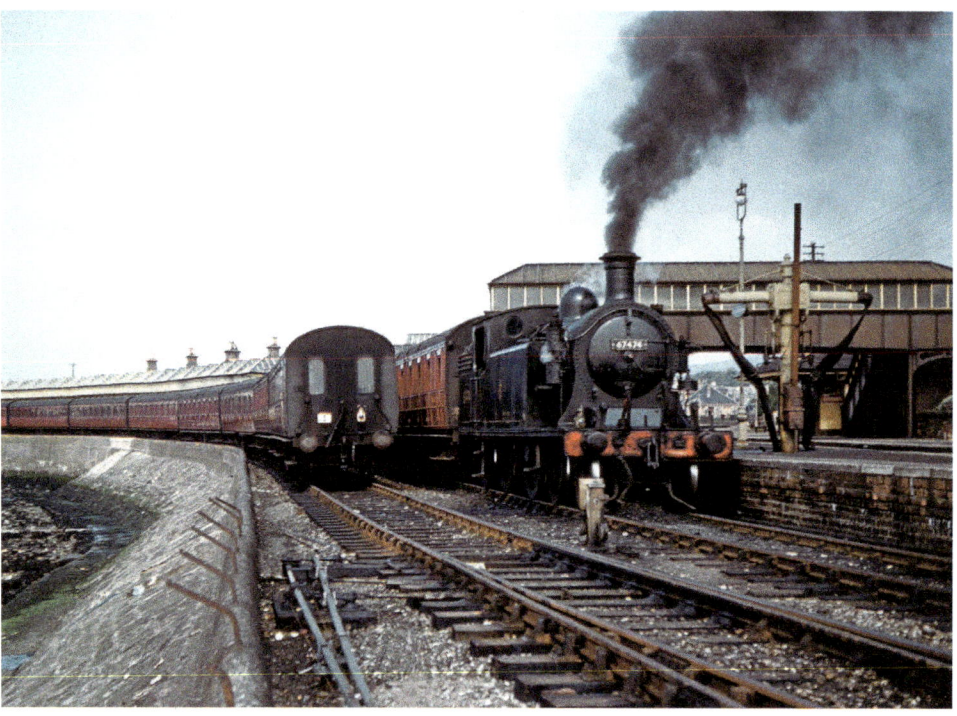

When seen at Helensburgh in the first few months of 1960, Class C15 No. 67474 had just weeks to go in service. (Strathwood Library Collection)

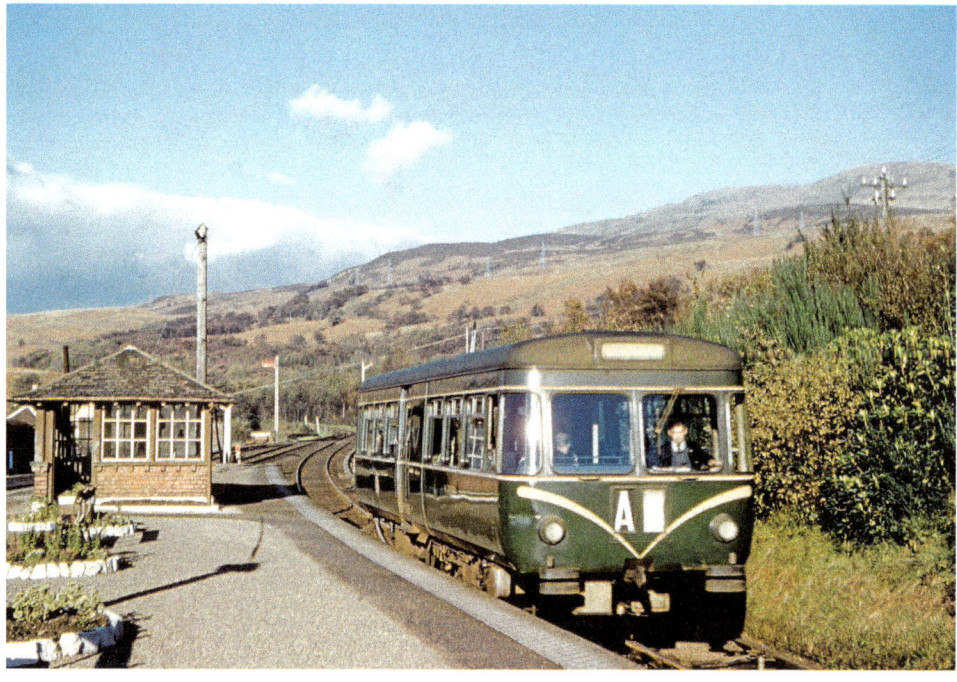

Among the bright ideas of the time were a number of lightweight railbus designs, including SC79974 from Park Royal seen at Garelochead. (Strathwood Library Collection)

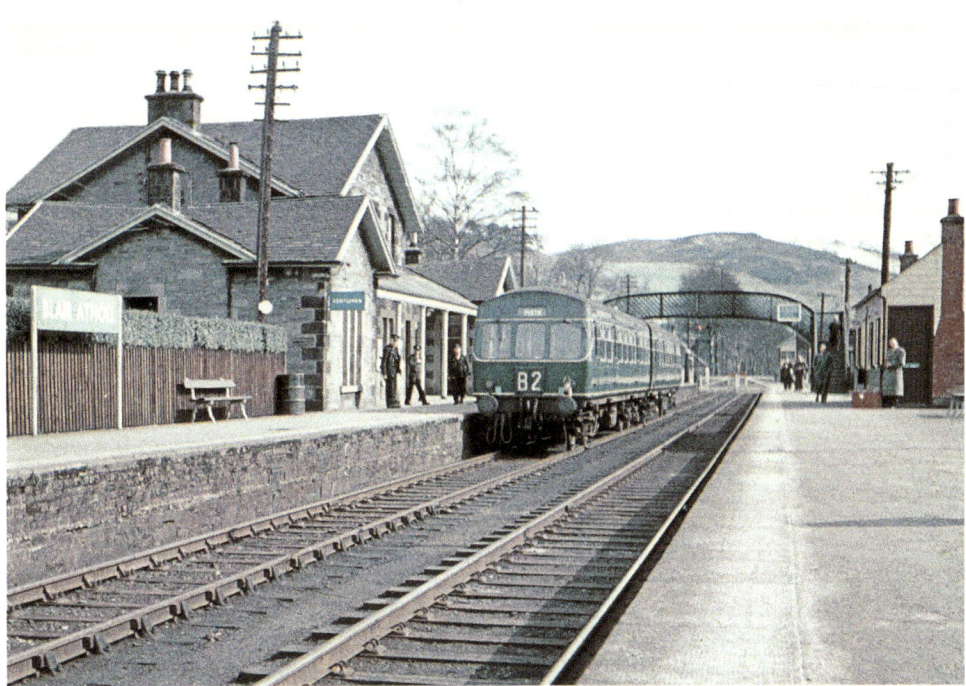

The numbers on the platforms at Blair Athol for the arrival of the 1.15 p.m. to Perth in April 1961 are boosted by several railway enthusiasts, here to see if the shed had anything to offer. (Late Vincent Heckford/Strathwood Library Collection)

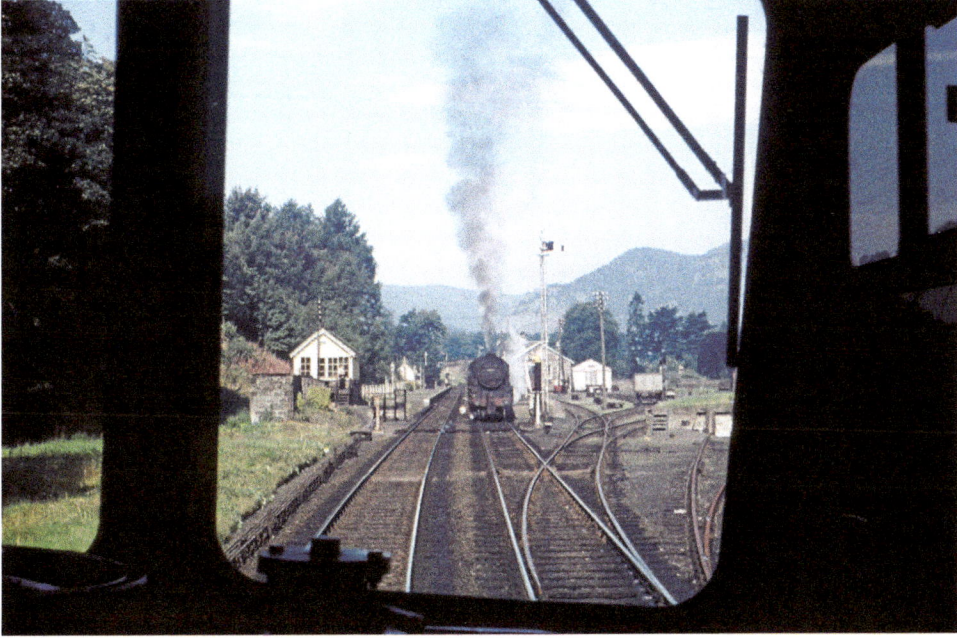

A position behind the driver's windows would always be popular with many passengers when travelling in a DMU, such as on board this Metropolitan Cammell unit nearing Dunkeld and about to pass Black Five No. 45179 on 1 September 1961. (Strathwood Library Collection)

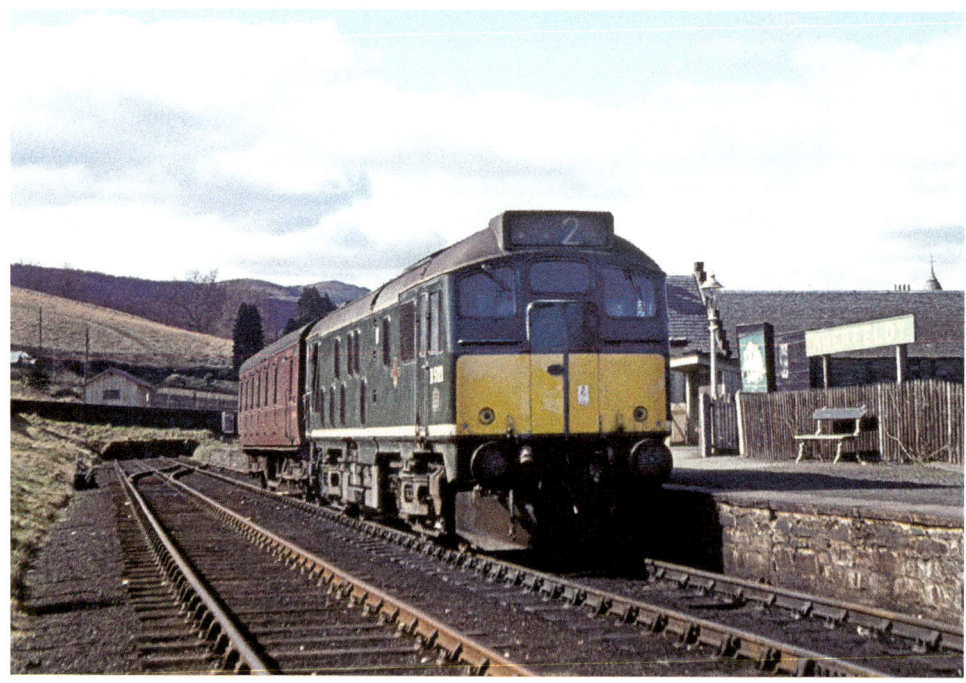

The ex-Caledonian Railway 0-4-4Ts gave way to British Railways-built Bo-Bos such as D5133 at Aberfeldy, which will hardly strain itself with the 12.17 to Ballinluig on 3 April 1965, the year of closure for this ex-Highland Railway branch. (Late Roy Hamilton)

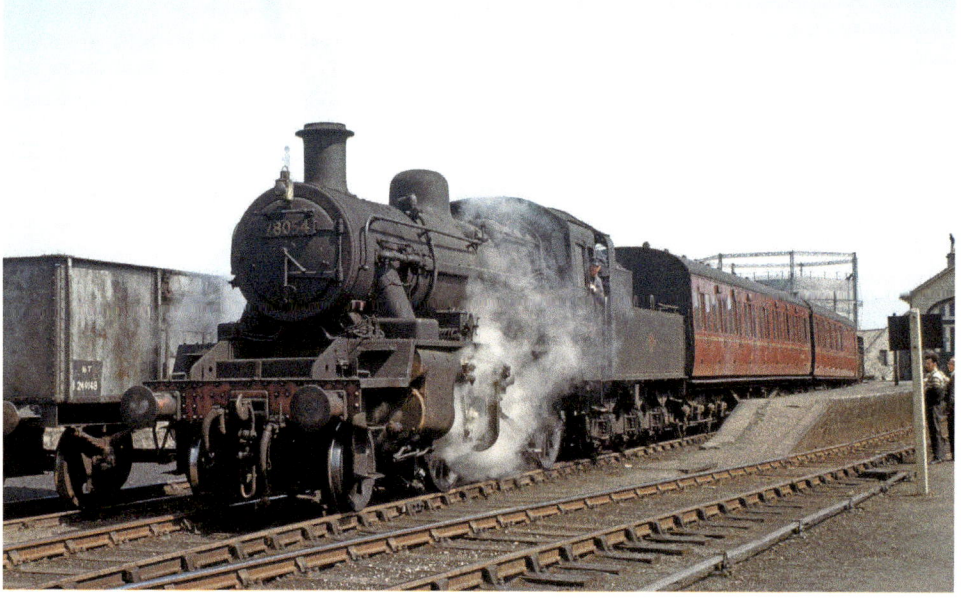

Standard 2MTs such as No. 78054 ousted the 0-4-4Ts on the ex-Great North of Scotland Railway's branch to Banff, as here on 28 May 1964. However in this the final year here the North British-built Bo-Bos were sometimes used. (John Rowe)

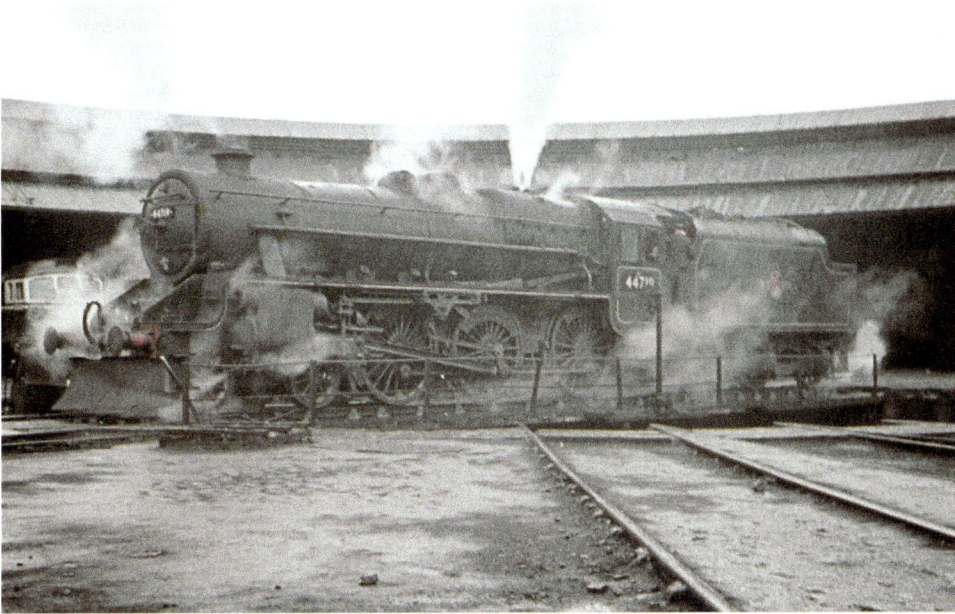

Typically dreich Highland weather at Easter 1961 greeted the party of spotters that travelled to the roundhouse at Inverness where Black Five No. 44719 was on the turntable outside with a good head of steam. Officially closed to steam on 12 January 1958, servicing facilities were transferred to the former Lochgorm Works premises until 1962, when the roundhouse shed closed completely. (Late Vincent Heckford//Strathwood Library Collection)

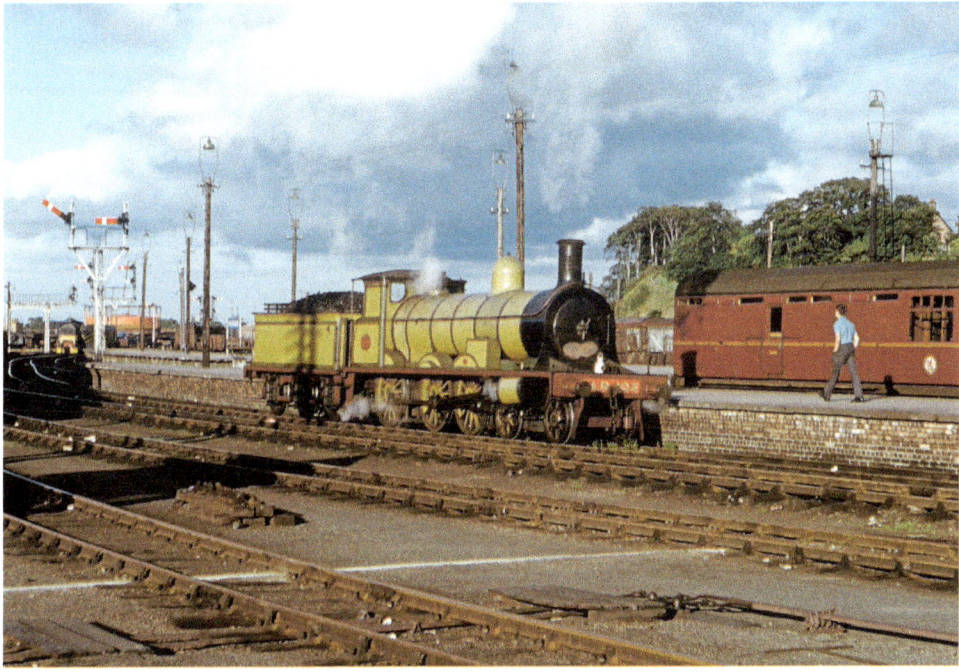

Evidence of some hard running on the smoke box of Highland Railway 103 at Inverness after a run from Perth on 21 August 1965 as it backs out for servicing. (Strathwood Library Collection)

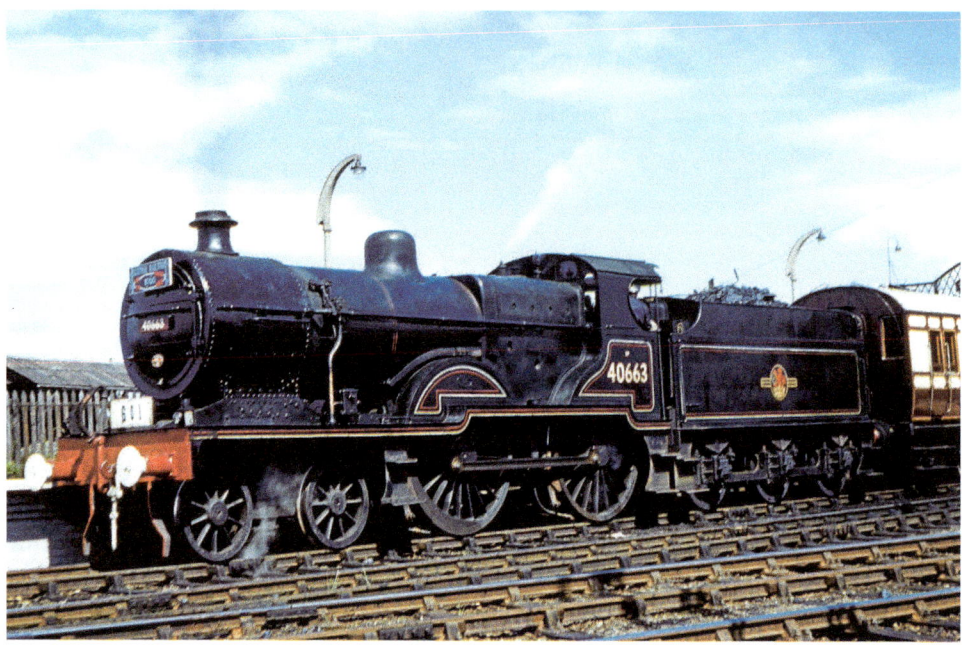

Fully bulled up for its duties within the five-day SLS and RCTS-organised Scottish Railtour in June 1960 was Class 2P No. 40663, standing for photographs at Forres. (Frank Hornby)

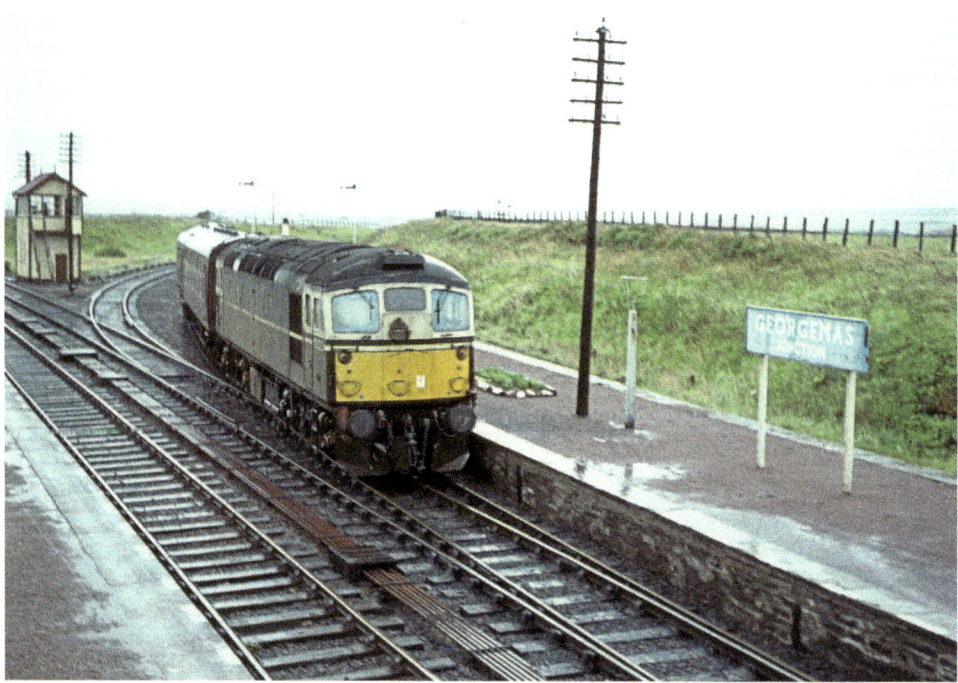

The wholesale dieselisation north of Inverness was completed early in the sixties, with the widespread use of Type 2 diesels from BRCW supplemented with others from British Railways and the workshops of North British. Arriving at Georgemas Junction from Thurso, once again in the rain, during August 1964 was D5325. (Winston Cole)

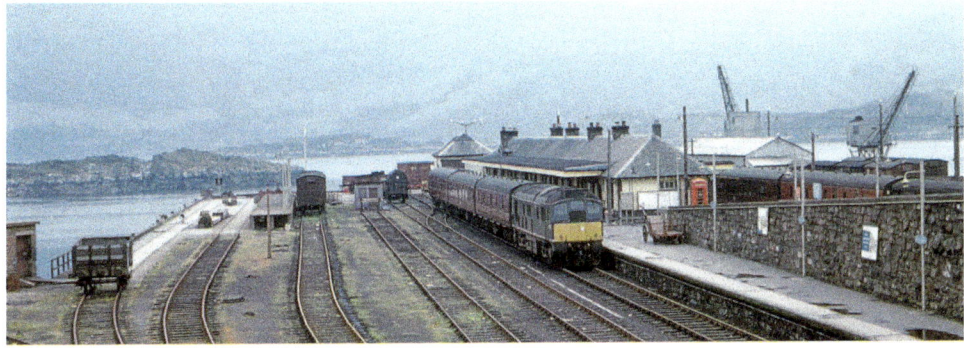

The next departure from Kyle of Lochalsh on 7 June 1964 would be behind D5128. (Strathwood Library Collection)

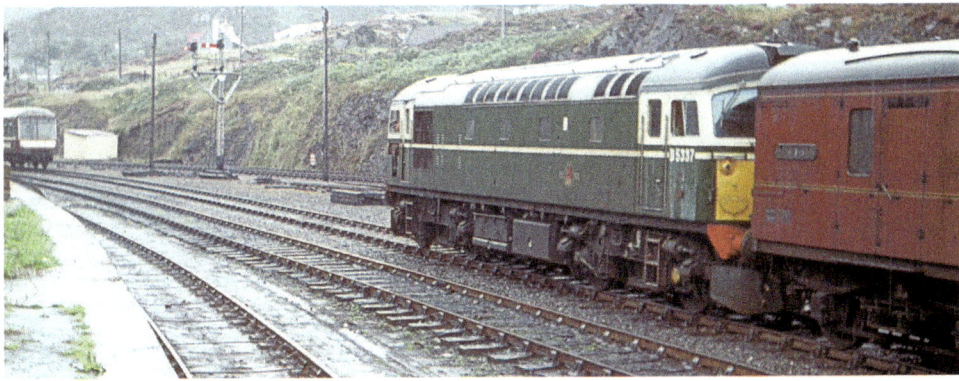

Wet weather persists in August 1964 for our cameraman's visit to Kyle of Lochalsh, with D5337 standing on the same road as the ex-Devon Belle observation coach. (Winston Cole)

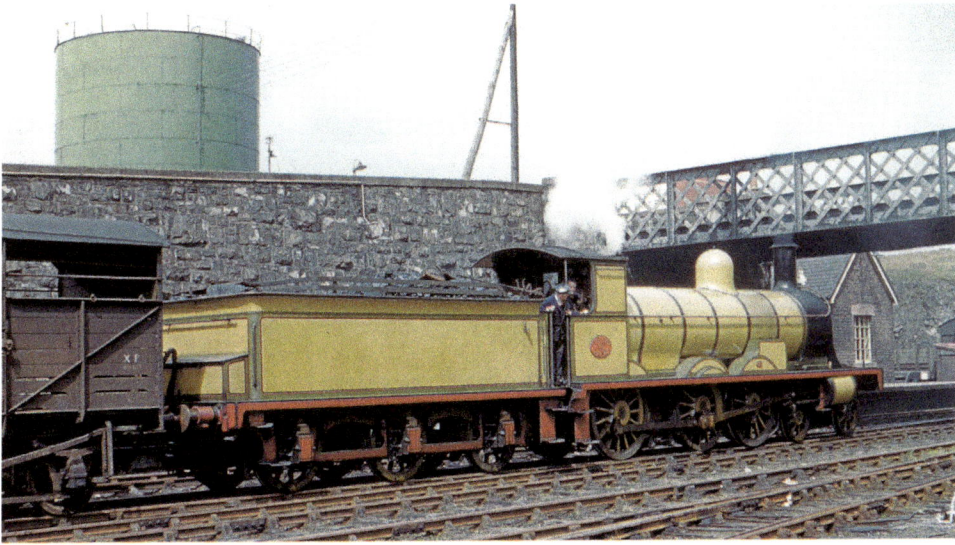

Aside from the British Railways-built cattle wagon this is how Kyle of Lochalsh might have looked in Highland Railway days, with the preserved 103 shunting stock in about 1960. (Strathwood Library Collection)

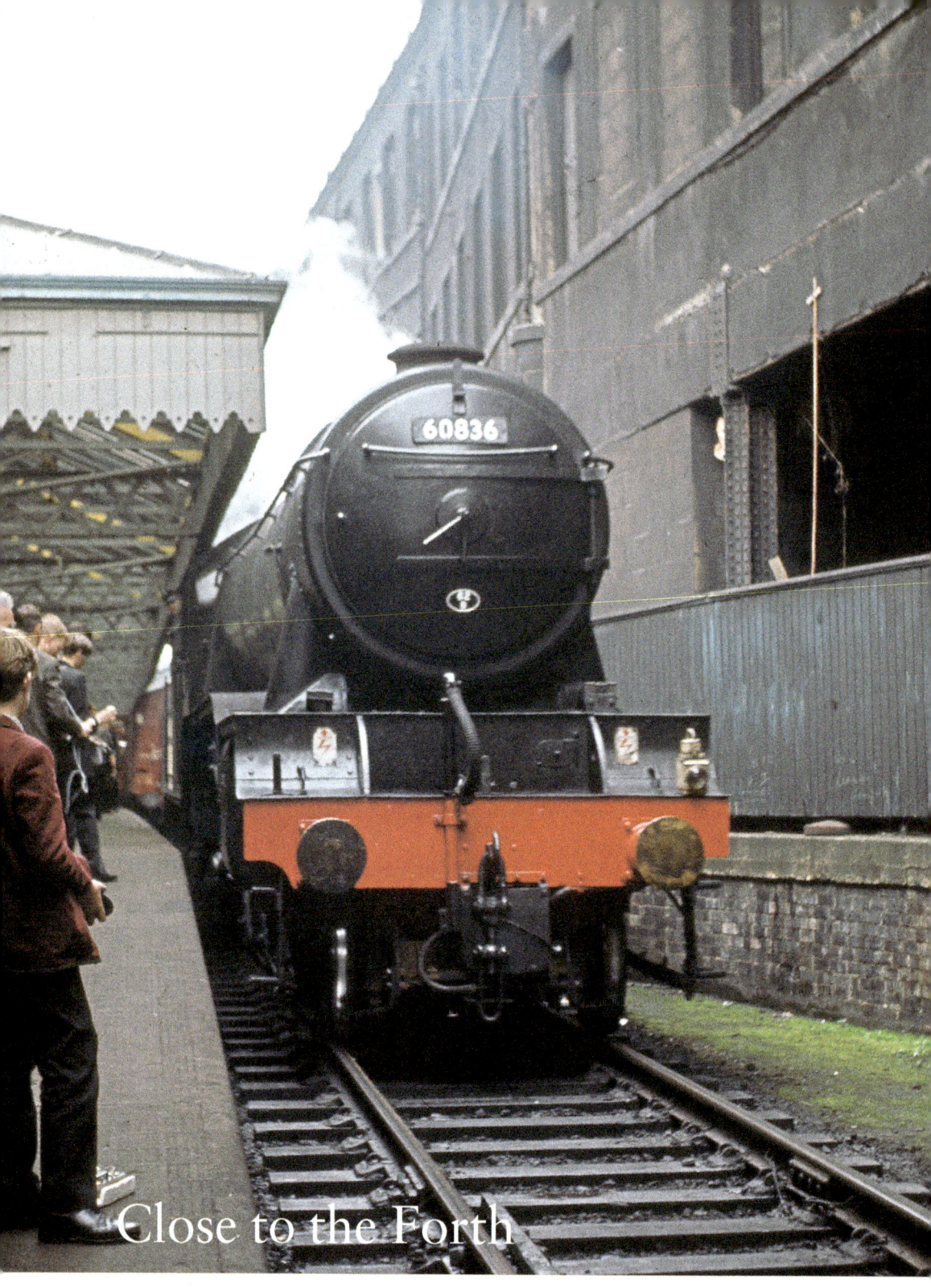

Close to the Forth

Class V2 No. 60836 comes off the Granite City special of 3 September 1966 in favour of Peppercorn A2 No. 60532 *Blue Peter*, which will take the train on from Edinburgh Waverley. (Strathwood Library Collection)

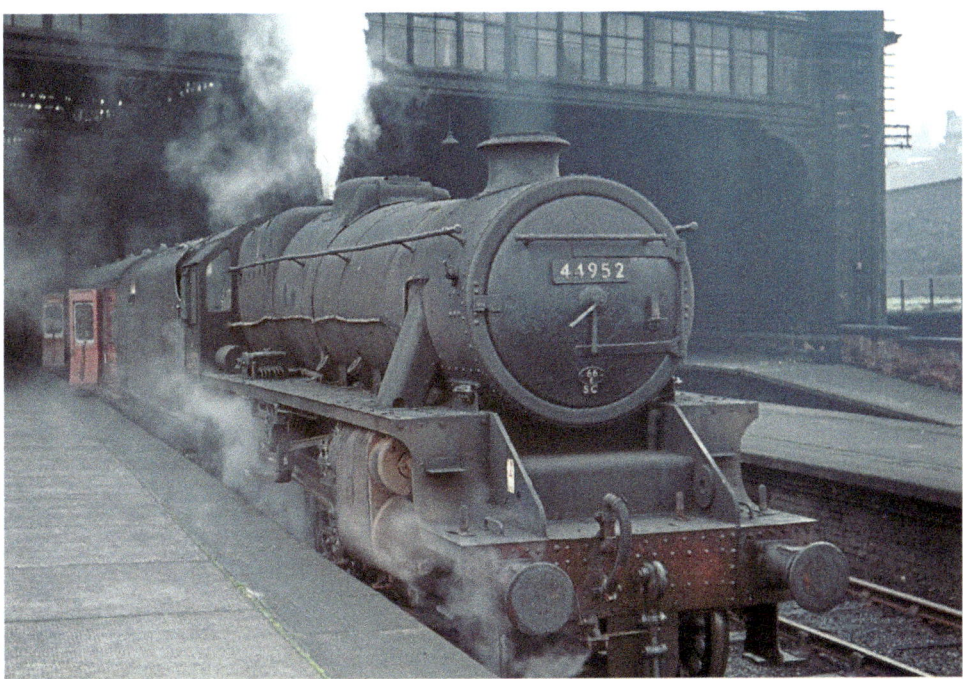

The original Edinburgh Princes Street station was closed by the North British Railway in 1868, leaving the Caledonian Railway's station to remain open until 1965. Shortly before closure Black Five No. 44952 awaits departure on 8 June. (Peter Coton)

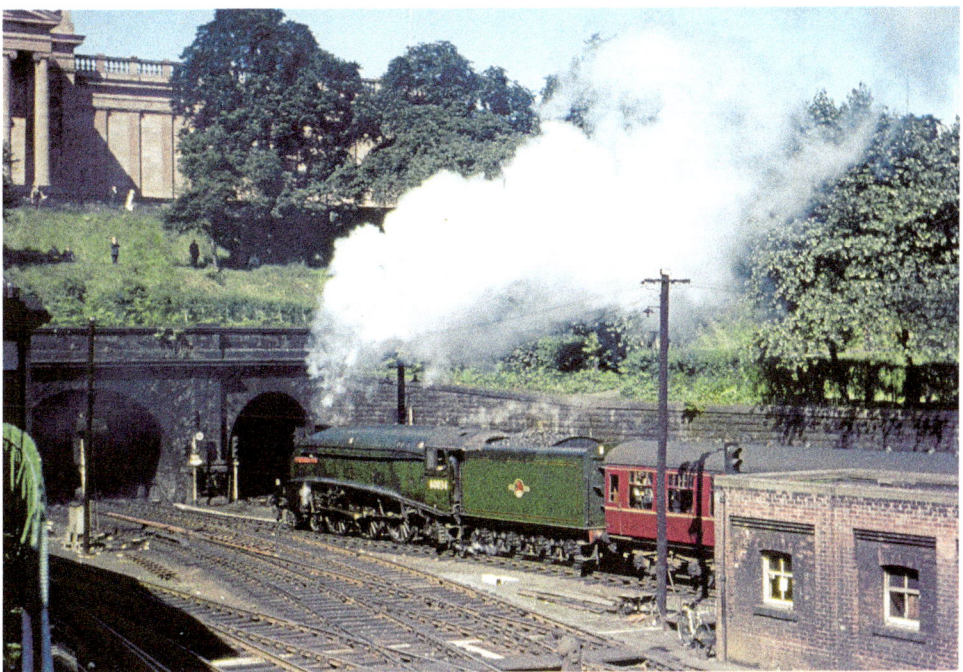

Striding away boldly into the tunnels at Edinburgh Waverley in July 1966 was No. 60034 *Lord Farringdon*. (Strathwood Library Collection)

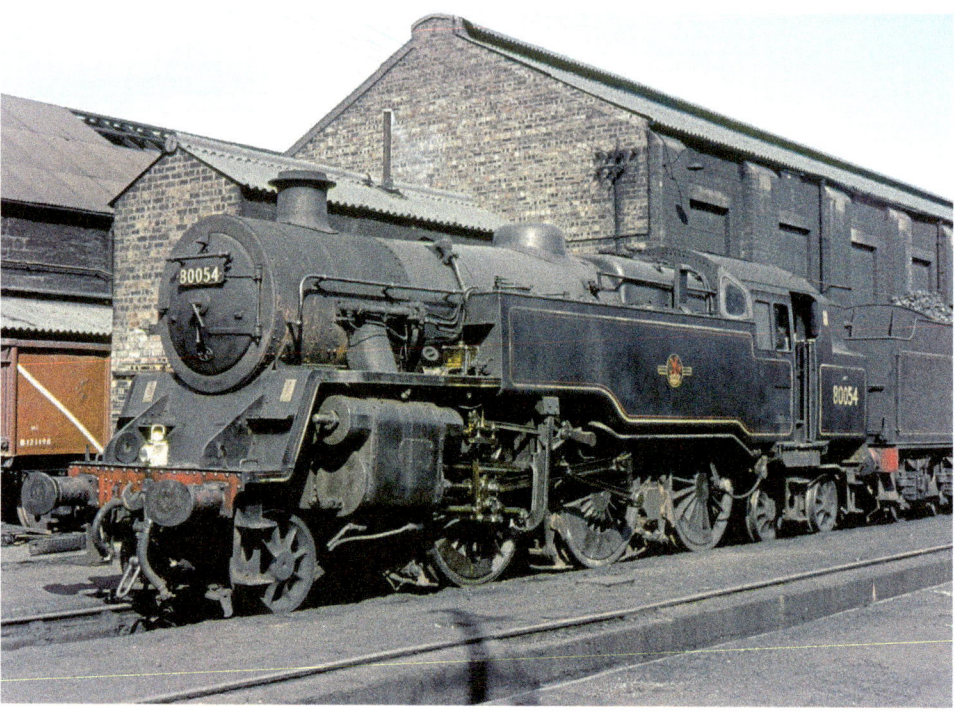

Among the nearby engine sheds to visit for the spotter was 64A (St Margarets), where we find Standard 4MT resting awhile during 1964. (Strathwood Library Collection)

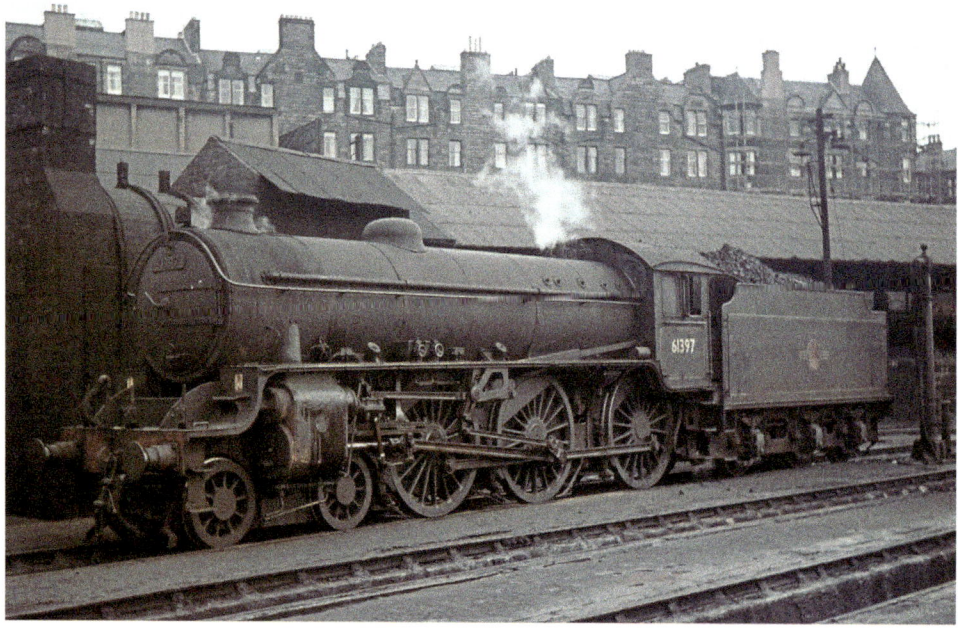

The shed here closed to steam in December 1966 and completely to all traffic six weeks later. On 4 June 1965 Class B1 61397, with unusually small cabside numerals, was present at St Margarets. (Peter Coton)

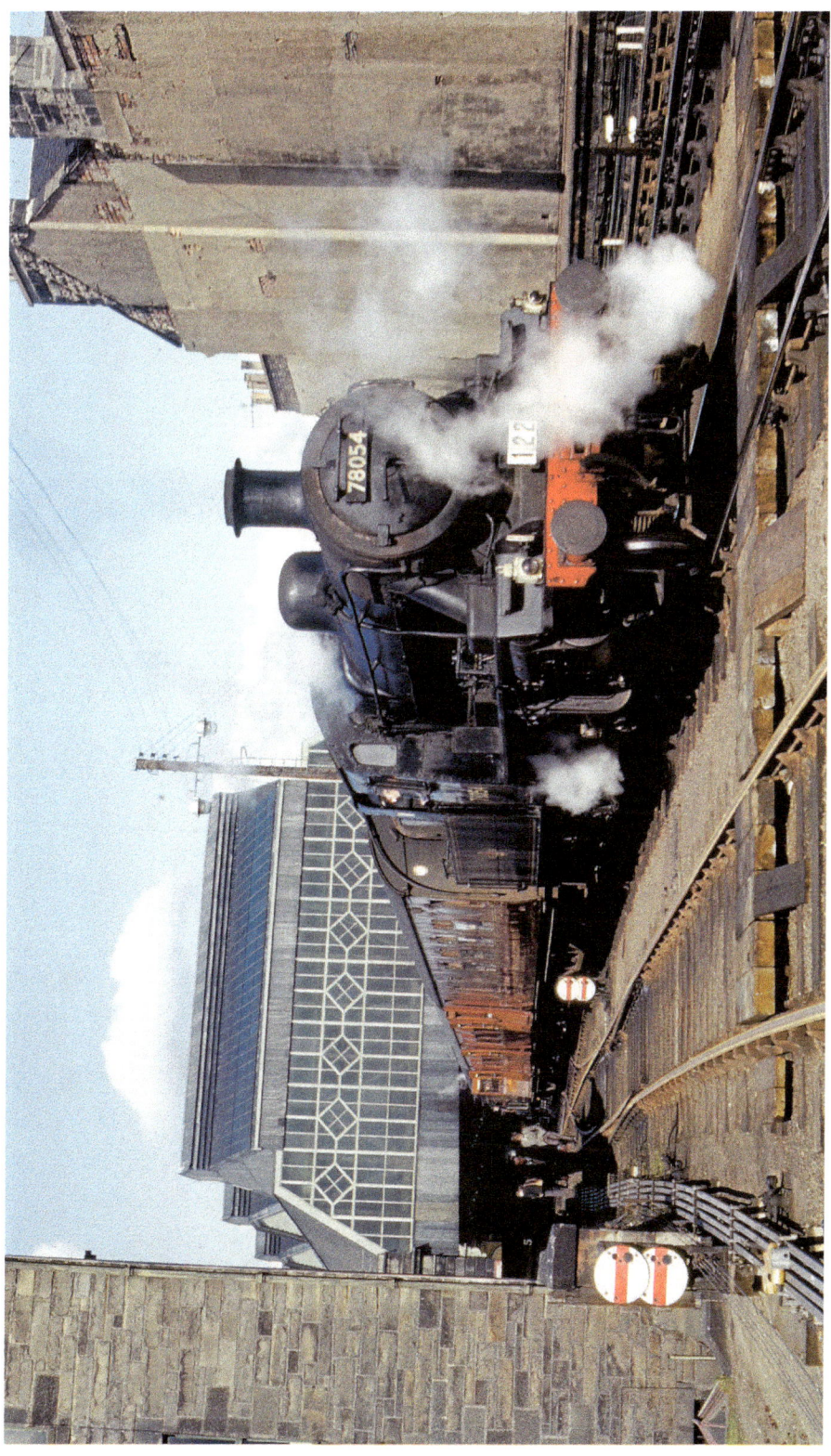

Leith Central was an ex-North British terminus closed in 1952 which proclaimed a return to passengers briefly for the visit of Standard 2MT No. 78054 on 1 April 1965. The overall roof made it an ideal place to stable DMUs after this and the occasional diesel locomotive until 1972. (Strathwood Library Collection)

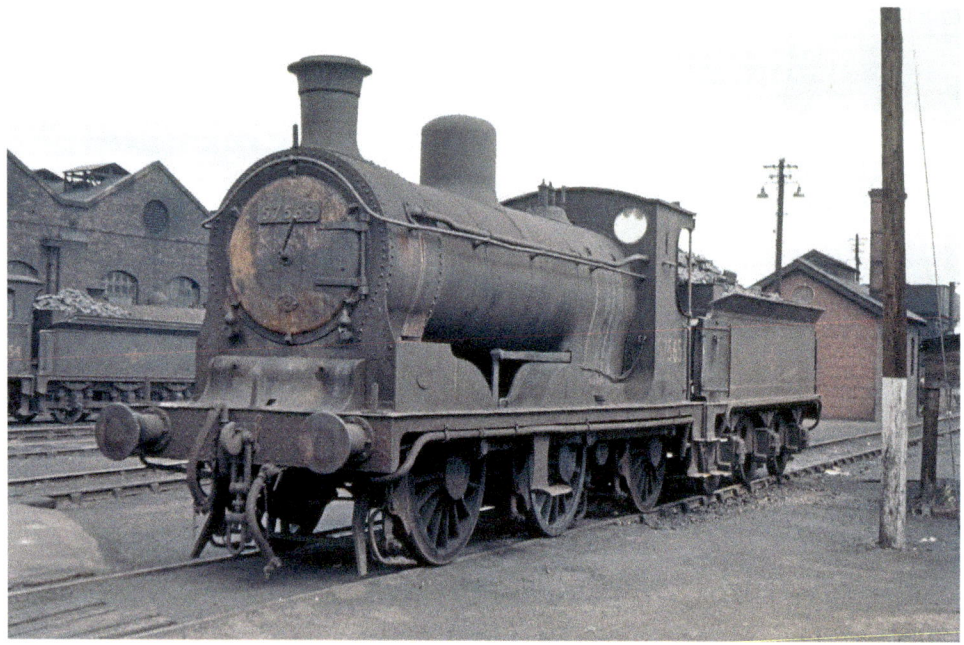

Always worth a visit, albeit for more humble locomotives, was 64C (Dalry Road), such as here on 12 June 1960 with McIntosh 3F No. 57565 standing cold, although her smoke box suggests some pretty hearty use previously. (Frank Hornby)

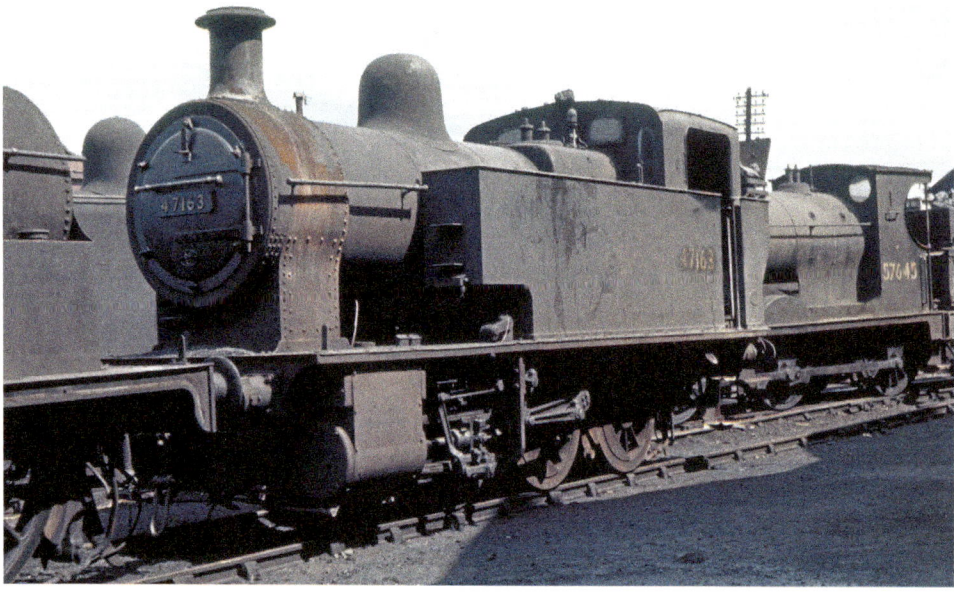

Also standing cold the same day on this visit was No. 47163, previously seen at Ladybank on page 24, which would cling on until December 1962 after further moves to Hamilton and Greenock. It passed to Campbell's in Airdrie as its last move, being scrapped in December 1963. (Frank Hornby)

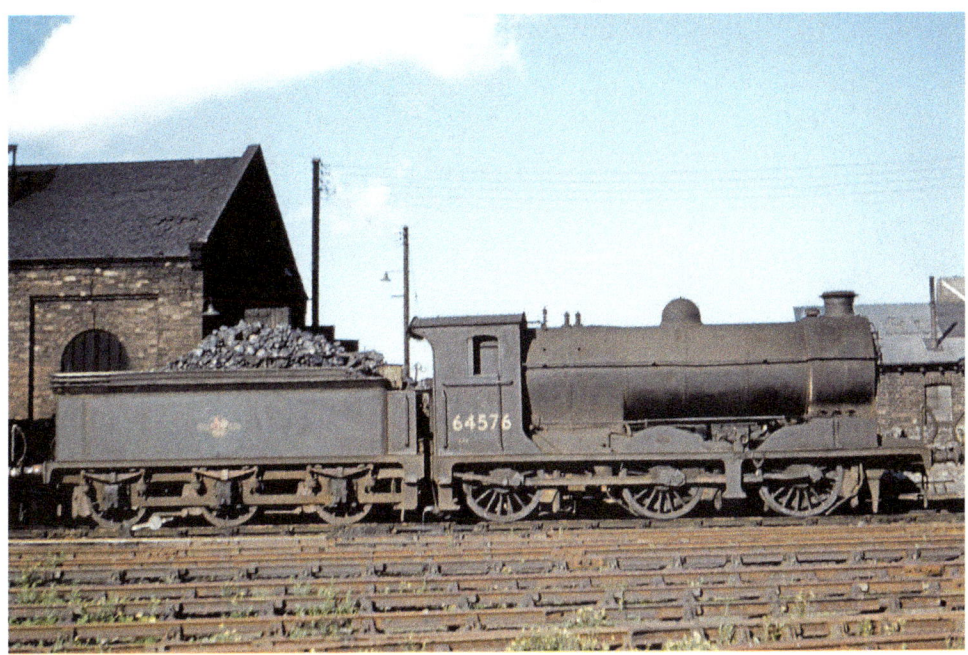

Another often forgotten engine shed was at Seafield, where we find Class J37 No. 64576 well coaled up and ready for action on coal trains once more in June 1960. In the hit parade was 'Cathy's Clown' from the Everly Brothers with seven weeks at number one, which was finally toppled by 'Three Steps to Heaven' by Eddie Cochran. (Frank Hornby)

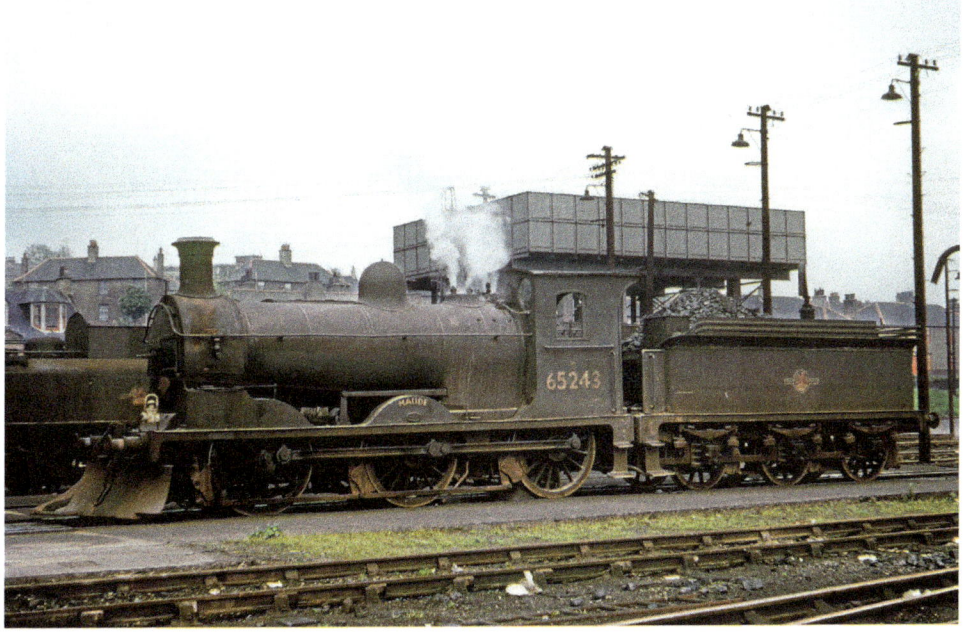

Unlike Seafield, which closed in September 1962, Bathgate remained open until late 1966, albeit to diesels only at the finish. But a visit on 7 June 1965 found Class J36 No. 65243 *Maude* soldiering on with two others into 1966. (Win Wall/Strathwood Library Collection)

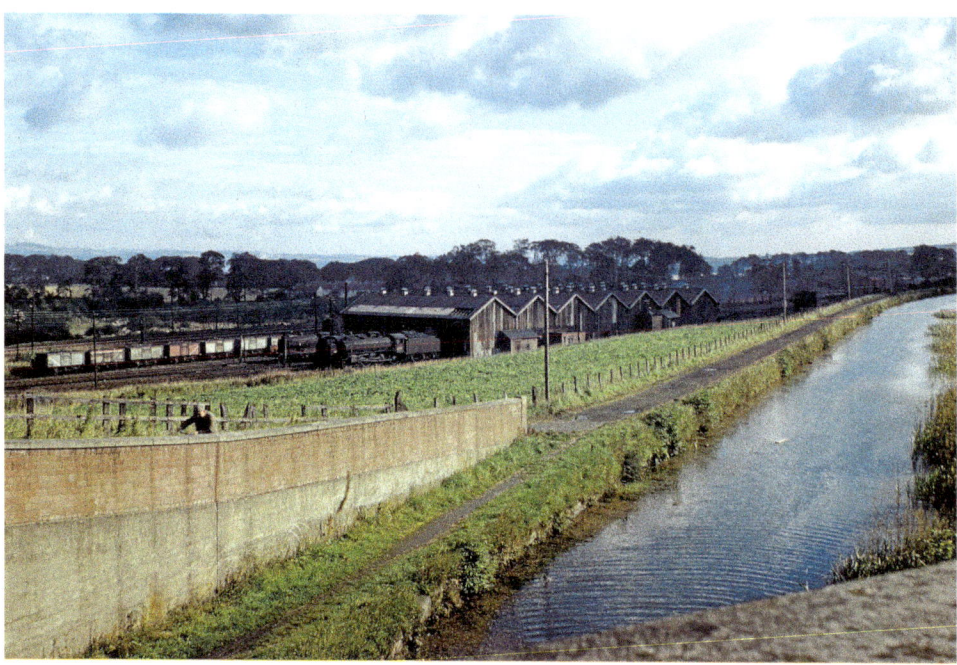

The Ian Allan *Shed Directory* offered simple guidance to the spotter on a visit to 65K (Polmont). The shed is on the south side of the line west of the station. The yard is visible from the line. Turn shape left outside the station along a cinder path running parallel to the line. Turn left over a railway bridge and right on to the canal towing path. A cinder path leads down to the shed from this towing path. Walking time 10 minutes. Simple directions here for the visitor from afar but the books provided a valuable resource to many throughout the fifties and sixties. (Chris Forrest)

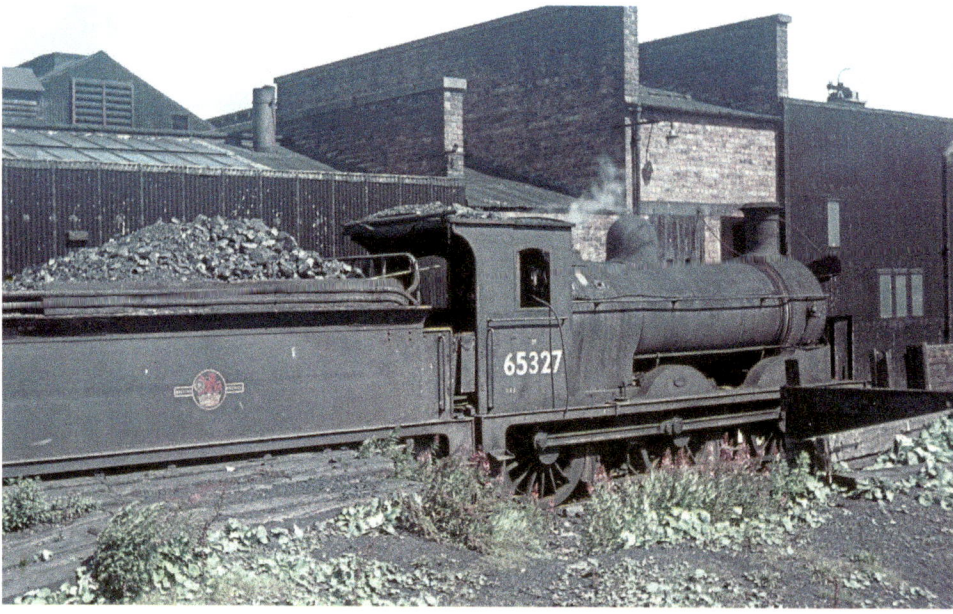

The years have left their sooty marks upon the buildings of Grangemouth when Class J36 No. 65327 sizzled quietly away in the sun on 1 August 1965, a few months before being withdrawn. (Dave Down)

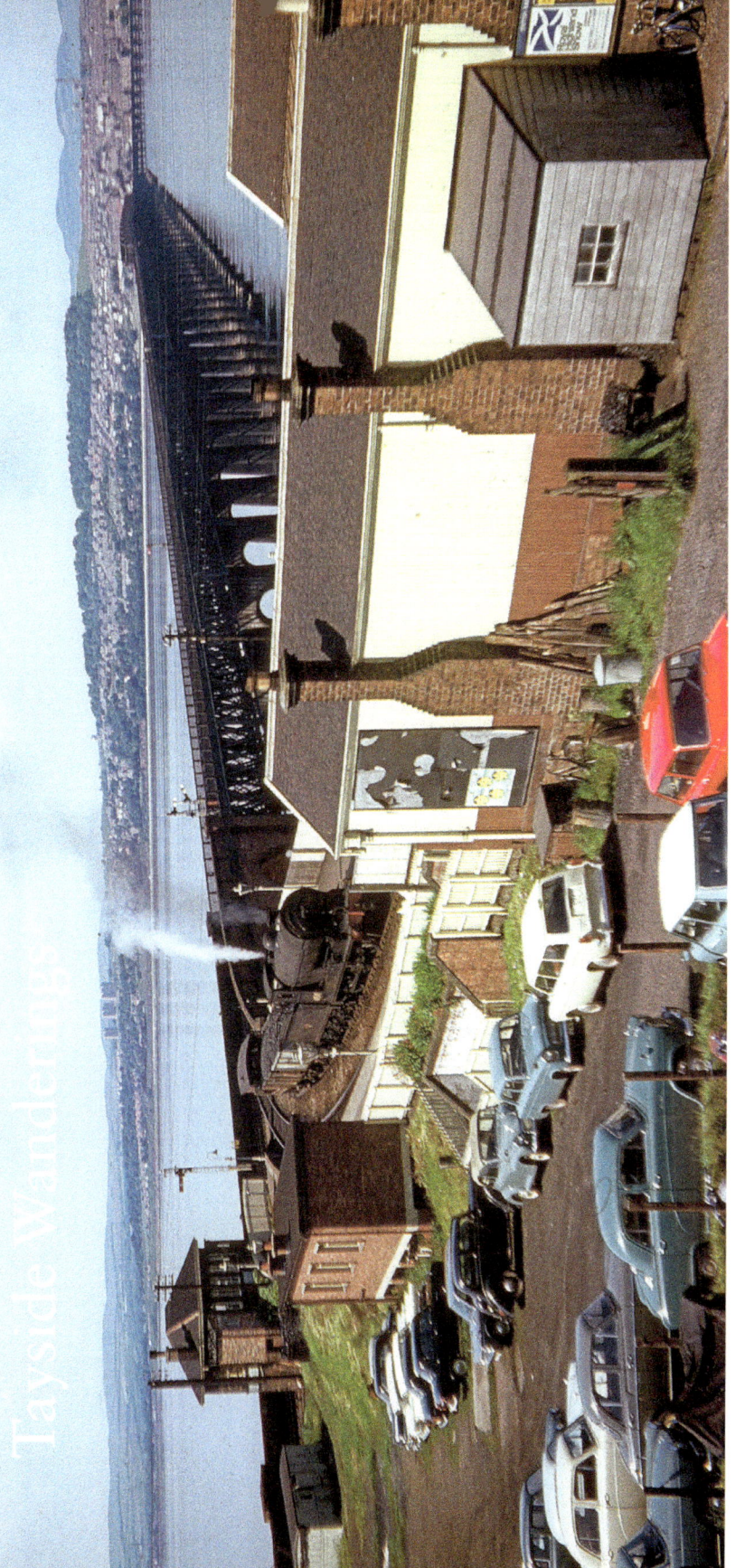

Tayside Wanderings

The second Tay bridge opened for traffic, after some rigorous testing, upstream of, and parallel to, the original bridge in 1887. The new bridge proposal was formally incorporated in July 1881 and the foundation stone laid on 6 July 1883. Construction involved 28,000 tons of concrete, 77,000 tons of iron and steel, 10 million bricks weighing 44,300 tons and 3 million rivets. Fourteen men lost their lives during its construction, most by drowning. On the southern side of the two-and-a-quarter-mile crossing of the Tay at Wormit station on 9 June 1965 was Class J37 No. 64547, waiting for the signal to enter the single track tunnel towards Newport-on-Tay West. (Micheal Beaton)

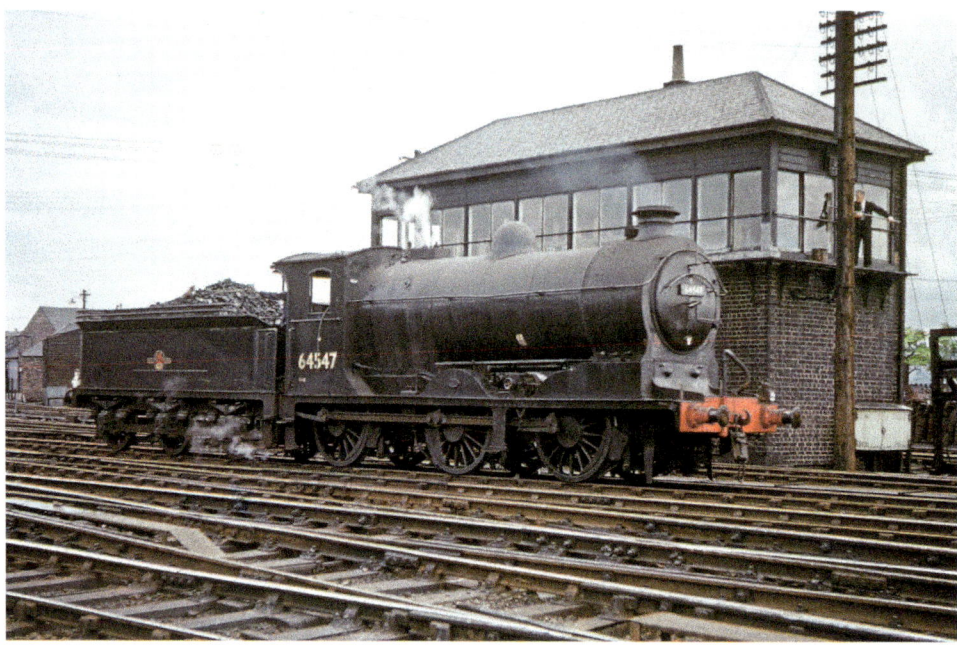

The signalman is out cleaning his windows on 5 June 1965 at Dundee as the same Class J37 from the previous shot four days before rolls by light engine. (Win Wall/Strathwood Library Collection)

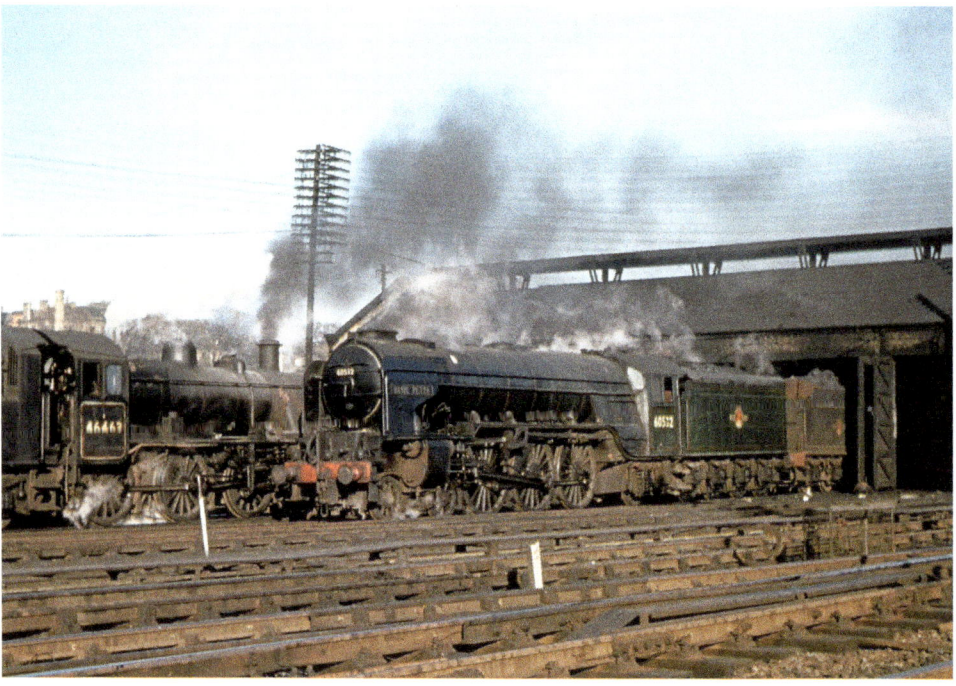

Dundee West became a works from 1953 until 1958, leaving 62B (Dundee Tay Bridge) as the main engine shed until April 1967 when Dundee West shed reverted to use as a shed for diesels. In 1965 Tay Bridge shed hosted No. 60532 *Blue Peter*; visitors at this time would find any one or more of the trio of A2s based here at the time standing at this point. (Strathwood Library Collection)

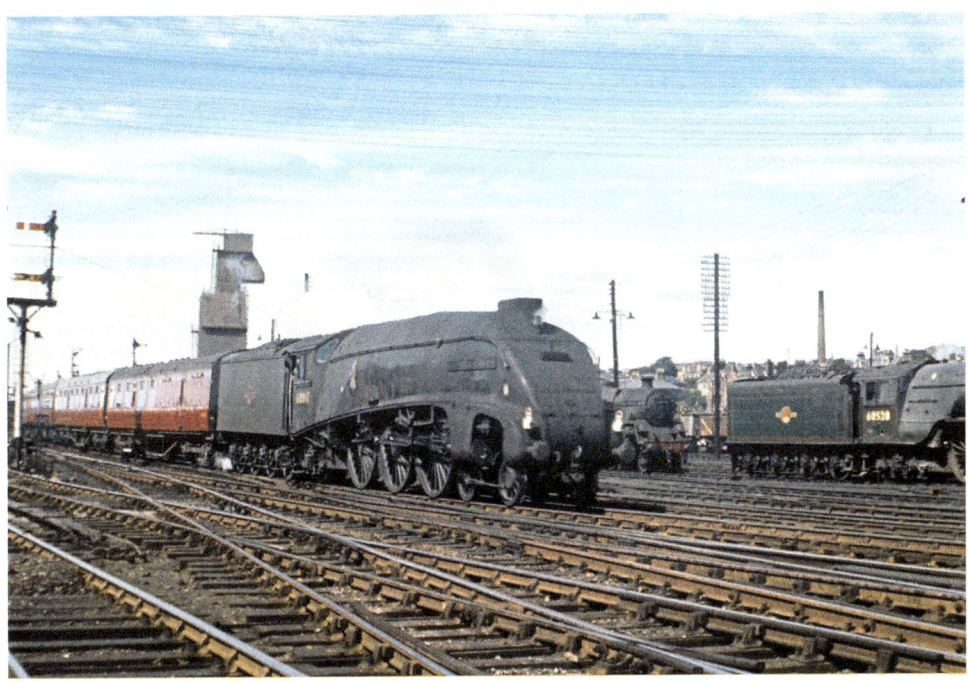

Passing Tay Bridge shed in 1964 was No. 60010 *Dominion of Canada* with Class A2 No. 60528 *Tudor Minstrel* amusing itself outside between turns. (Douglas Paul)

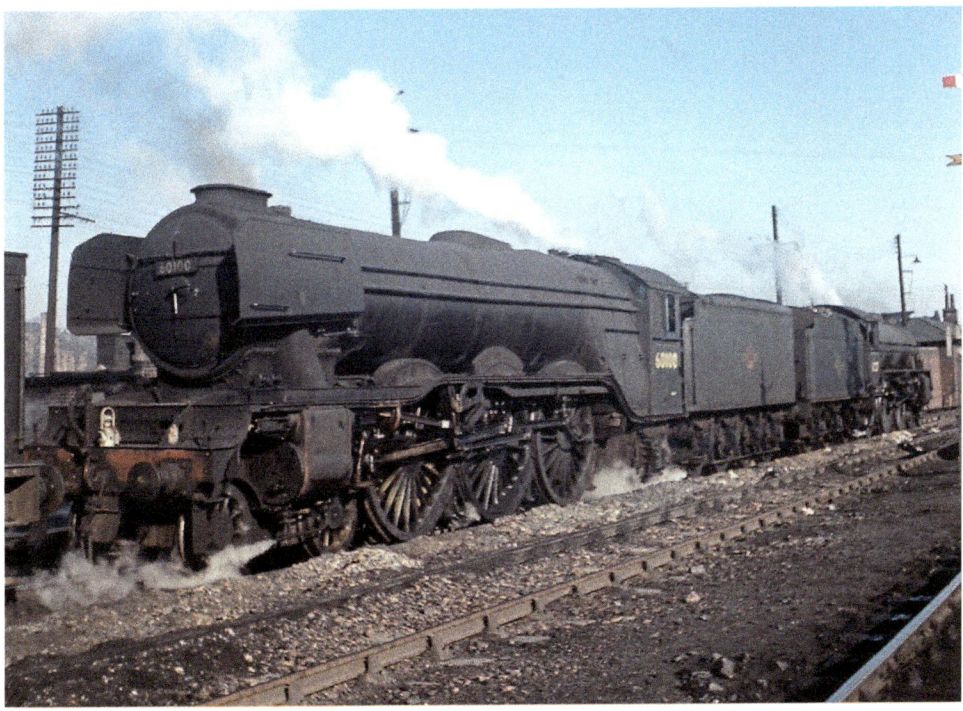

Fitted with a double chimney and smoke deflectors was Gresley A3 No. 60100 *Spearmint*, hissing away on shed at Dundee Tay Bridge in 1963. (Douglas Paul)

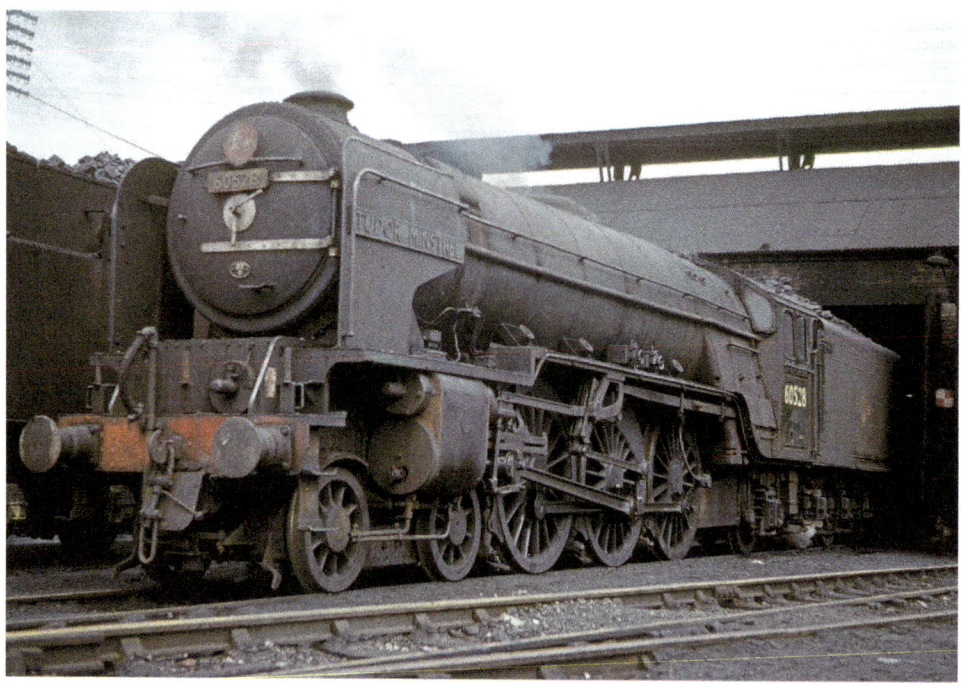

Much dirtier by June 1965, Peppercorn A2 No. 60528 *Tudor Minstrel* patiently waits outside for her next duty at Tay Bridge. This Doncaster-built Pacific entered service in February 1948 with the infant British Railways. (Win Wall/Strathwood Library Collection)

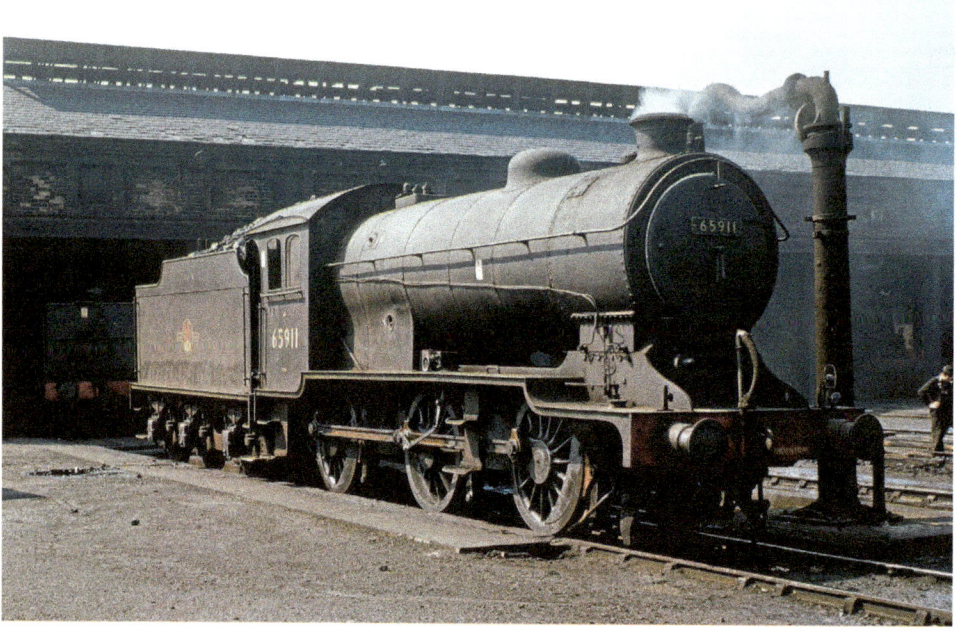

One of Gresley's Class J38s, No. 65911, has been prepared for the road outside the running shed at Tay Bridge in September 1964. All thirty-five of the class went into traffic in the first five months of 1926 from Darlington Works. (John Rowe)

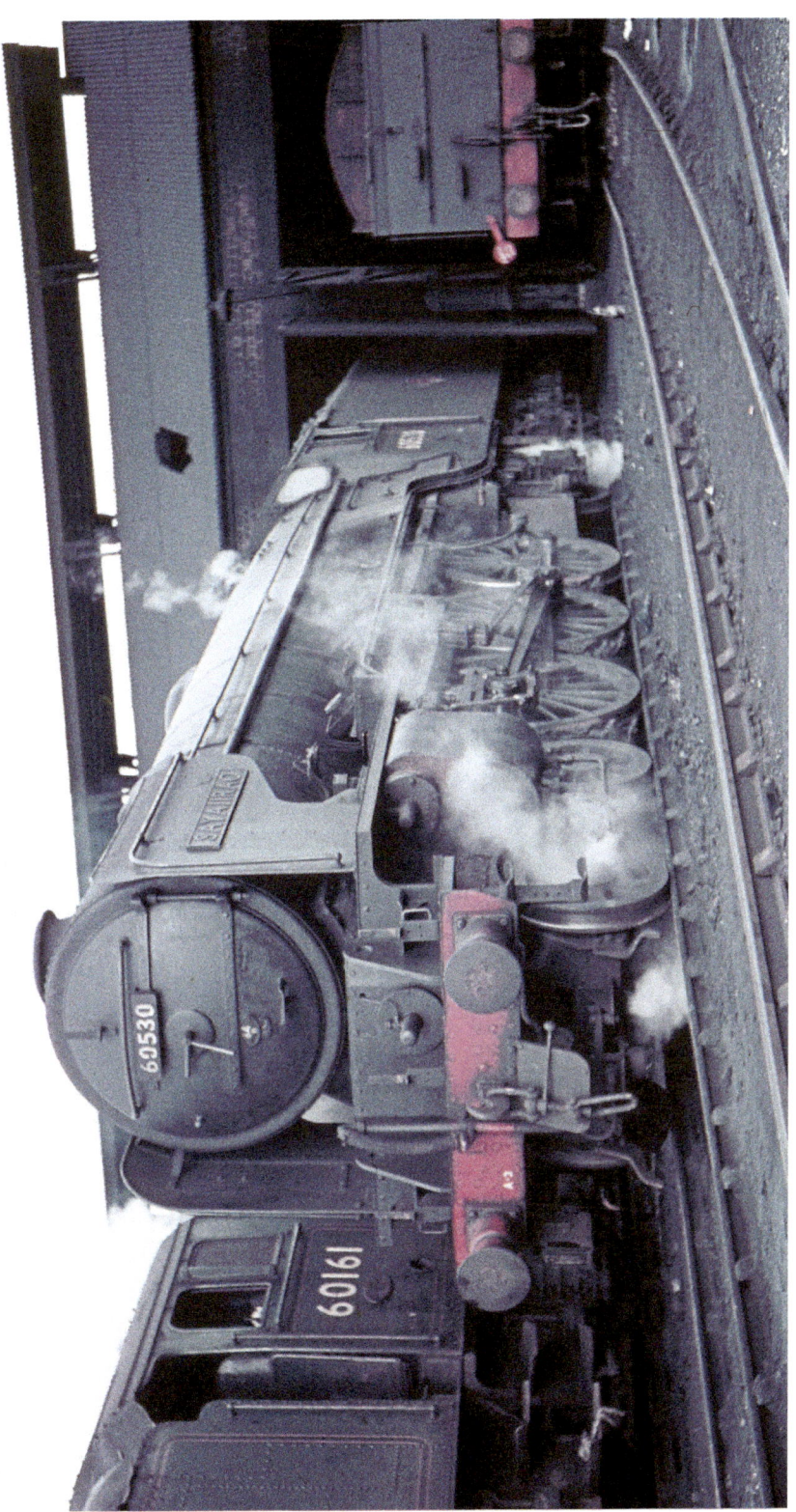

In April 1961 Thompson A1 60161 *North British* kept company with Peppercorn A2 No. 60530 *Sayajirao* outside Tay Bridge. (Late Vincent Heckford/Strathwood Library Collection)

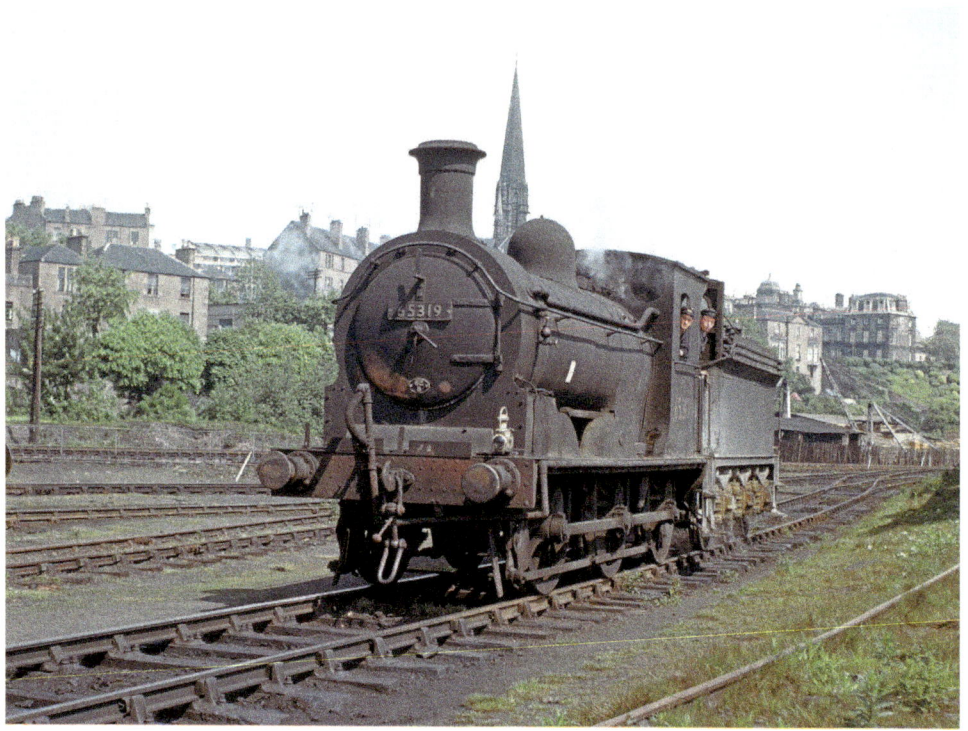

A jolly crew look out from their tender cab-fitted Class J36, No. 65319, at Dundee in September 1964. (John Rowe)

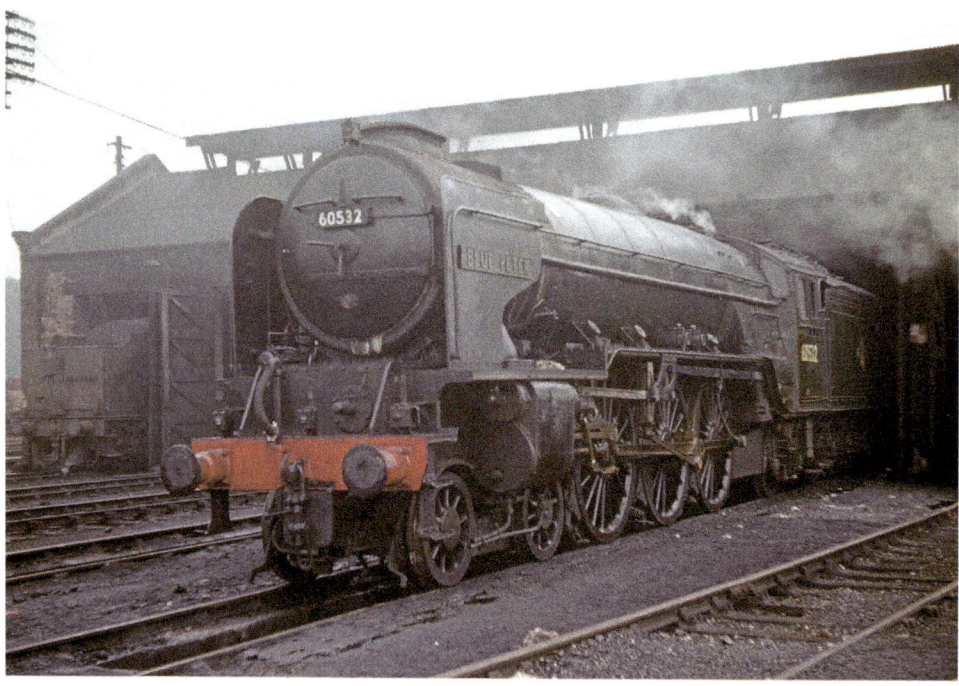

Standing proud outside at Tay Bridge on 8 June 1965, we find No. 60532 *Blue Peter* flying the flag for the shed's A2s. (Michael Beaton)

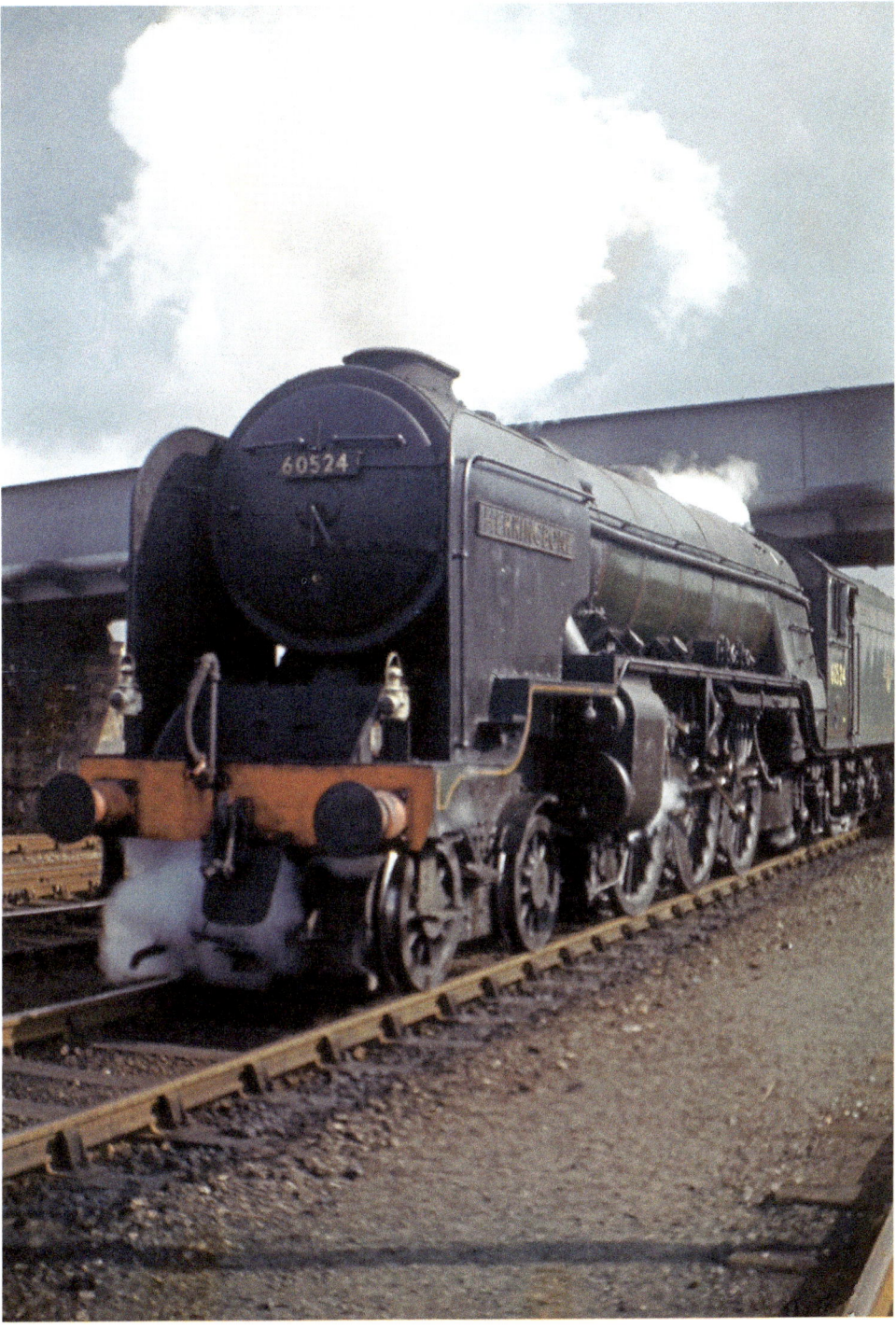

Peppercorn's Class A2/3 development of the earlier Thompson Class A2/2 brought fifteen locomotives including No. 60524 *Herringbone* into traffic from 1946. 'Herringbone' was the name of the winning horse of the 1943 1,000 Guineas and the St Leger the same year and was owned by Lord Derby; it is seen breaking into a canter at Bridge of Dun on 13 April 1963. (Douglas Paul)

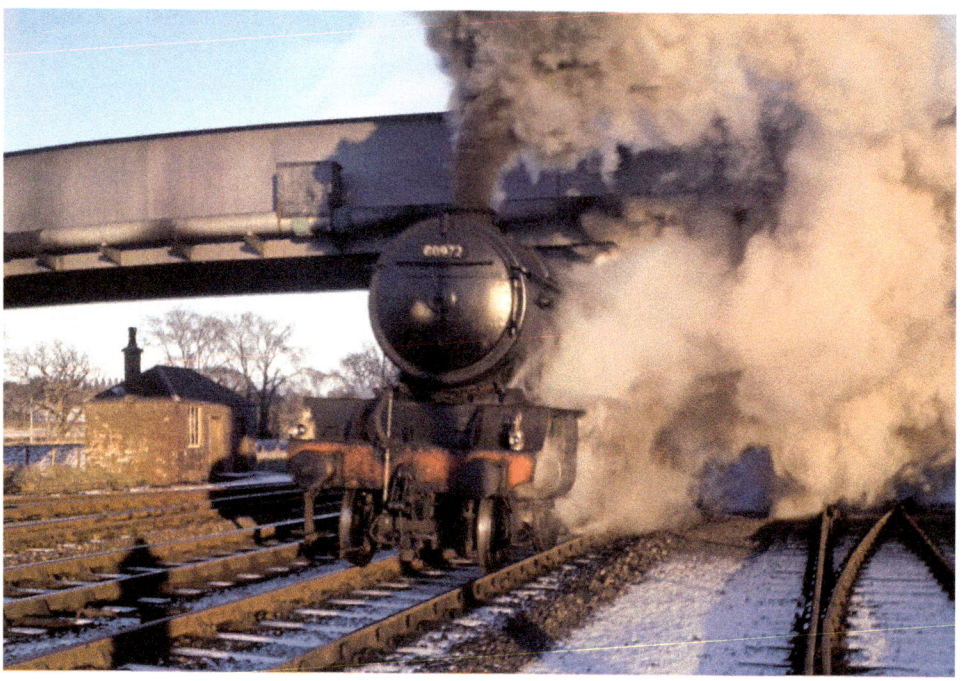

It is a cold and frosty morning after light snow in January 1963 as Gresley V2 No. 60972 makes a fuss on departing from Bridge of Dun. (Douglas Paul)

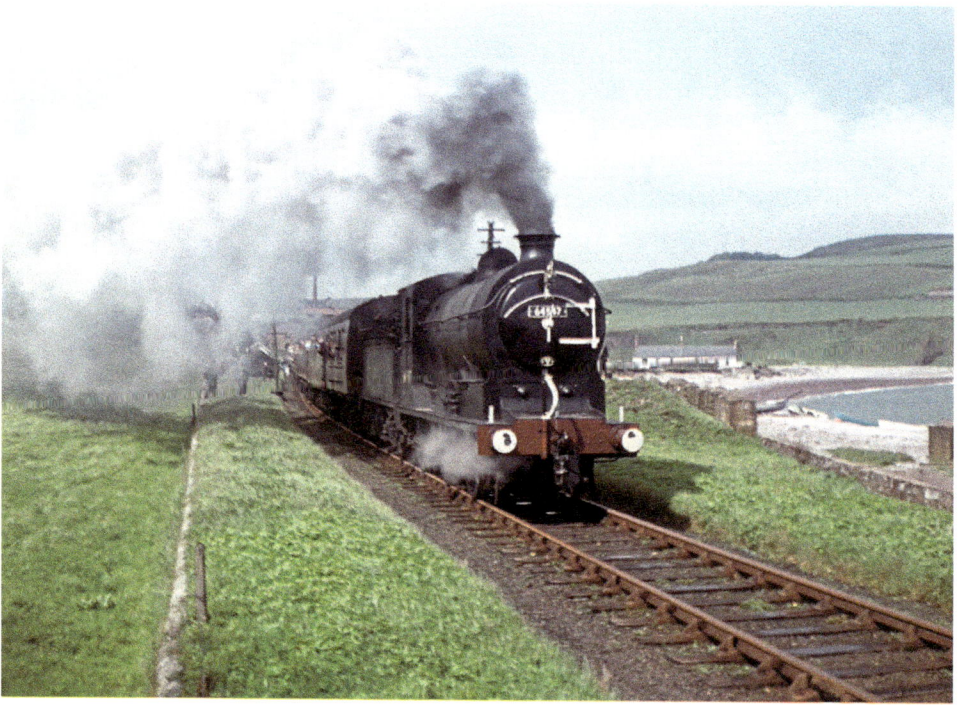

Also making a fruity exhaust was Class J37 No. 64547 with the last train to Inverbervie on 21 May 1966. (Douglas Paul)

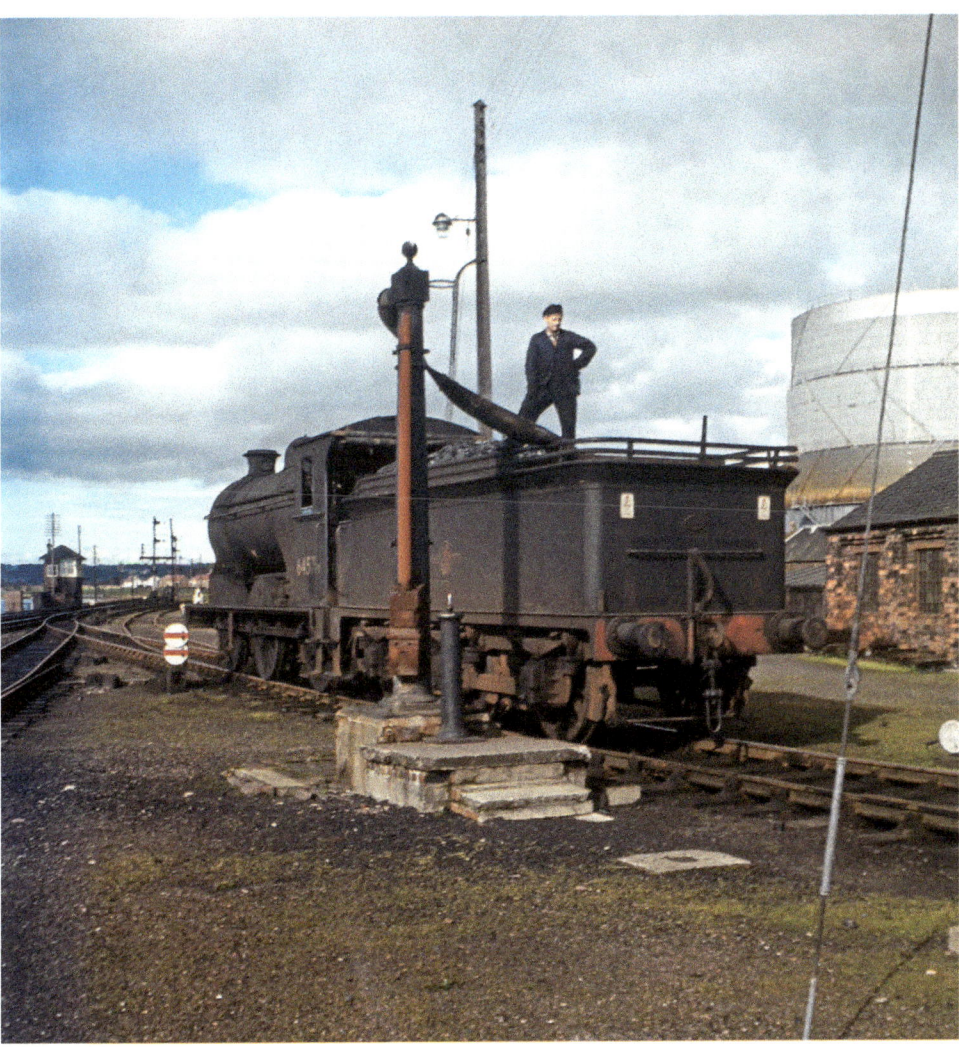

The fireman of Class J37 No. 64576 waits for the water crane to be turned on at Montrose during 1963. This decade of changing ideas and values saw George C. Wallace become Governor of Alabama in 1963. In his inaugural speech, he defiantly proclaimed, 'Segregation now, segregation tomorrow, and segregation forever!' Concerns this side of the Atlantic were to motivate 70,000 marchers from Aldermaston to London to demonstrate against nuclear weapons with a 'ban the bomb' campaign. (Douglas Paul)

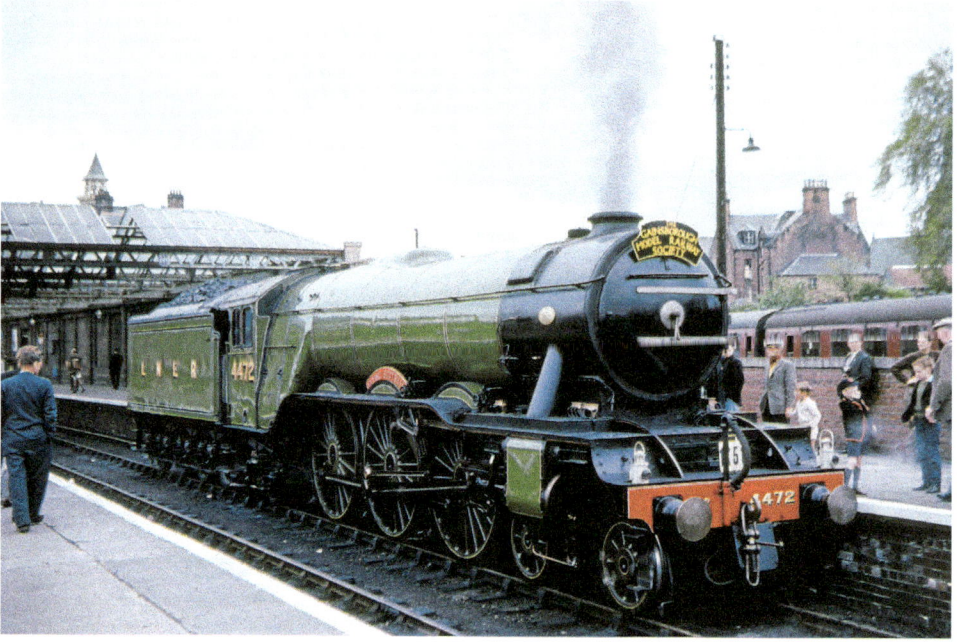

Specials

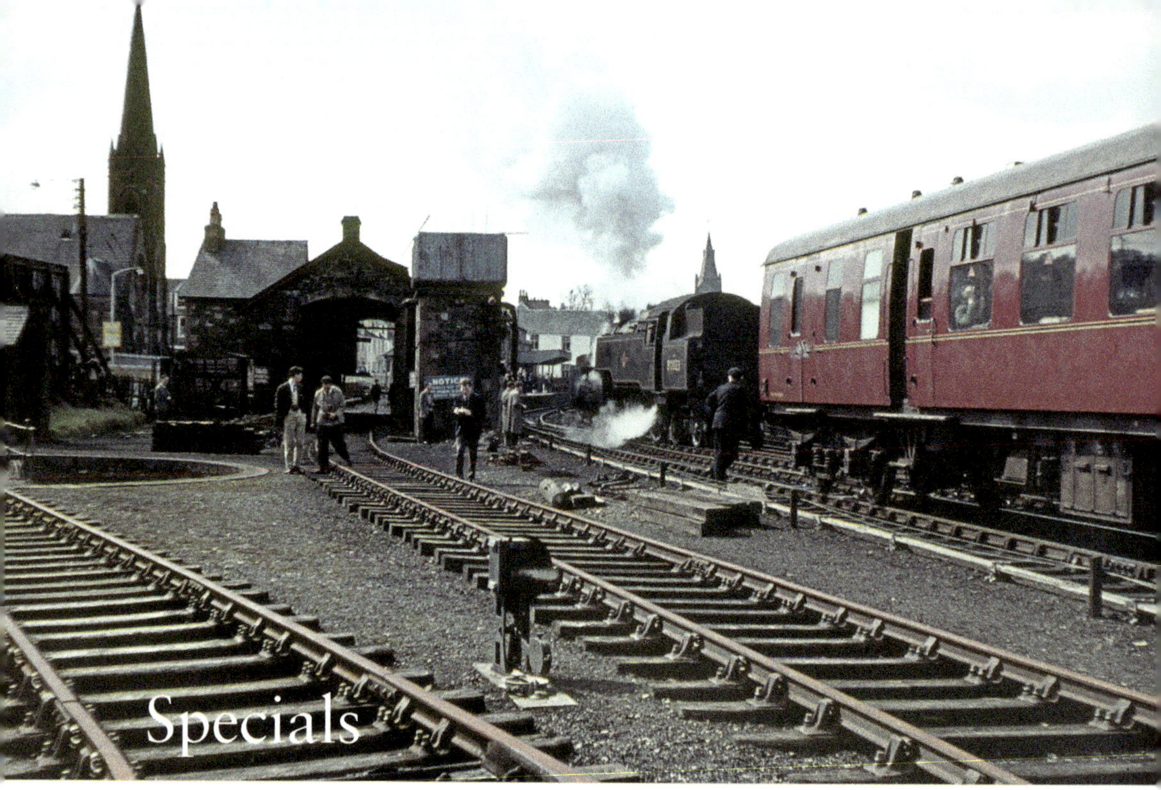

The branch from Castle Douglas where we left No. 45588 *Kashmir* on page 39 was covered by Standard 4MT No. 80023 to Kircudbright and back on 15 April 1963, where the tank comes off to run round by the small shed and turntable at the terminus. (Richard Icke)

The Gainsborough Model Railway Society ran a large number of tours through the sixties, most involving the use of No. 4472 *Flying Scotsman*, including this one which has brought the A3 to Dumfries. (Strathwood Library Collection)

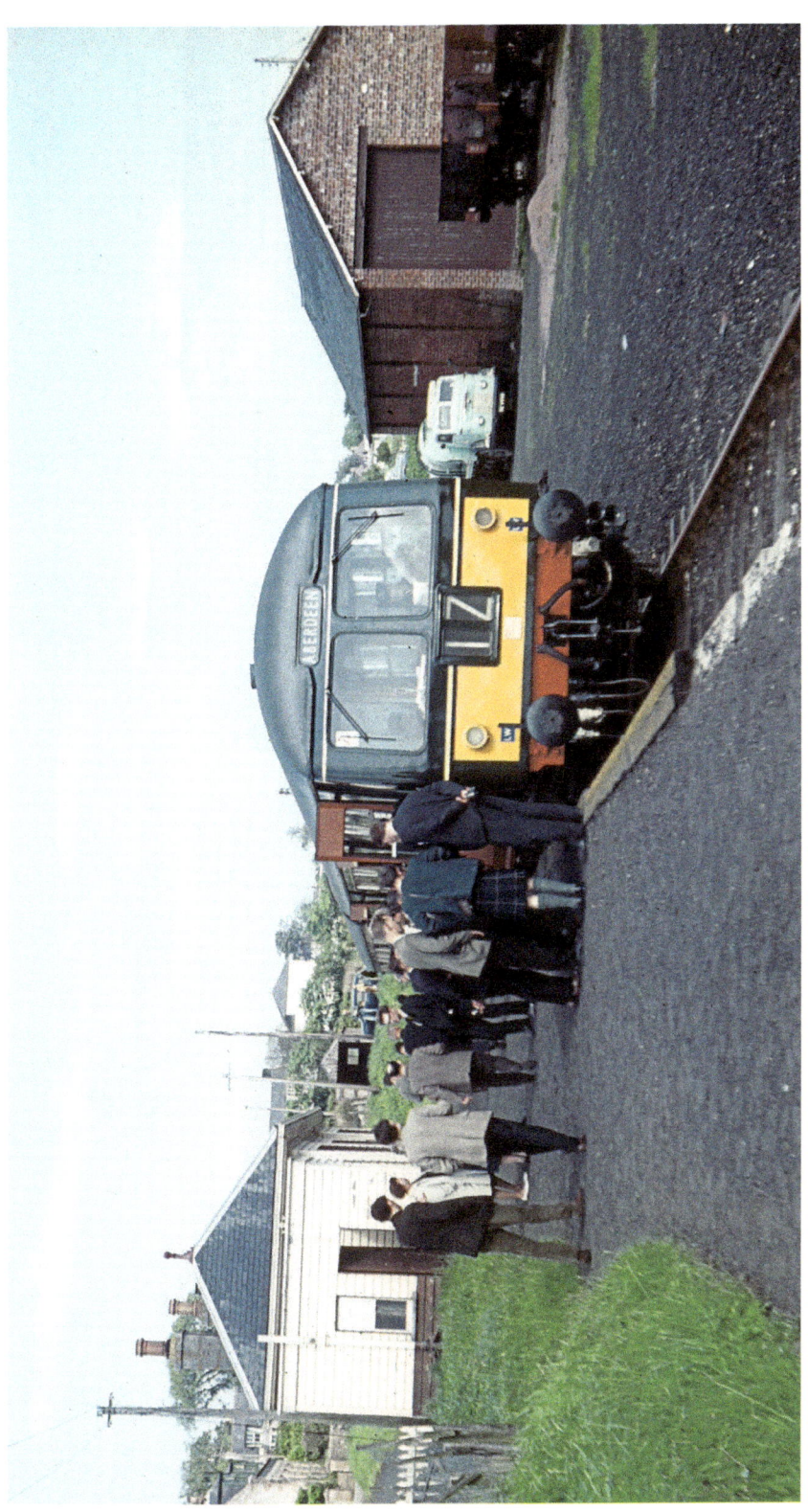

Just over five miles long was the branch from Inverurie to Old Meldrum, which opened for services in 1856 and was operated by the Great North of Scotland Railway, who tried using one of their two steam railmotors on the branch in 1905 without success. The LNER gave up on passenger trains in 1931 although goods workings continued as late as 1966. This allowed the Branch Line Society to arrange a visit using a Cravens-built DMU to the remarkably well preserved terminus as part of their Aberdeenshire Railtour on 5 June 1965. (Late Roy Hamilton)

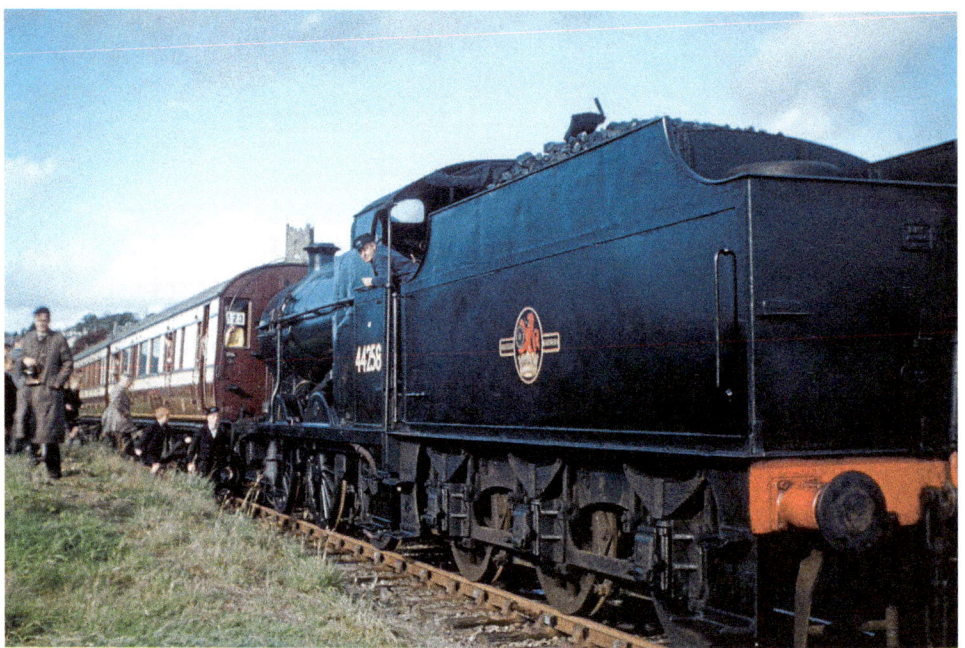

The preserved ex-Caledonian Railway coaches have been incorporated in this special visiting the terminus at Bankfoot from Stanley Junction near Perth behind Fowler 4F No. 44258. Passenger services having been removed by the LMS in 1931, a sparse goods traffic for the supply of seed potatoes lasted until 1964. (Strathwood Library Collection)

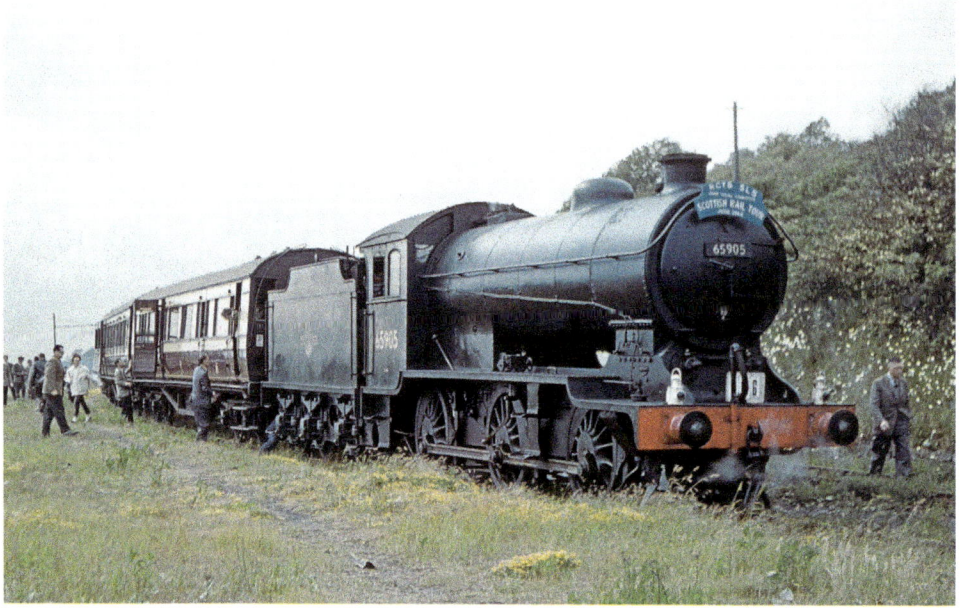

Once again in view are the two Caledonian Railway coaches providing a splash of pre-Grouping colour to Charlestown on 19 June 1962. Twenty-two steam locomotives were used during this incredible eleven-day Scottish Rail Tour organised by the RCTS and the SLS, including Class J38 No. 65905. (Frank Hornby)

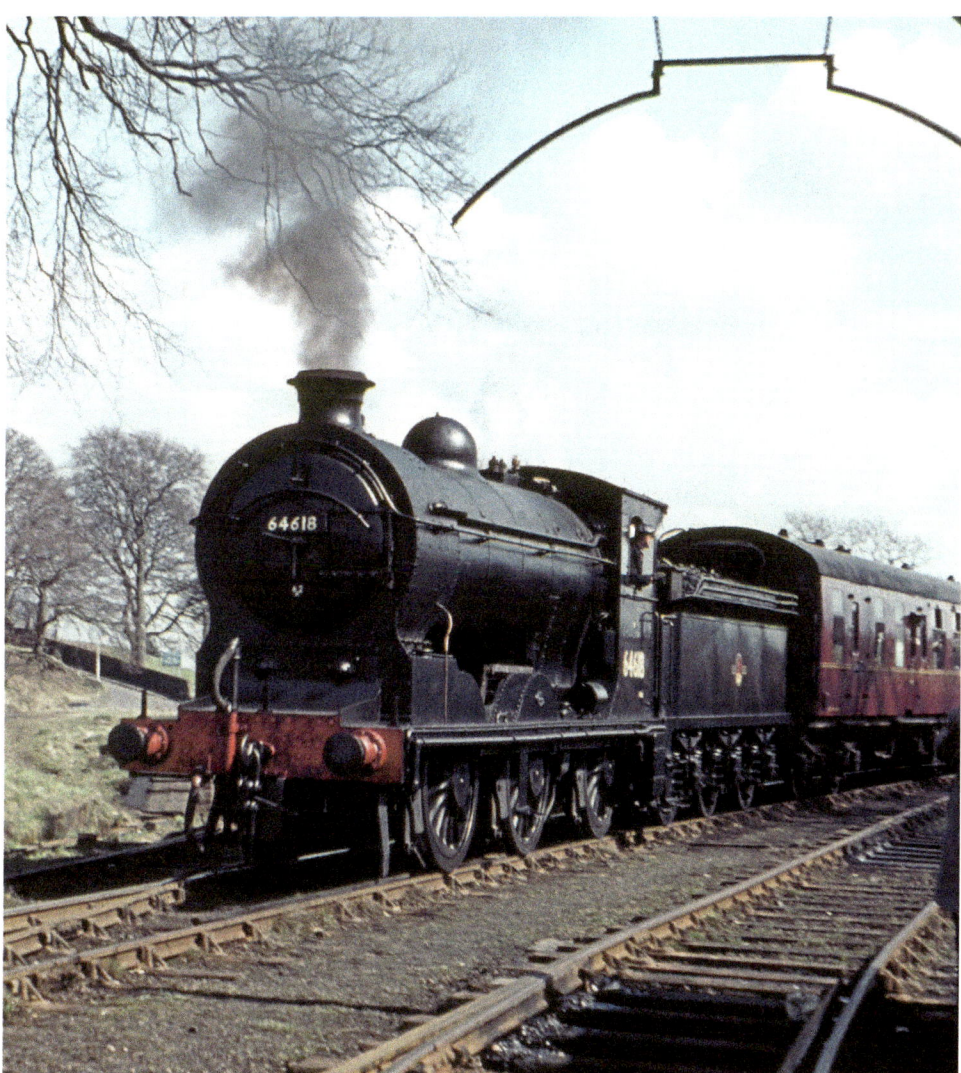

A more modest fourteen steam locomotives took part in the SLS and BLS-arranged Scottish Rambler No. 2 including Class J37 No. 64618, which was well spruced up for the run down the Leslie branch on day two of this four-day excursion over Easter 1963. The branch was opened in 1857 as part of the North British Railway's empire with seven trains a day at the time of the Grouping. Under the LNER services were withdrawn to passengers in 1932; the carriage of freight traffic continued until 1967 with diesel shunters being used at the end. (Richard Icke)

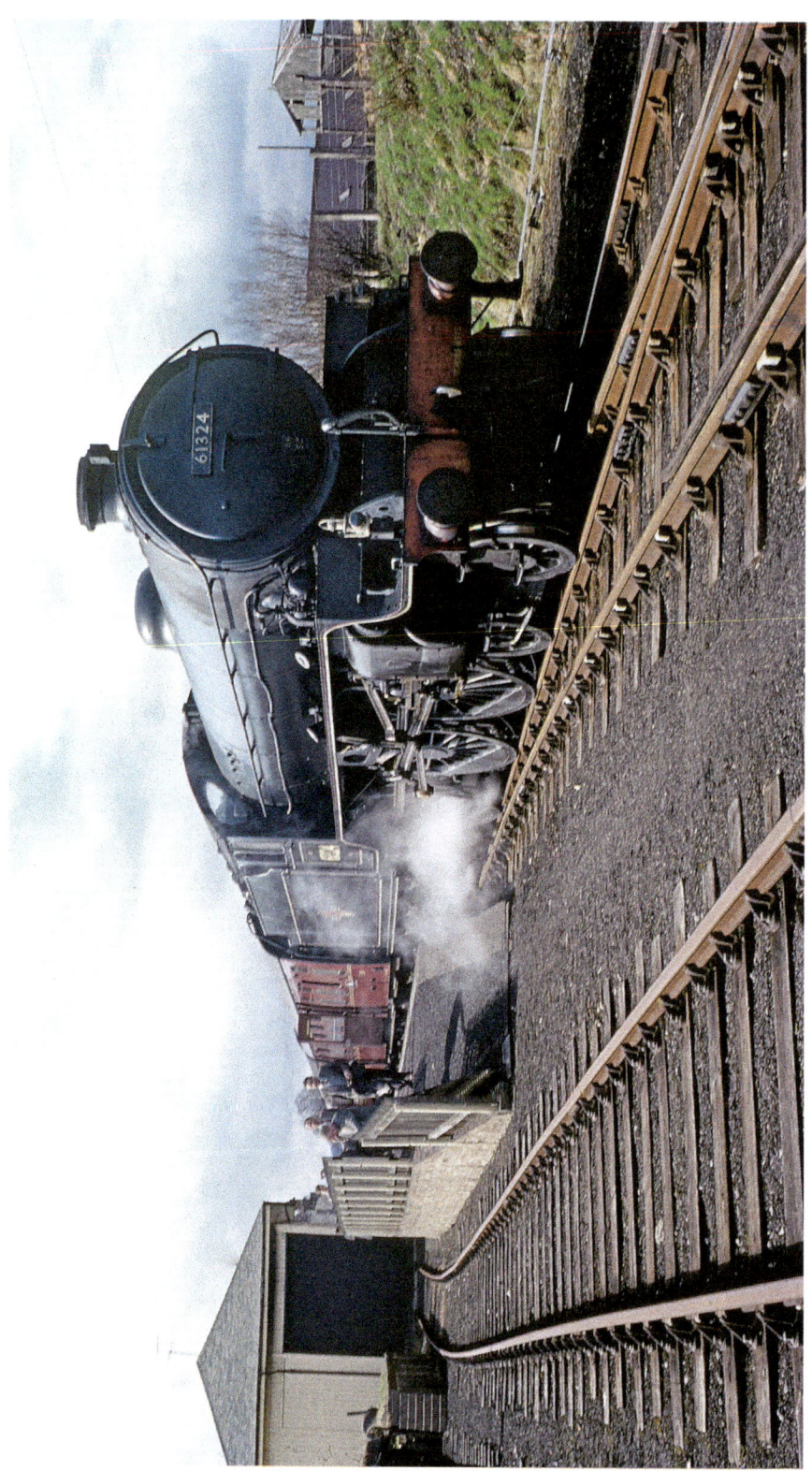

Another locomotive from this same tour was No. 61324, halted at Chirnside as part of the leg from Edinburgh Waverley along the ECML to Reston, thence to Duns and back before heading for Tweedmouth and Coldstream. The line from Duns to Greenlaw was washed out on 12 August 1948 during terrible floods in the area and was never reinstated. (Strathwood Library Collection)

Shedbashing Glasgow

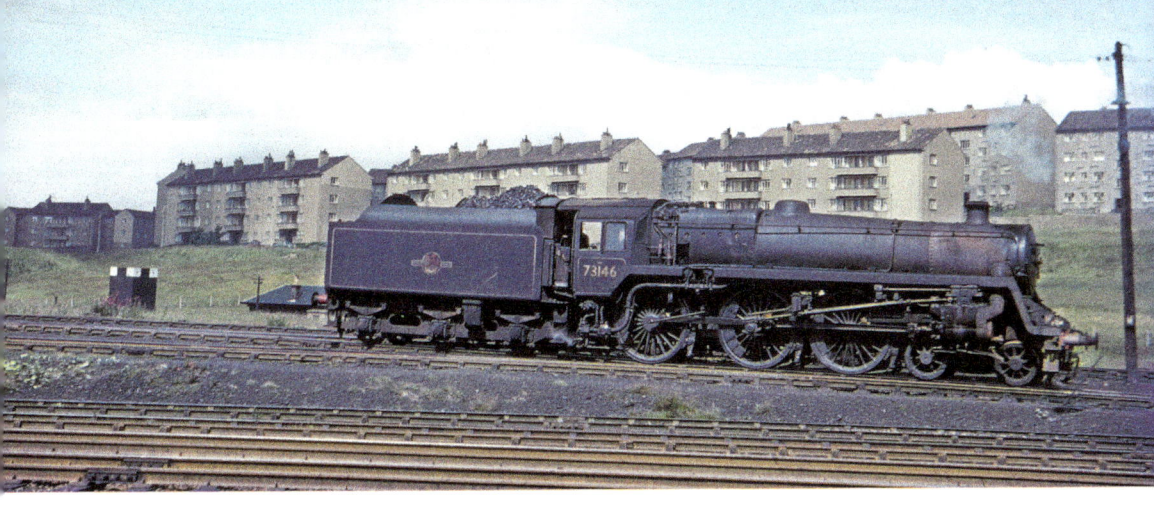

One of the Caprotti-fitted Standard 5MTs, No. 73146, runs light down the bank at Balornock in August 1965. Built at Derby Works in 1957, this engine was only allowed to give ten years' service to the Scottish Region before being withdrawn. (Strathwood Library Collection)

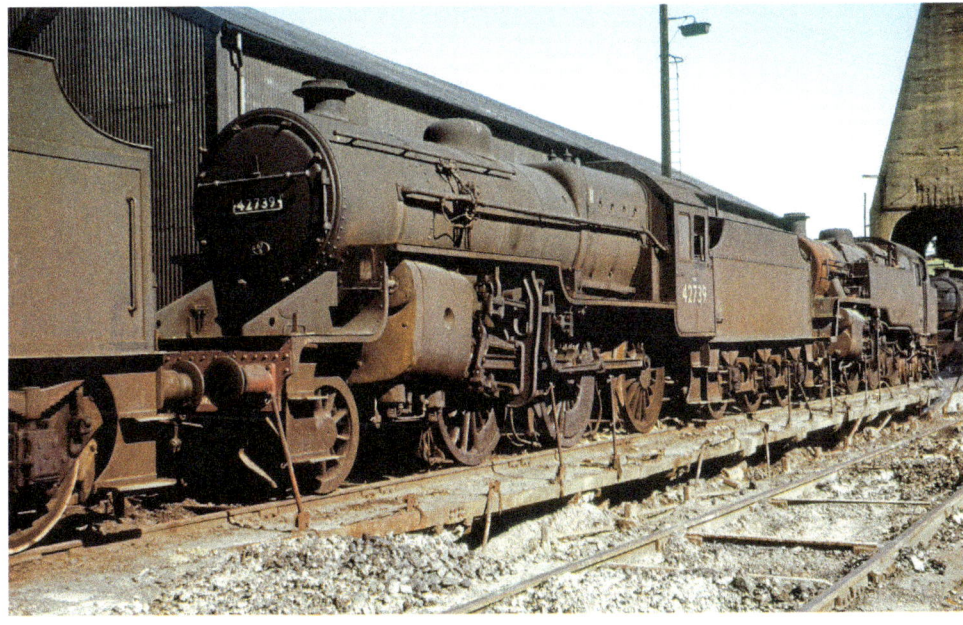

Standing amongst the discarded ash at Eastfield on 24 July 1966 was Crab No. 42739, six months from being withdrawn but with at least seventeen years' service under its belt. This was a bumper year for fans of Carry On films with *Carry on Screaming!* and *Carry On Don't Lose Your Head* being released. (Strathwood Library Collection)

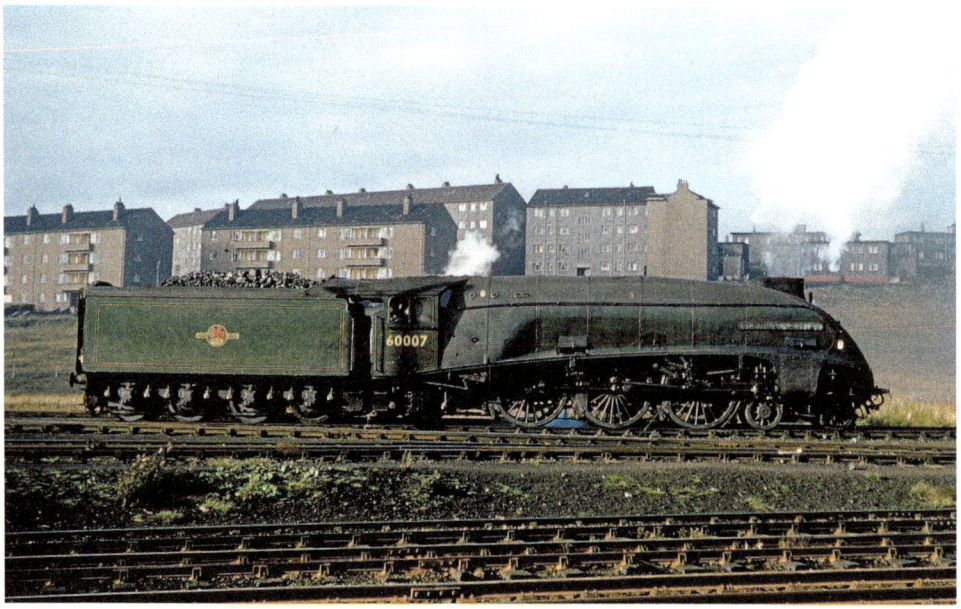

Next to pass our unknown cameraman at Balornock in September 1964 this time was No. 60007 *Sir Nigel Gresley*, running light engine. (Strathwood Library Collection)

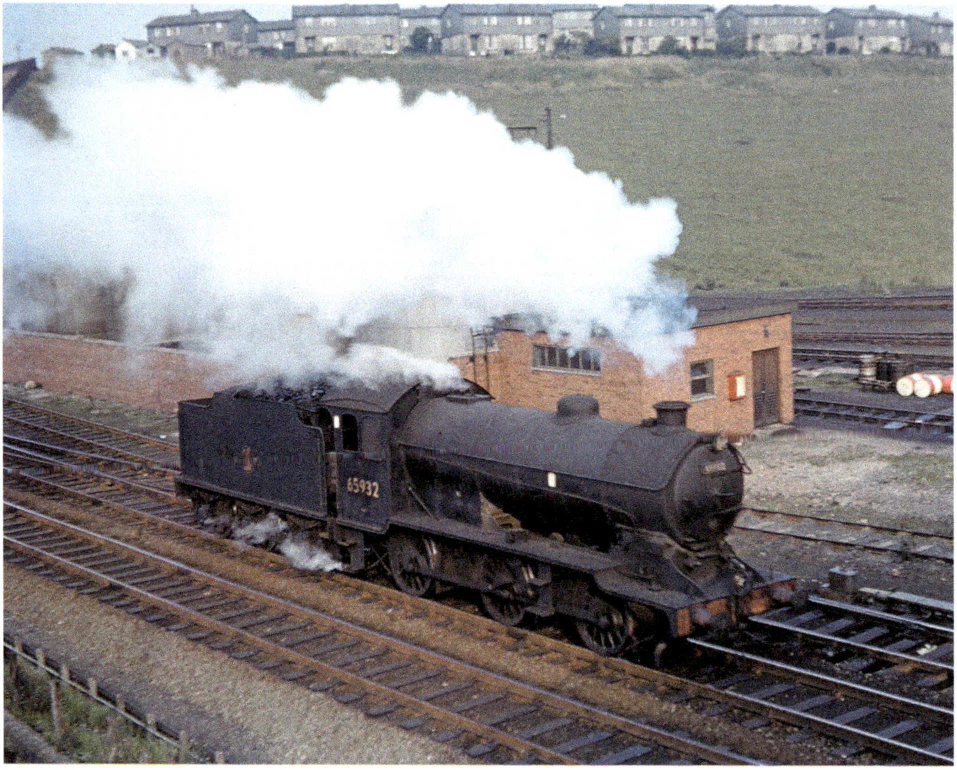

Another light engine movement brings Class J38 No. 65932 past the recently constructed fueling point for diesels at Eastfield in October 1964. (Strathwood Library Collection)

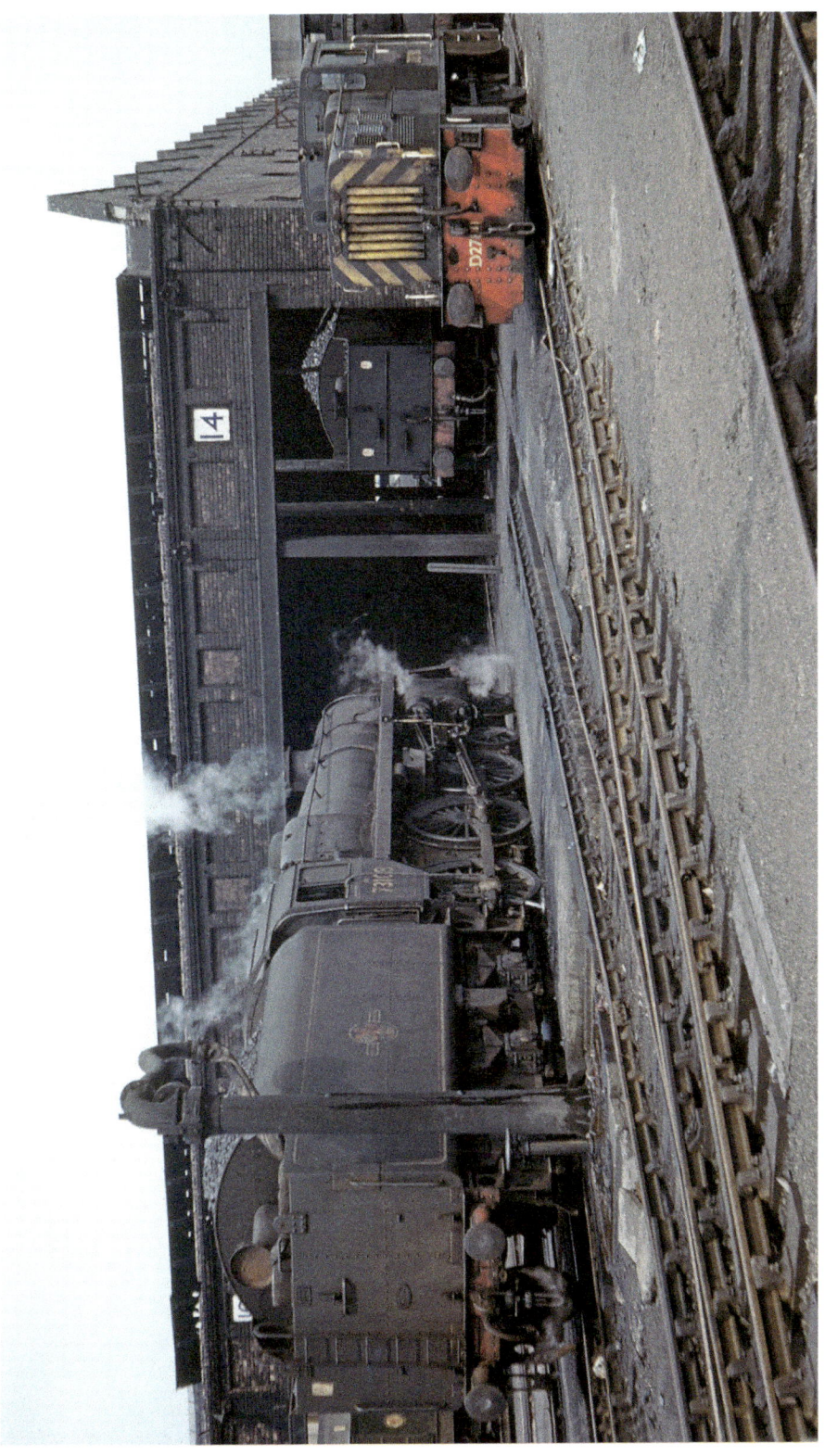

The rebuilding process at 65A (Eastfield) would not be complete until the early seventies, with diesels sharing accomodation with the dying steam fleet in June 1965 when Standard 5MT 73108 was taking a breather. (Win Wall/Strathwood Library Collection)

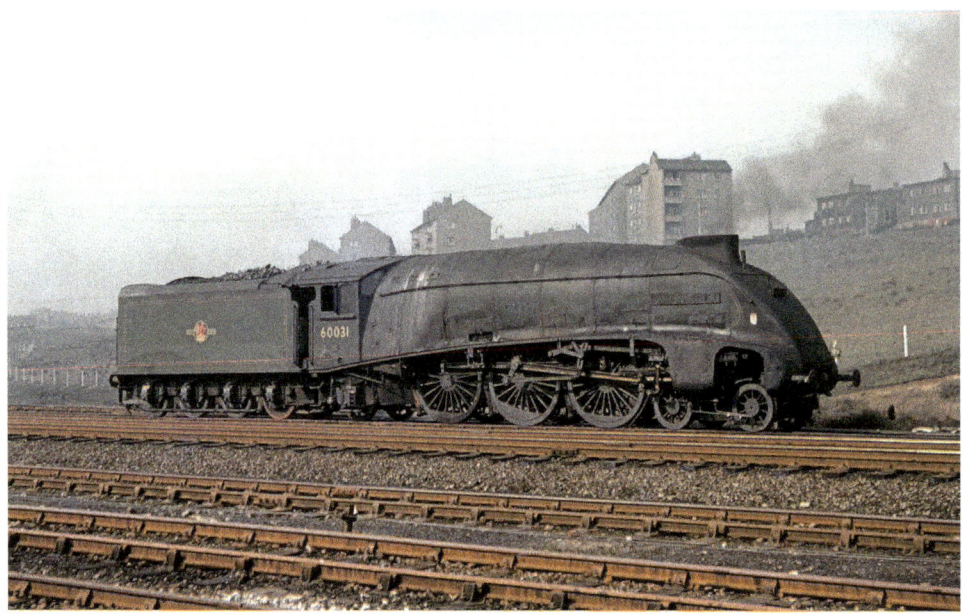

In April 1963 No. 60031 *Golden Plover* had been transferred to nearby 65B (St Rollox) from 64B (Haymarket) for just over a year now and was clearly not receiving the regular attentions of any cleaners since its move. (Strathwood Library Collection)

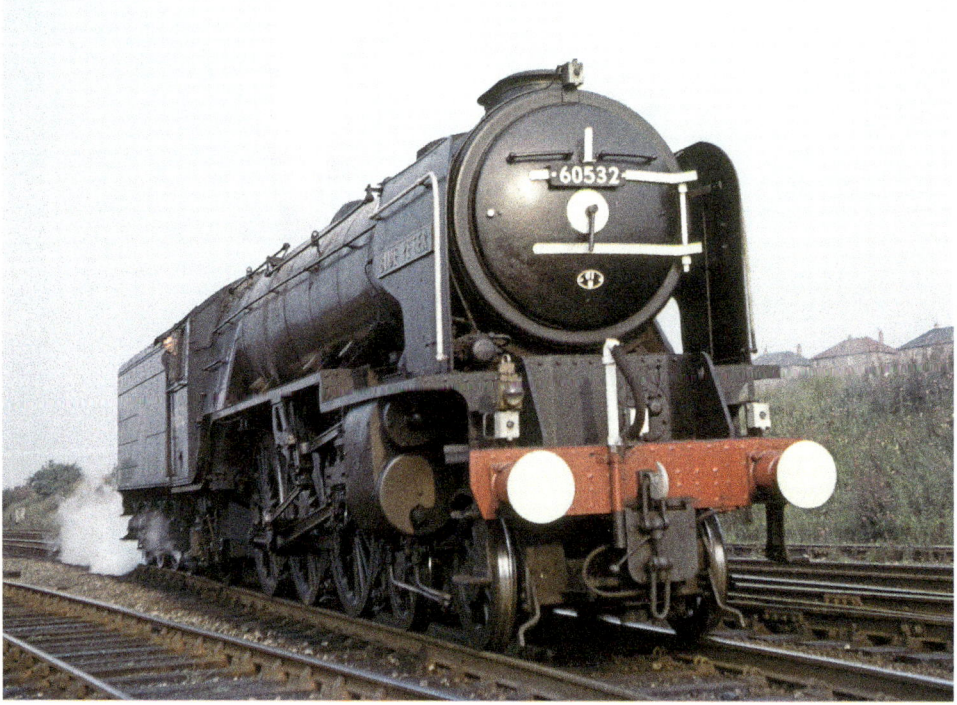

Making its way light engine also near St Rollox was No. 60532 *Blue Peter* which, although cleaner, had seen much activity from a whitewash brush to work a Railtour in October 1966. (Strathwood Library Collection)

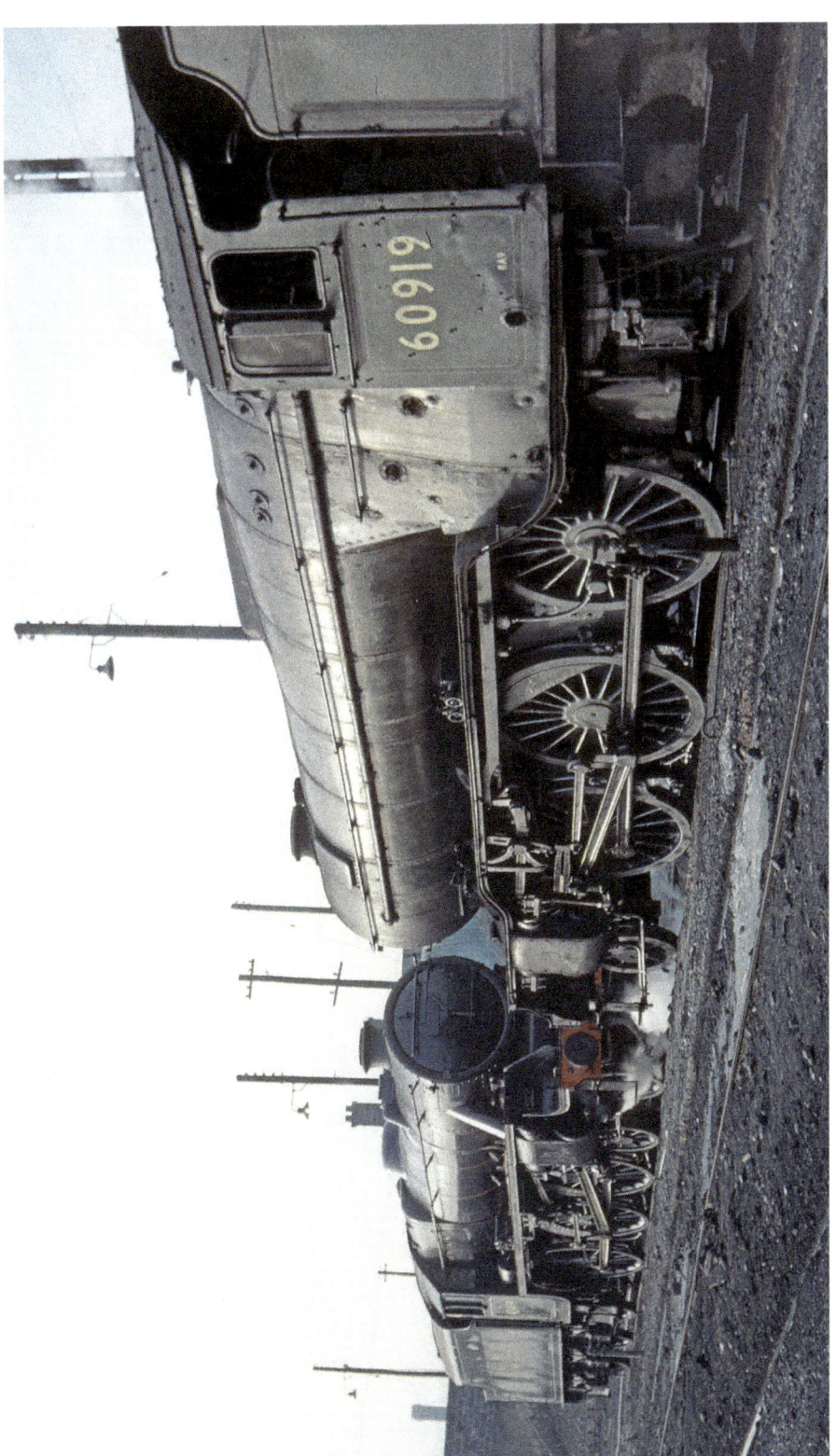

There is no use of white paint for picking out the numbers on the smoke box plate of Black Five No. 45455, face to face with Gresley V2 No. 60919 at St Rollox in March 1963. (Strathwood Library Collection)

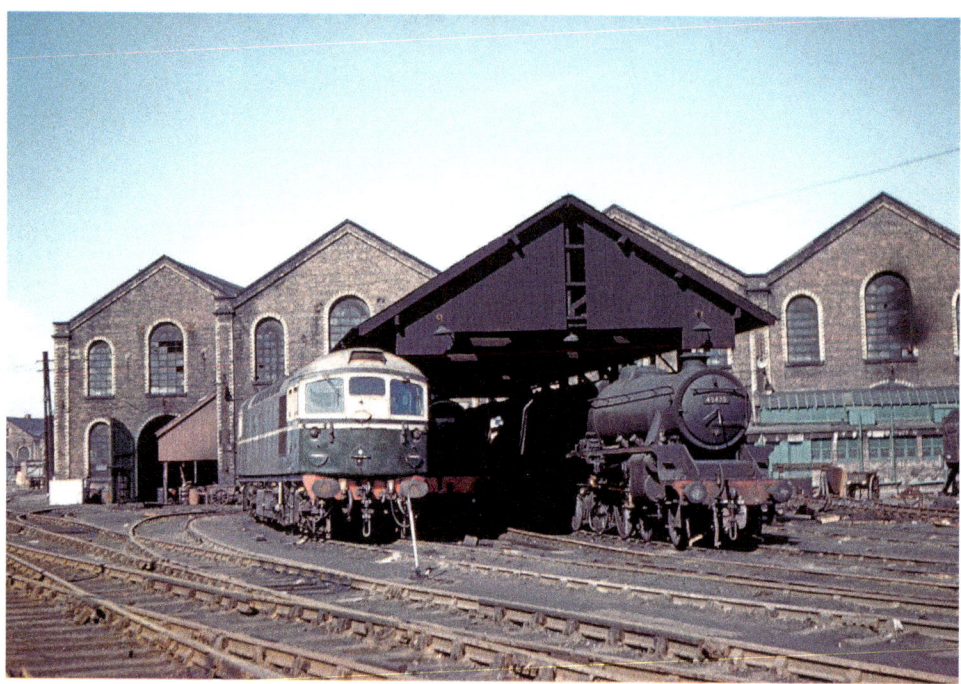

The first built of the BRCW Type Two diesel D5300 keeps company with another Black Five, No. 45475, outside St Rollox Works on 19 June 1960. The diesel and a number of its classmates had just transferred to the Scottish Region, having entered service allocated to 34B (Hornsey) during 1958 and 1959. (Frank Hornby)

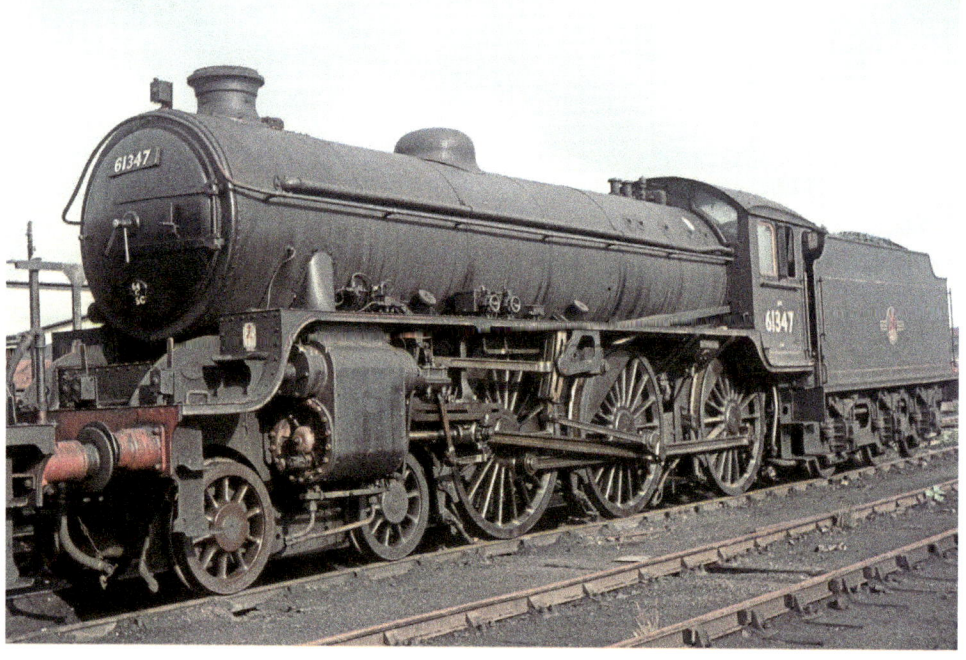

Arriving at Cowlairs Works in July 1965 for attention was No. 61347. The B1 would give another twenty-two months' active duty before being set aside for scrapping. (Dave Down)

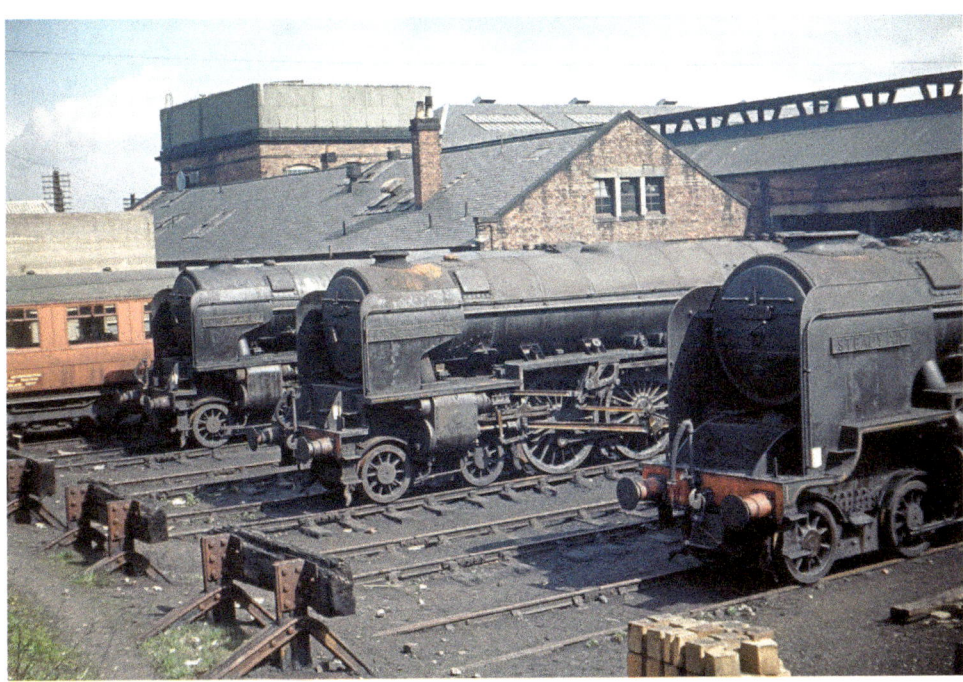

LNER designs would not carry much favour at Polmadie, so it was little wonder that they quickly set aside No. 60512 *Steady Aim*, No. 60535 *Hornet's Beauty* and No. 60527 *Sun Chariot* in 1965. (Len Smith)

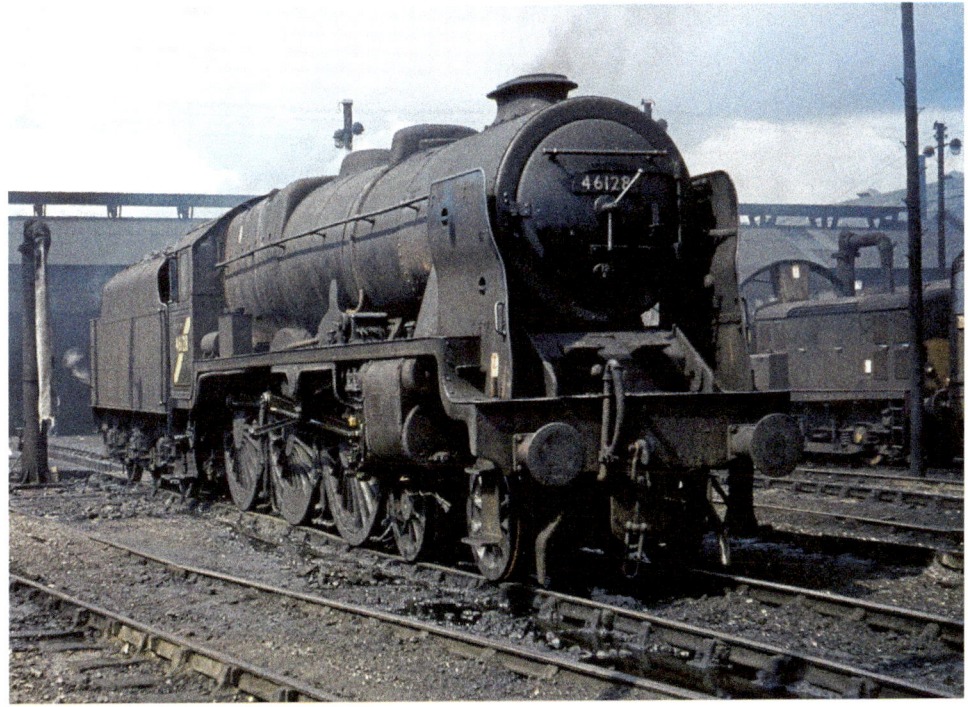

The men of Polmadie would be fond of their beloved Royal Scots, though, such as No. 46128 *The Lovat Scouts*, on shed on 10 August 1964. (Strathwood Library Collection)

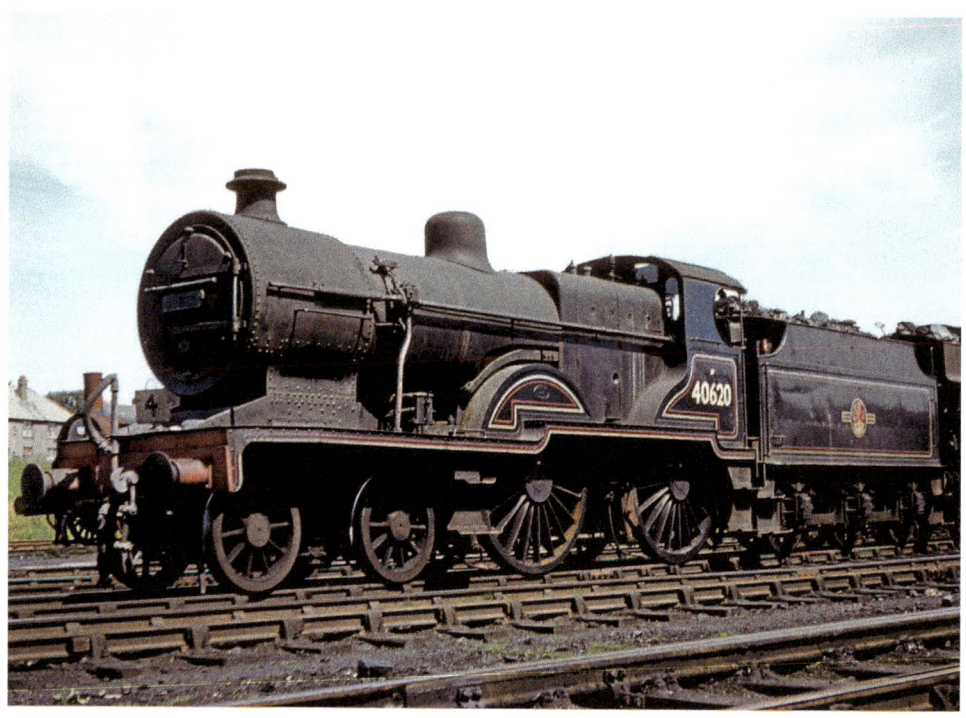

Just over a year further in traffic remained for Class 2P No. 40620, standing at Corkerhill on 19 June 1960. (Frank Hornby)

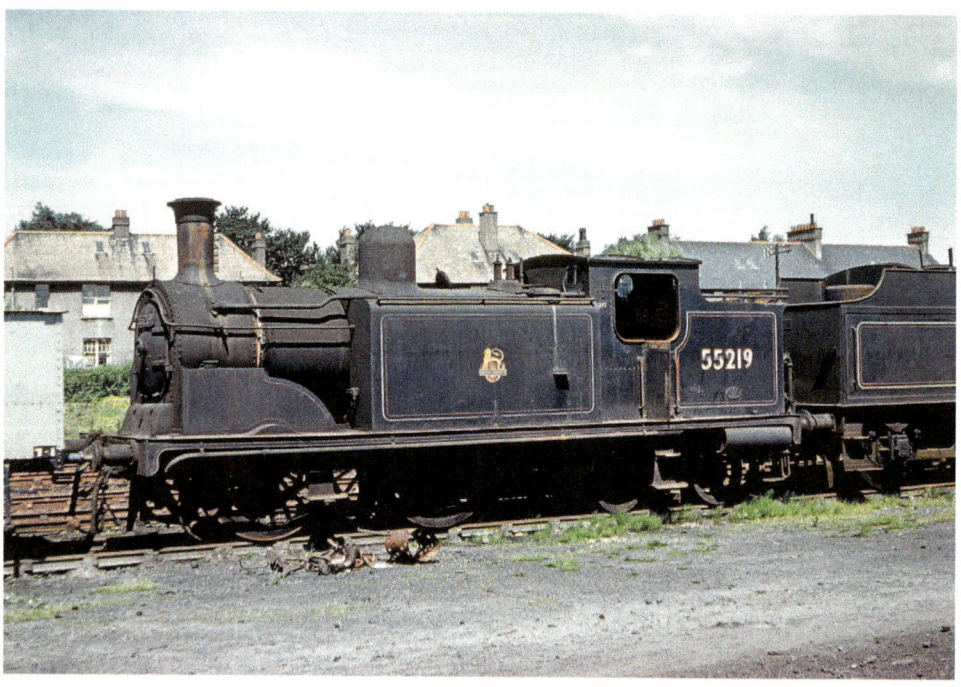

Whereas McIntosh 2P No. 55219, also at Corkerhill the same day, only has the trip to the breakers to look forward to. (Frank Hornby)

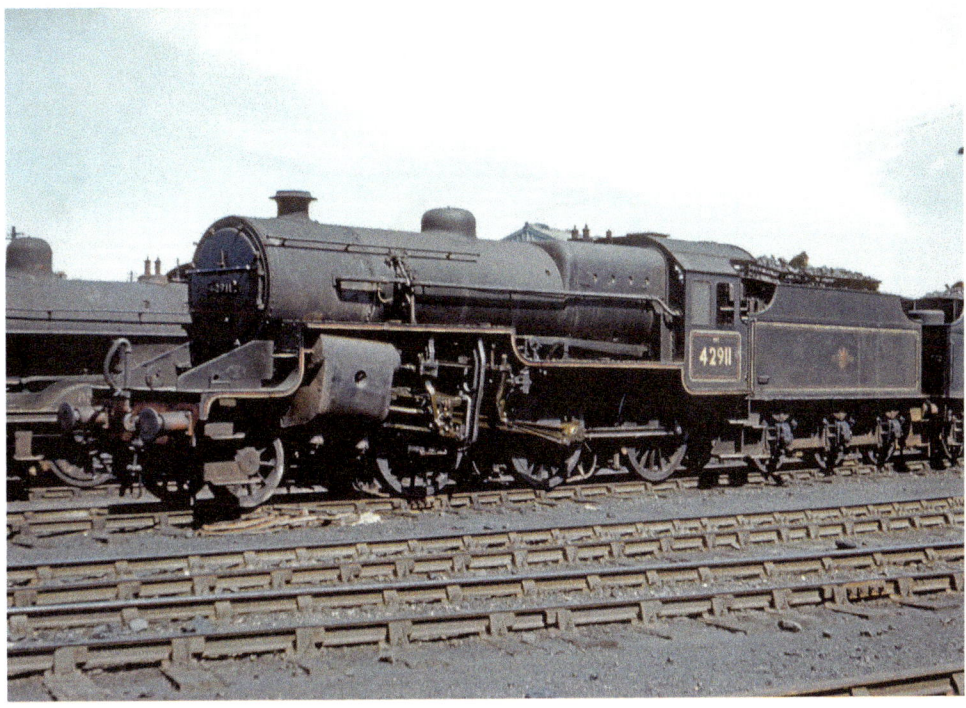

Also taking in the June sunshine at Corkerhill was Crab No. 42911 in 1960. Coded 67A, it closed to steam on 1 May 1967, being turned over to diesels and DMUs thereafter. (Frank Hornby)

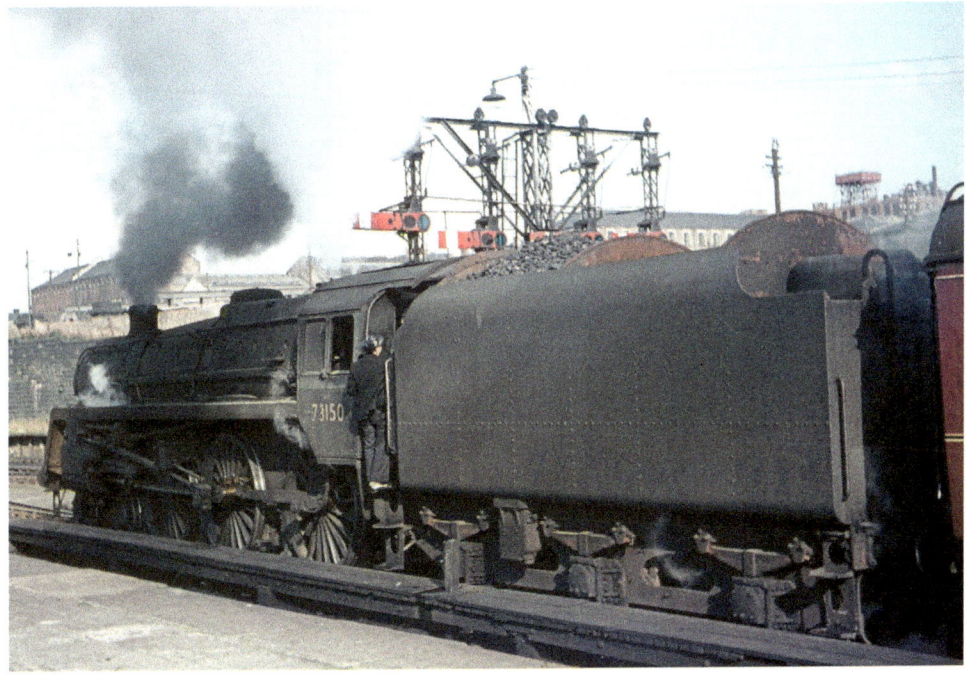

Taking our leave of Glasgow for now, we arrive at Buchanan Street station in search of A4s in 1966 to find the young crew member climbing back on board Caprotti-fitted Standard 5MT No. 73150. (Peter Coton)

Indian Summer
for the A4s

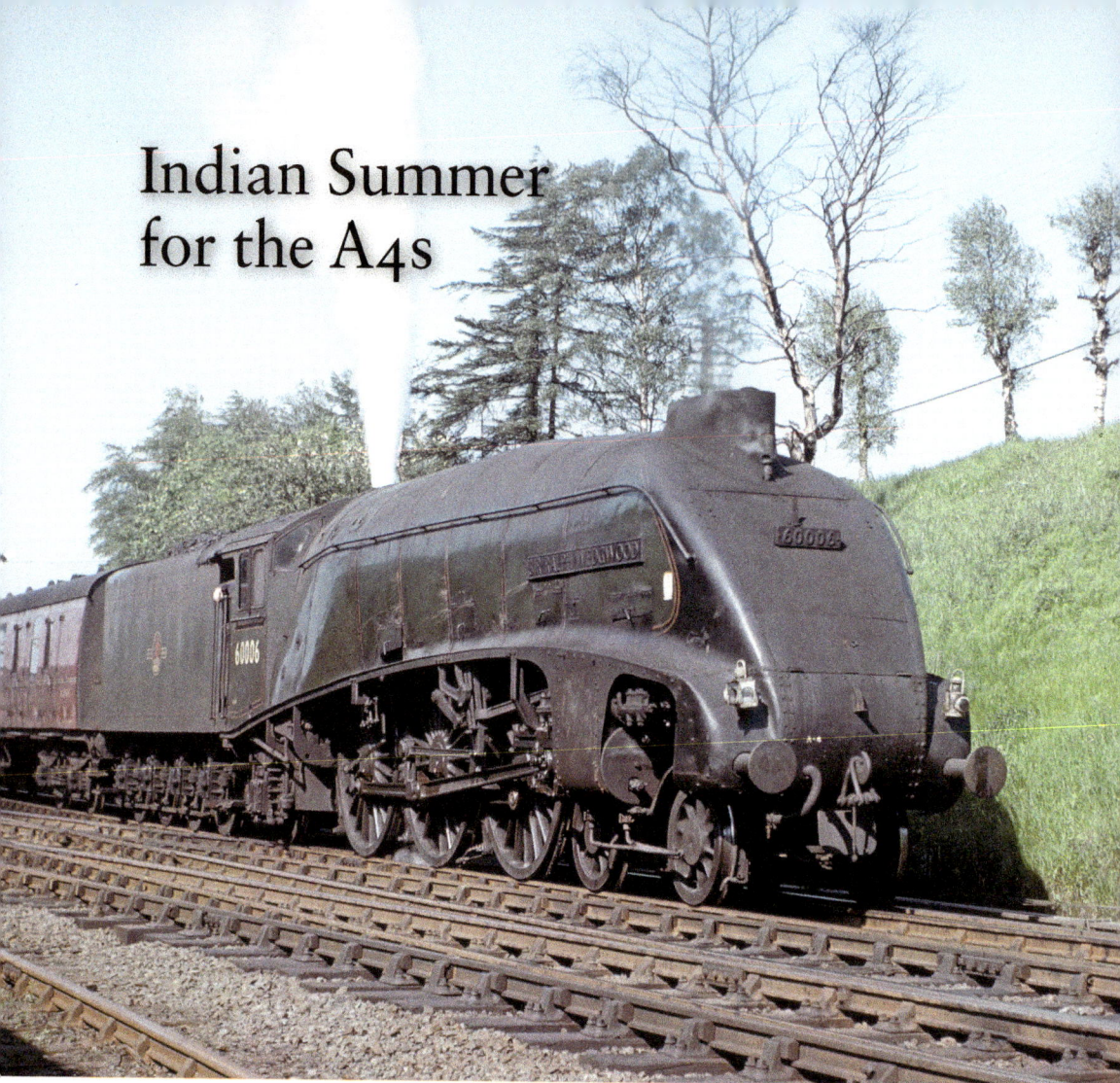

The use of these fine Gresley Pacifics on the Glasgow to Aberdeen route in the mid-sixties was a major draw for eager enthusiasts to enjoy some everyday haulage behind A4s now they had disappeared from the East Coast Main Line. At the head of an Aberdeen to Glasgow express in 1964 was No. 60006 *Sir Ralph Wedgwood*, blowing off furiously during the Gleneagles stop. The Beatles, Cilla Black, Roy Orbison, The Searchers and The Rolling Stones all managed to take two hits each to number ones in the British charts during 1964. (John Rowe)

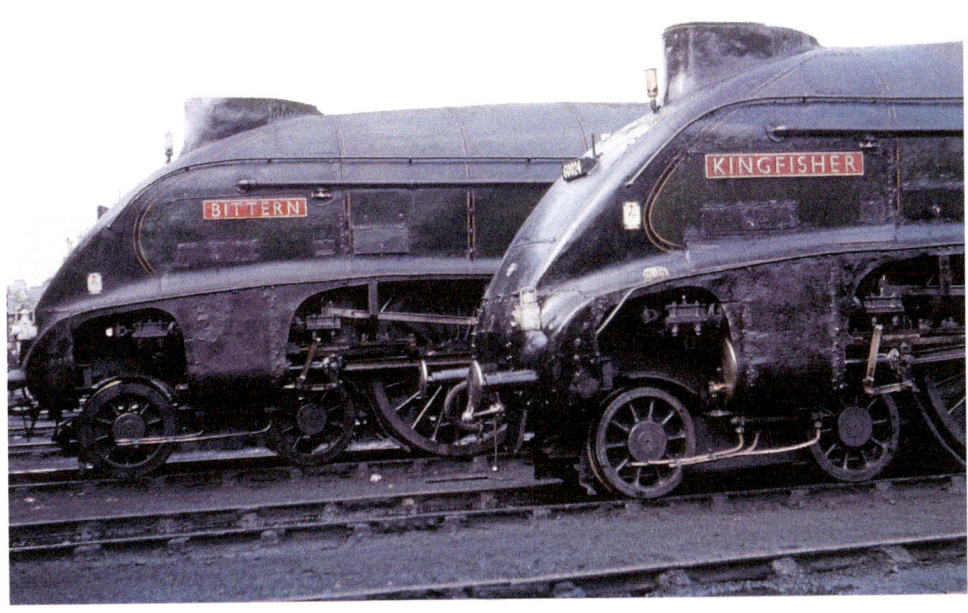

At Aberdeen Ferryhill in 1966 No. 60019 *Bittern* and 60024 *Kingfisher* compare chimney flarings. (Strathwood Library Collection)

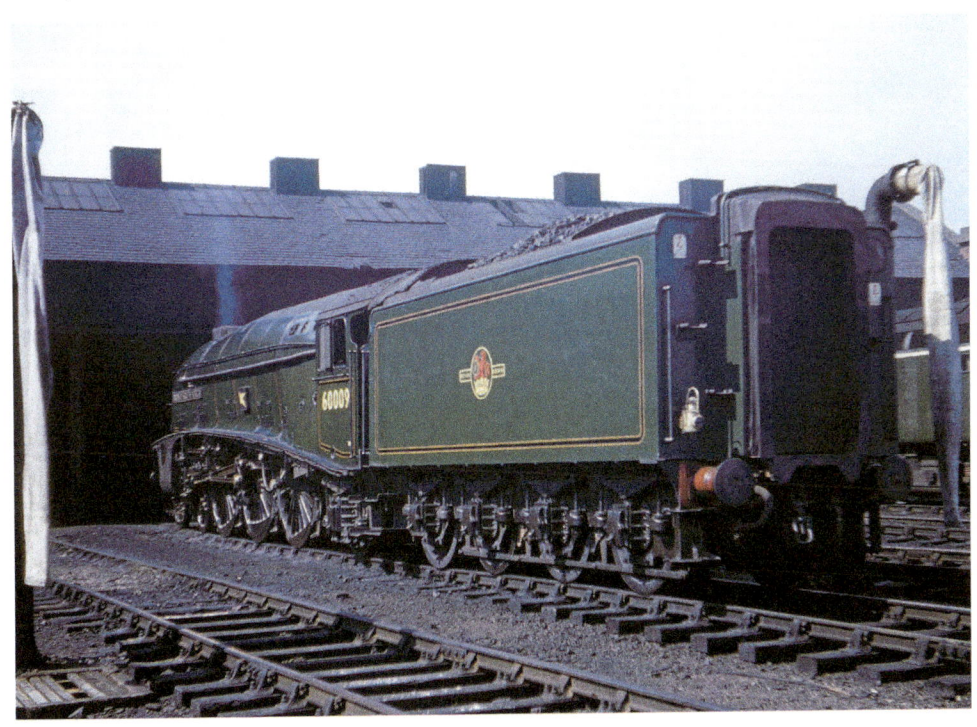

One of the corridor tenders is fitted to No. 60009 *Union of South Africa*, again at Ferryhill on 5 June 1965. (Michael Beaton)

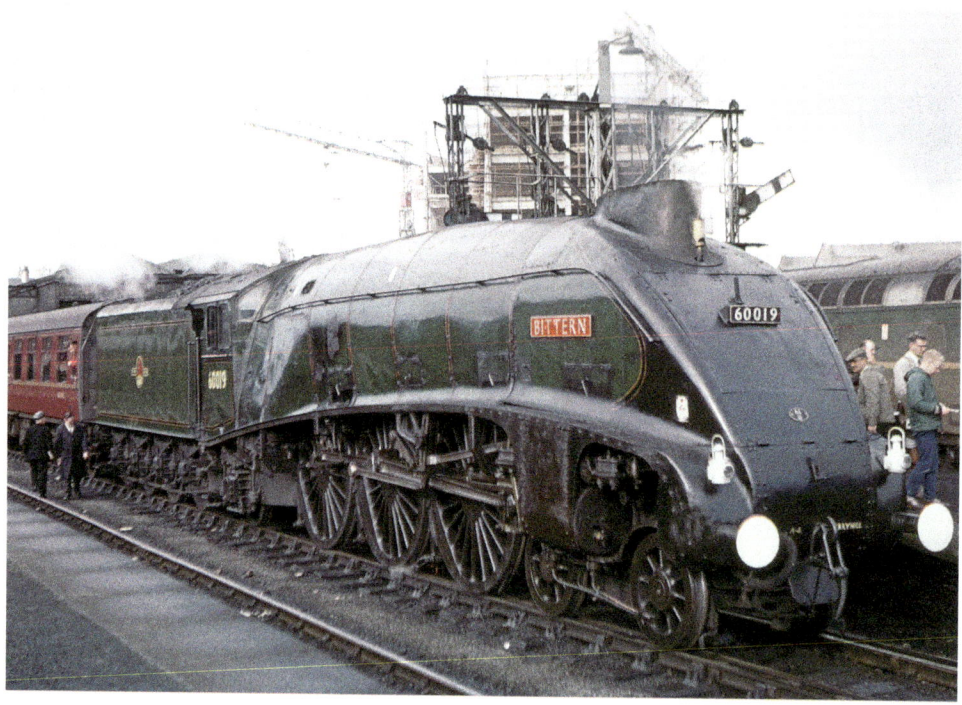

Freshly bulled up buffers adorn No. 60019 *Bittern* at Buchanan Street in 1966. (Strathwood Library Collection)

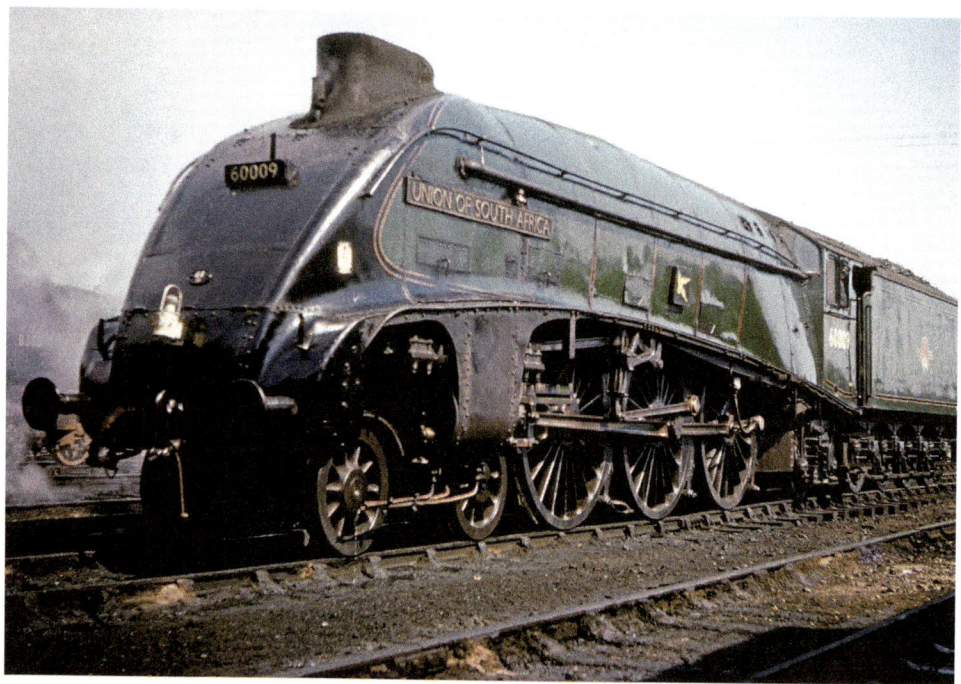

Particularly impressive from low angles, Gresley's superb designs capture the imagination, such as No. 60009 *Union of South Africa* during June 1965 at Ferryhill between turns on a steady roster of specials mixed into runs on the expresses to Glasgow. (Win Wall/Strathwood Library Collection)

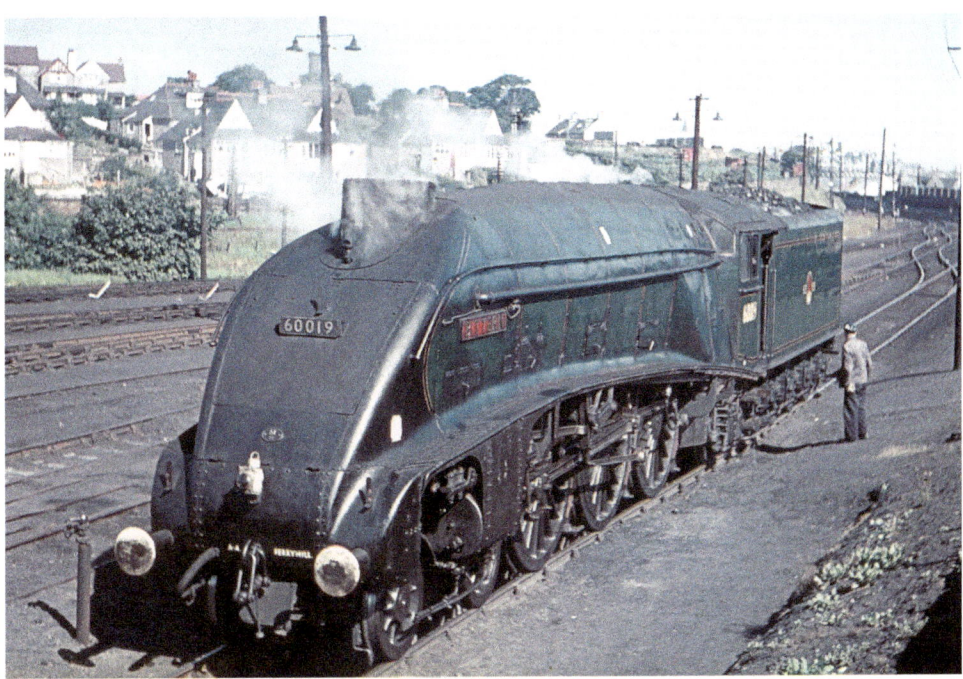

Really, those elegant curves look good from almost every angle, such as on 6 August 1966 with No. 60019 *Bittern* being prepared at Ferryhill. (Peter Coton)

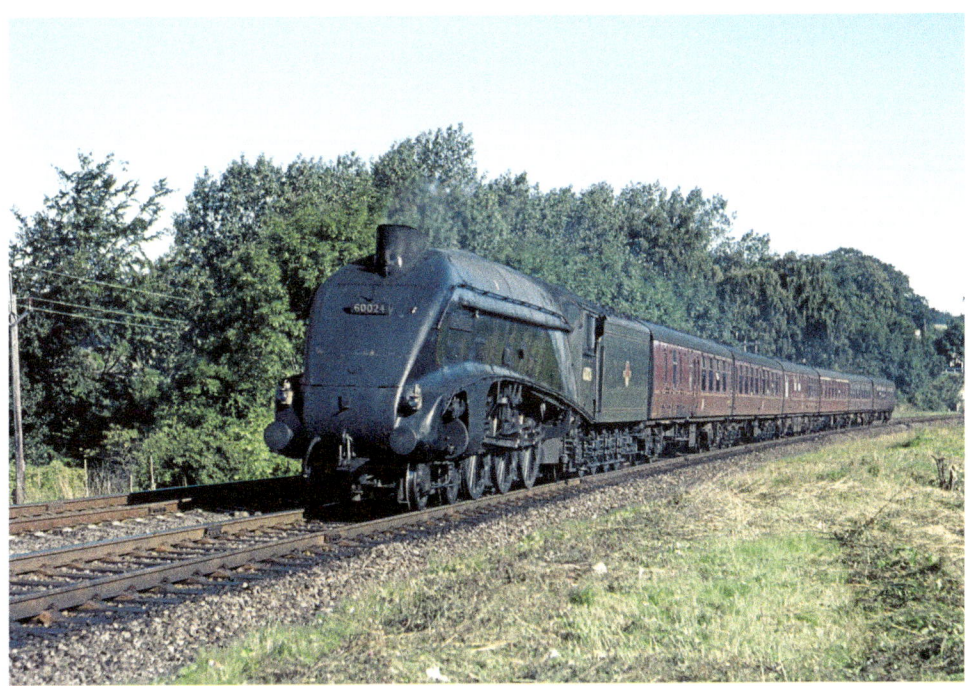

Critics would argue that they should fly when only loaded with six coaches as here at Bridge of Allan behind No. 60024 *Kingfisher*, although there are records of the class making fabulous runs with huge trains likewise to dispel their critics. (Strathwood Library Collection)

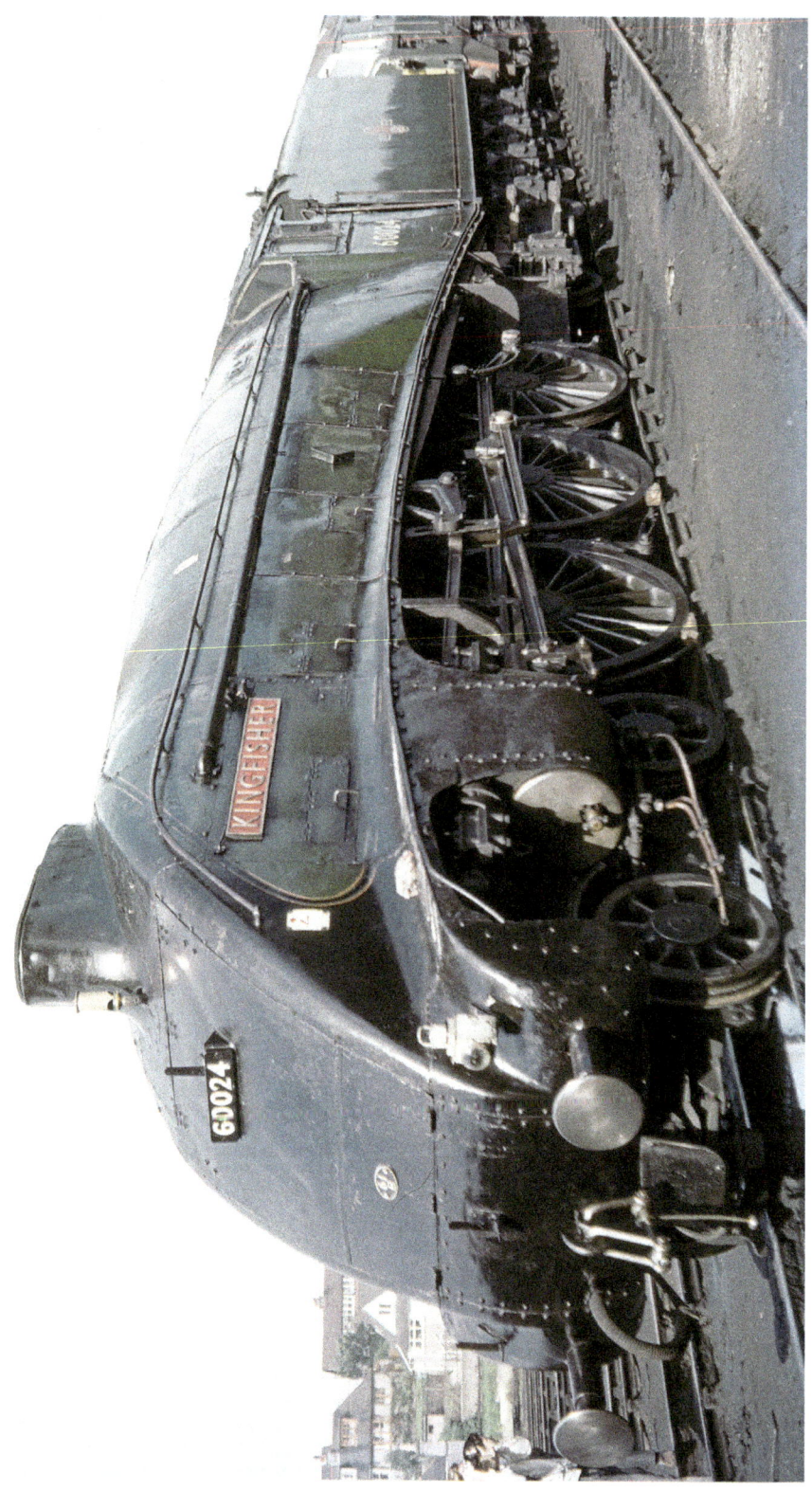

The buffers are even burnished as No. 60024 *Kingfisher* glistens in the sun outside at Ferryhill in September 1966, just days before being taken out of service. At the start of 1965 there were twelve of the A4s available; this number fell to just six to start into 1966, with *Kingfisher* and *Bittern* being the last two withdrawn in September. (Strathwood Library Collection)

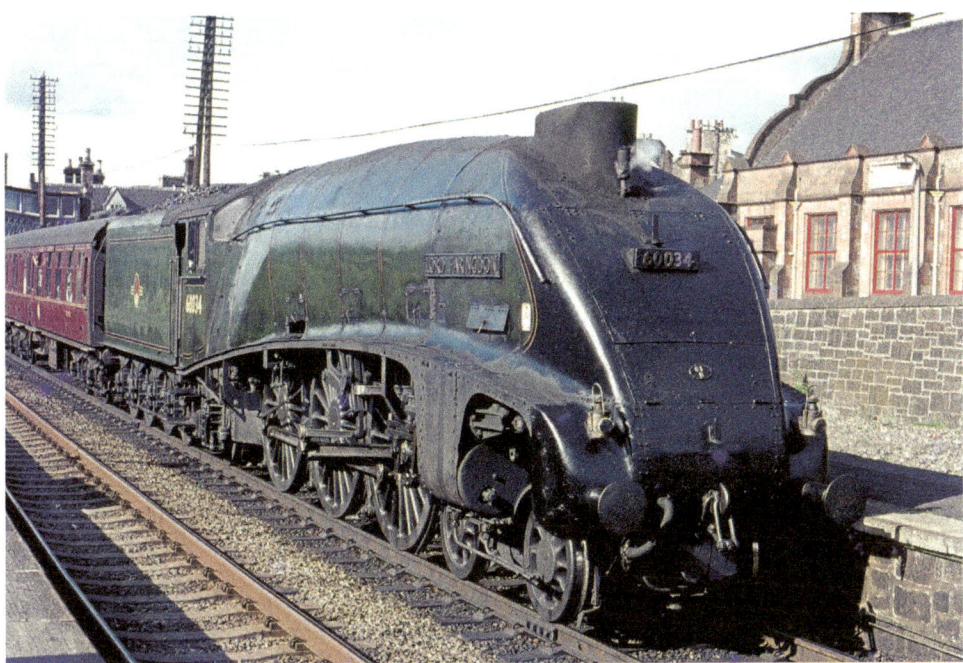

Generally the survivors in the last couple of years were well kept, such as No. 60034 *Lord Farringdon* at Dunblane in 1965. This was the last of the A4s to be renamed in early 1948, giving up its previous name *Peregrine* in favour of the name of the former Chairman of the Great Central Railway from 1889 to 1922. During the First World War he founded the British Trade Corporation, serving as its first Chairman. He was created a baronet in 1902 and a baron in 1916. At his death in 1934 the administration of his estate gave rise to Henderson Global Investors, which became a public company in 1983 and by the Millenium reported assets of £83 billion. (Strathwood Library Collection)

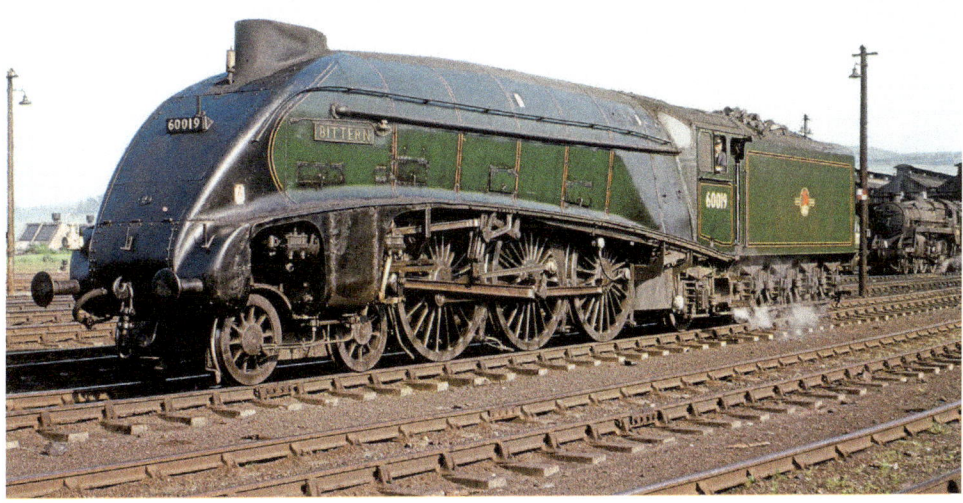

Pottering about the shed yard at Perth in September 1964 was a very clean 60019 *Bittern*. (John Rowe)

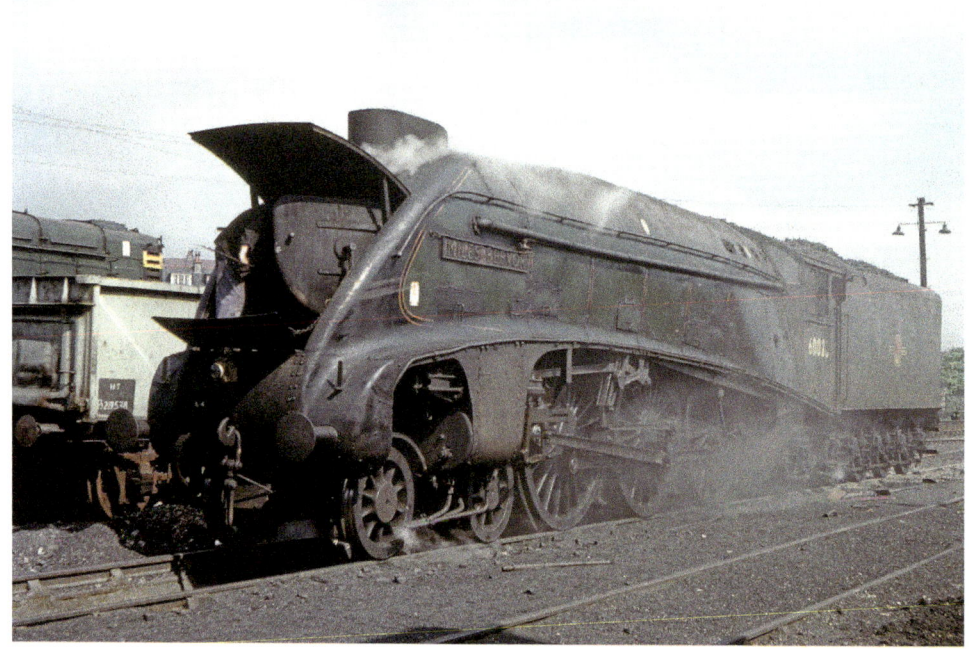

A slightly more work weary No. 60028 *Miles Beevor* has its smoke box swept out, adding to the dusty appearance of this Pacific in its last six months in service on 5 June 1965. (Win Wall/Strathwood Library Collection)

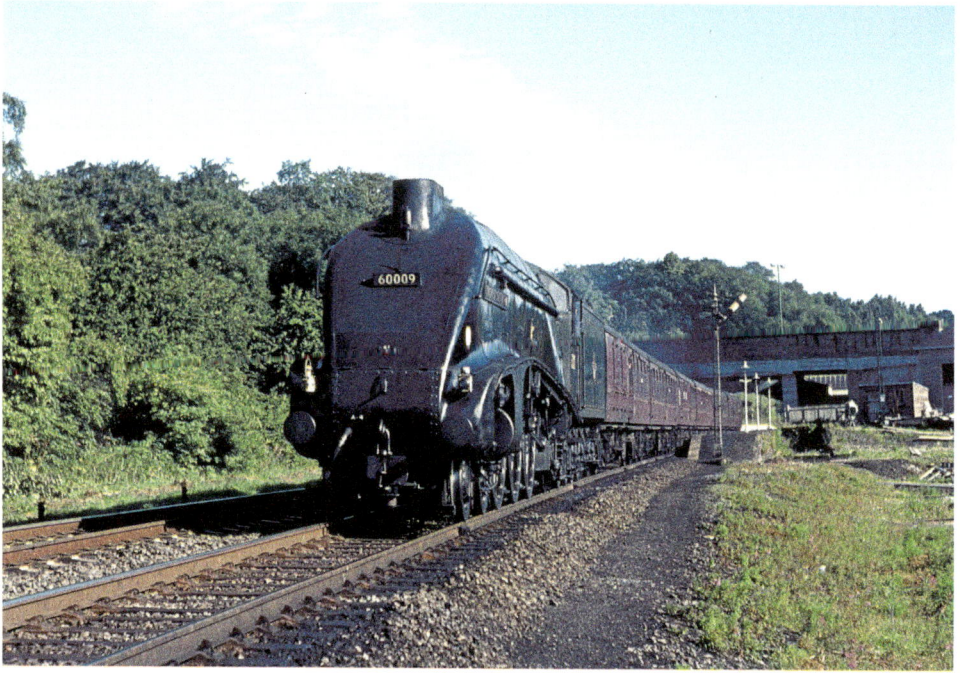

Respectably clean again is No. 60009 *Union of South Africa*, departing Bridge of Allan in 1965. (Strathwood Library Collection)

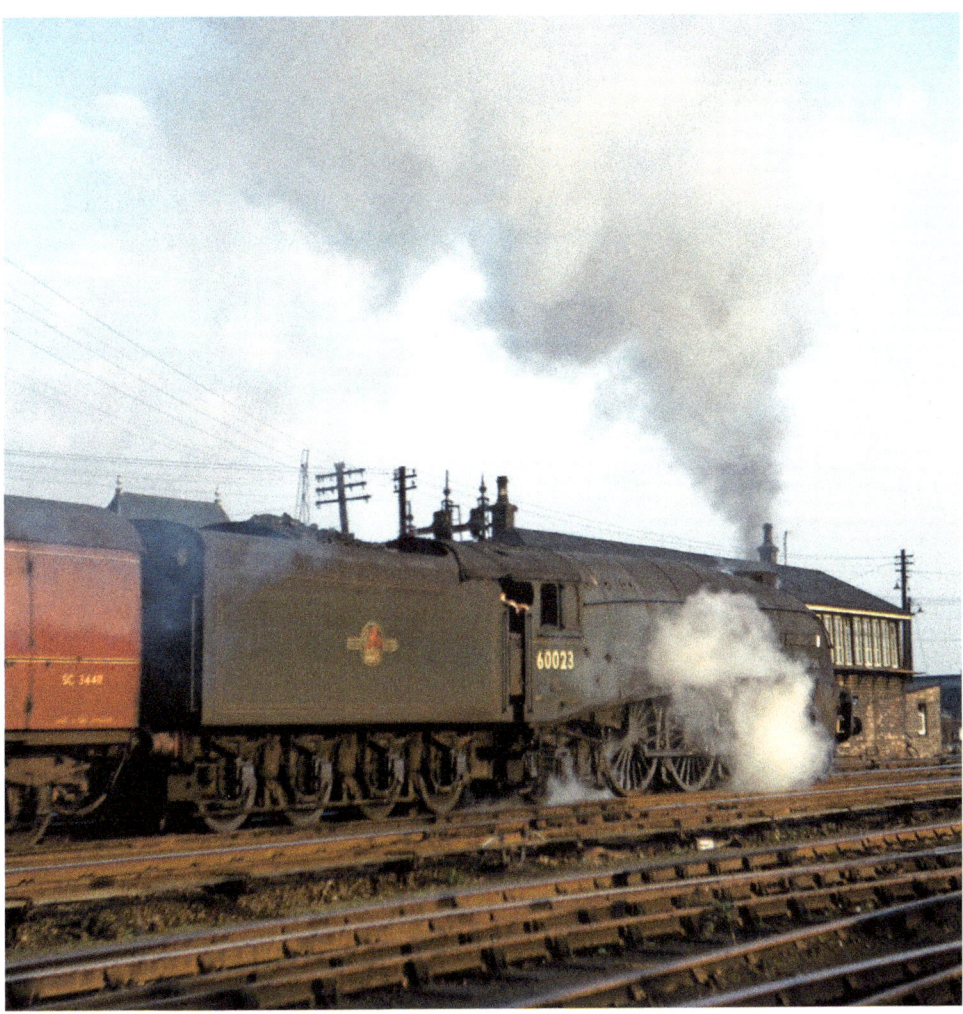

Evidence of work through its last summer in 1964 was letting down the appearance of No. 60023 *Golden Eagle*, getting underway once more at Stirling during October a few days before being withdrawn. During the same month Nikita Krushchev was deposed in the USSR by Leonid Brezhnev and Kosygin, whilst in this country Labour won the general election, winning power with a very small majority; Harold Wilson as Prime Minister assumed power. (Strathwood Library Collection)

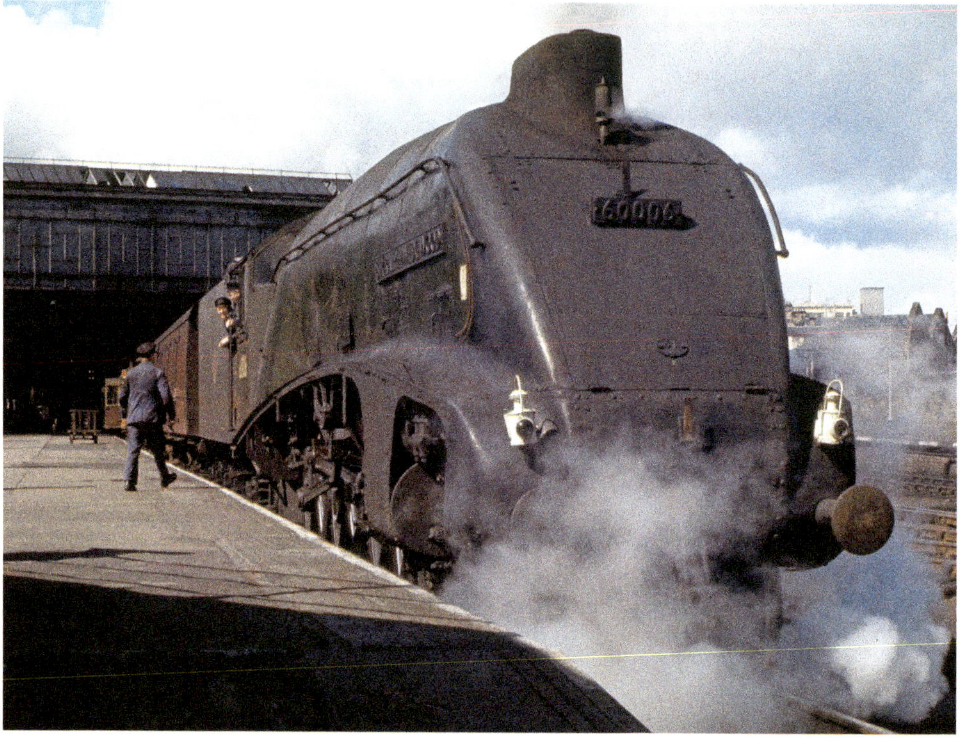

Another lightweight load for No. 60024 *Kingfisher* at Perth on 28 June 1966. During the previous month two heavyweights had fought for the world boxing title when Cassius Clay beat Henry Cooper in the sixth round of their bout at the Arsenal football ground, at Highbury, North London. (Michael Beaton)

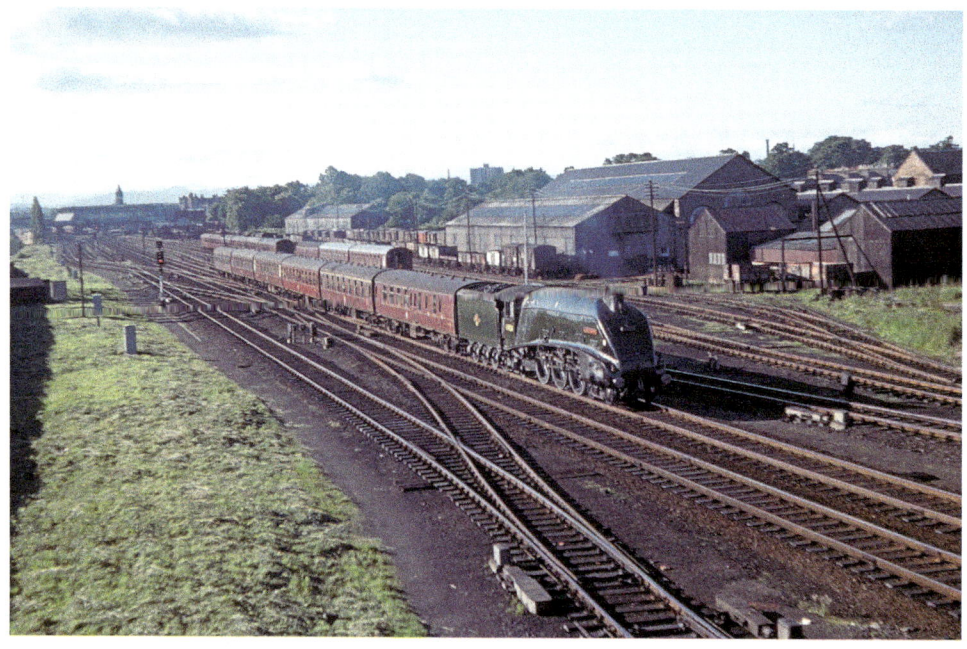

The crew of No. 60006 *Sir Ralph Wedgwood* look out at Perth in 1965. (Strathwood Library Collection)

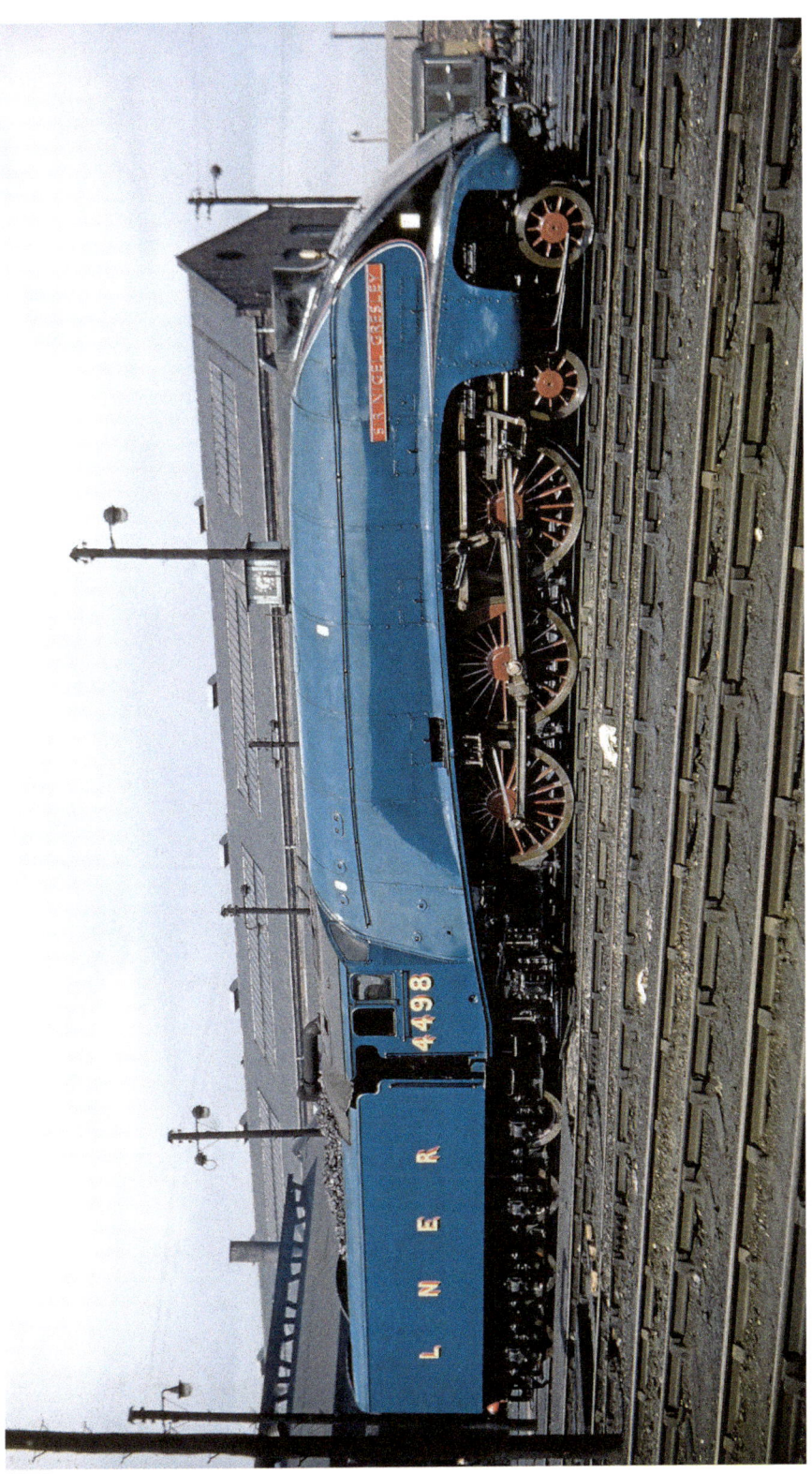

The nose of a Clayton pokes out behind the now preserved No. 4498 *Sir Nigel Gresley*, restored to LNER livery, at Polmadie in 1967. In 1937 the 100th Gresley Pacific was built by the London and North Eastern Railway, and the railway honoured her designer by giving the locomotive his name. *Sir Nigel Gresley* the locomotive was saved from scrapping in 1966 by a small group, who set up the A4 Preservation Society to secure the engine's future. (Strathwood Library Collection)